P. WILLIAMSON

REGIONAL TRAMWAYS

THE NORTH WEST OF ENGLAND POST 1945

REGIONAL TRAMWAYS

THE NORTH WEST OF ENGLAND POST 1945

PETER WALLER

Regional Tramways: The North West of England

Published in 2017 by Pen & Sword Transport
an imprint of
Pen & Sword Books Ltd
47 Church Street, Barnsley, South Yorkshire, S70 2AS

ISBN 978 1 47386 207 4

Printed and Bound in China by Imago

Pen & Sword Books Ltd incorporates the imprints of Pen & Sword Archaeology, Atlas, Aviation, Battleground, Discovery, Family History, History, Maritime, Military, Naval, Politics, Railways, Select, Transport, True Crime, and Fiction, Frontline Books, Leo Cooper, Praetorian Press, Seaforth Publishing and Wharncliffe.

For a complete list of Pen & Sword titles please contact
PEN & SWORD BOOKS LIMITED
47 Church Street, Barnsley, South Yorkshire, S70 2AS, England
E-mail: enquiries@pen-and-sword.co.uk
Website: www.pen-and-sword.co.uk

CONTENTS

ABBREVIATIONS

BEC	British Electric Car Co, Trafford Park, Manchester
EE	English Electric
EMB	Electro-Mechanical Brake Co
ERTCW	Electric Railway & Tramway Carriage Works
GEC	General Electric Co
LCC	London County Council
M&T	Maley & Taunton
MBROT	Manchester, Bury, Rochdale & Oldham Tramways
MCW	Metropolitan-Cammell-Weymann
MTPS	Merseyside Tramway Preservation Society
NTM	National Tramway Museum
SHMD	Stalybridge, Hyde, Mossley & Dukinfield Tramways & Electricity Board
SLT	South Lancashire Tramways
Starbuck	Starbuck Car & Wagon Co
VAMBAC	variable automatic multinotch brakes and acceleration control
UDC	Urban District Council
UEC	United Electric Car Co

KEY TO MAPS

- Passenger lines
- Lines closed before 1 January 1945
- Non-passenger lines
- Lines of neighbouring operators – open at 1 January 1945
- Lines of neighbouring operators – closed at 1 January 1945
- Passenger lines built opened after 1 January 1945
- Lines under construction at 1 January 1945 – never completed

PREFACE

This is the third in a series intended, ultimately, to cover all the tramways of the British Isles. It focuses on those tramway systems in north-west England that operated after 1945. However, it also gives an overview of tramway development from the horse-tram era onwards in the region. Individual chapters deal with each of the first-generation tramways that survived into 1945 with a map showing the system as it existed at 1 January 1945 and a fleet list of all the trams operated after that date. Coverage also includes the two second-generation tramways in the area.

One of the facets of the tramways of this region was the interlinked nature of many of the systems. It was possible to travel from the Pier Head in Liverpool to the Pennines via tram; the journey needed numerous changes but the network of tramways stretching across the region was unique in Britain

The majority of illustrations in the book are drawn from the collection of Online Transport Archive (OTA); I would like to express my gratitude to Barry Cross, the late Alan Donaldson, the late Stanley Eades, Les Folkard, the late Philip Hanson, the late Harry Luff, Martin Jenkins, the late R.W.A. Jones, the late J. Joyce, the late F.N.T. Lloyd-Jones, John Meredith, the late J.H. Roberts, the late Ronnie Stephens, the late Phil Tatt, the late F.E.J. Ward, the late Peter N. Williams, and the late R.L. Wilson – all of whose negatives or collections are now in the care of OTA – and the National Tramway Museum, which now houses the collections of Maurice O'Connor, W.A. Camwell and Bob Parr. Martin Jenkins has been a great help in tracking down certain images and giving information, particularly on the Liverpool system. Every effort has been made to ensure complete accuracy; unfortunately the records available are not always consistent and, with the passage of time, the number of those with detailed knowledge is sadly gradually declining. Likewise every effort has been made to ensure the correct attribution of photographs. It goes without saying that any errors of fact or attribution are the author's and any corrections should be forwarded to him care of the Publisher.

Peter Waller
Shrewsbury,
August 2016

INTRODUCTION

It was in this region that the tramway age reached the British Isles, when, on 30 August 1860, the American George Francis Train introduced the first horse tramway to Birkenhead. The Birkenhead Street Railway Co operated over a four-mile 5ft 2in gauge route, which was converted to standard gauge in 1864, and the original fleet of eight double and single-deck cars was imported from the US. Operating the line passed to the Birkenhead Tramways Co on 23 July 1877.

The Birkenhead Tramways Co also took over a second horse tramway, the Hoylake & Birkenhead Rail & Tramway Co, on 12 October 1879; this standard-gauge line opened its 2½-mile route on 6 September 1873 and operated a fleet of eight Starbuck-built double-deck trams.

Control of the Birkenhead Tramways Co passed to Birkenhead Corporation in 1889 and the inherited lines were subsequently leased to the Birkenhead United Tramways, Omnibus & Carriage

The first horse trams in the region were operated by the Birkenhead Street Railway Co from August 1860. Initially the fleet comprised two open-top double-deck cars: Nos.1 and 2 (the latter illustrated here). Barry Cross Collection/Online Transport Archive

The Hoylake & Birkenhead Rail & Tramway Co was operated by eight open-top double-deck horse trams supplied by Starbuck. Barry Cross Collection/ Online Transport Archive

Co from 15 August 1890. A total of eleven route miles was operated by a fleet of twenty-seven cars inherited from the company and ten new cars acquired from Milnes. Birkenhead United took over operating a further company, the Wirral Tramway Co, in May 1900 pending the line's electrification. The three-mile standard-gauge line originally opened on 28 March 1877. Birkenhead United operated the route from 16 May 1900 through to electrification on 22 January 1901. Operating the Birkenhead United system passed to Birkenhead Corporation in 1901 and the last horse trams operated on 8 November of that year.

Birkenhead United, Tramways Omnibus & Carriage Co No.12 pictured on the Prenton line at Woodside. This was one of a number of double-deck trams supplied by Milnes in 1890. Martin Jenkins Collection/Online Transport Archive

A Wirral Tramways Co tram seen alongside the company's New Ferry depot. The company operated twelve horse trams; the car illustrated is one of seven single-deck trams acquired for the line's opening. These were built originally for the Wirral Tramway Co by Starbuck in 1877. Martin Jenkins Collection/Online Transport Archive

Apart from the horse tramways in Birkenhead, there was a separate standard-gauge system serving neighbouring Wallasey. Extending for just over 3¼ route miles, the Wallasey Tramways Co began operation on 30 June 1879. Operating the line passed to the Wallasey United Tramways & Omnibus Co on 8 May 1891. The line was taken over by Wallasey Urban District Council (UDC) on 1 April 1901 and the final horse tram operated on 19 March 1902.

Another early horse tramway operated across the River Mersey from 2 July 1861 to either late 1861 or early 1862; the tracks were removed during summer 1862. Known as the Old Swan Tramway and operated by the Liverpool Road &

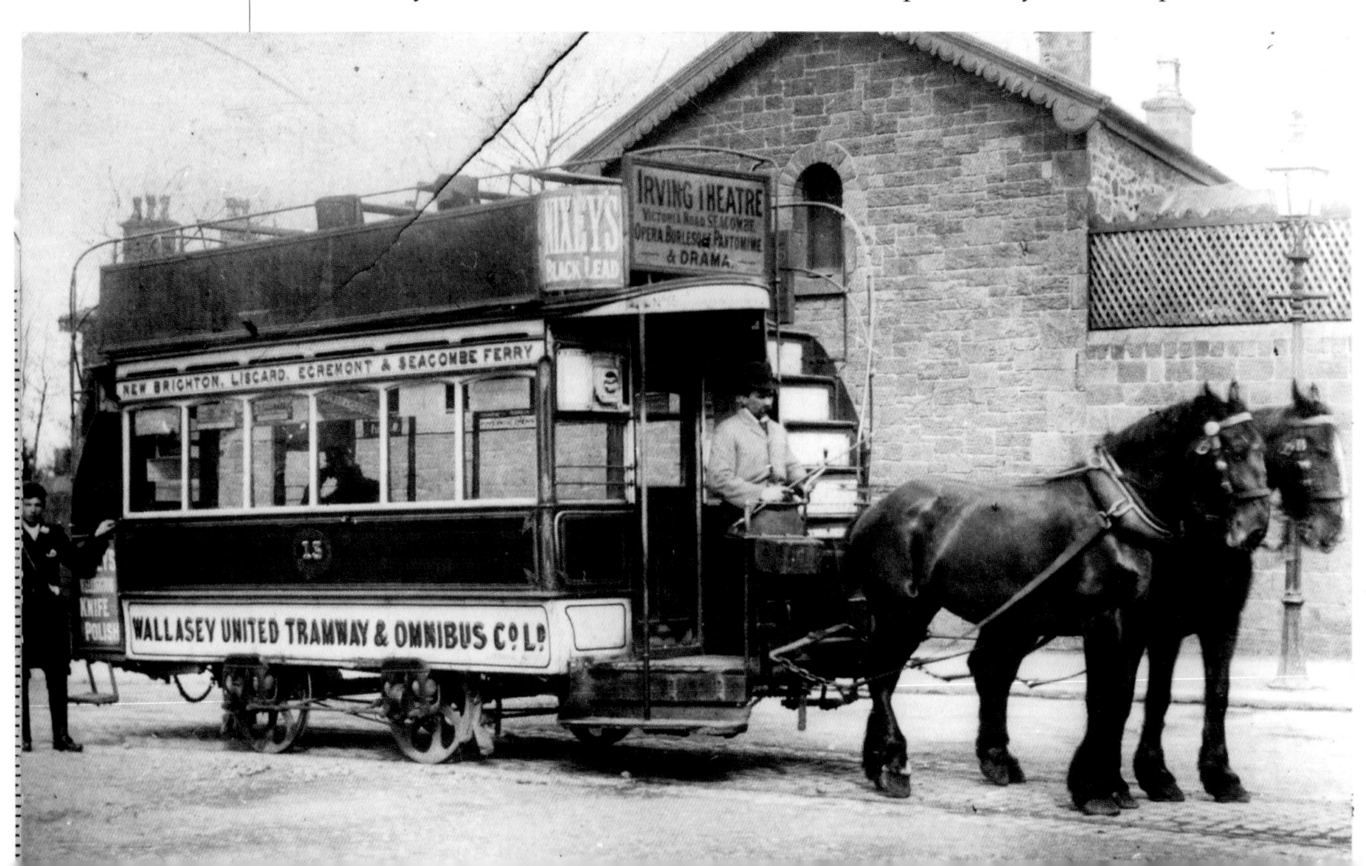

The Wallasey United Tramway & Omnibus Co owner supplemented its existing fleet by acquiring a further seven cars, Nos.6, 7, 10-14, from Milnes. Barry Cross Collection/ Online Transport Archive

The Liverpool Street Tramways Co was independent for some seven years before it merged with the Liverpool Omnibus & Tramways Co to form the Liverpool United Tramways & Omnibus Co. Barry Cross Collection/Online Transport Archive

Rail Omnibus Co, the standard-gauge tramway extended for just over 1¼ miles and was operated by a single double-deck car supplied by Oldbury Carriage Works.

A second horse tramway opened in Liverpool on 1 November 1869. Operated by the Liverpool Tramways Co and extending over almost seven route miles, this company merged with the Liverpool Road & Rail Omnibus Co in 1876 to form the Liverpool United Tramways & Omnibus Co.

Following the merger, the Liverpool United Tramways & Omnibus Co

Trams belonging to the Liverpool United Tramways & Omnibus Co are recorded at the Quadrant, Lime Street. Note the tip horse on the nearest car, which was needed to tackle hill sections and possibly remained in harness as far as Old Swan. Martin Jenkins Collection/Online Transport Archive

ultimately operated a network of 42¾ route miles. Operation continued until 1897; Liverpool Corporation acquired the tramway on 1 January 1897 and took over operation from 1 September. A total of 281 horse trams passed to the corporation with the final horse trams operating in the city on 25 August 1903.

Another early tramway was the Salford Tramways Co. Following the successful launch of the tramway in Birkenhead, John Greenwood proposed a similar scheme for Salford. In late 1860 an experimental section of line was laid. An agreement was then made in June 1861 and the route from Pendleton to the town centre opened in stages. Although not wholly successful, the line was operational from 1861 until 1872.

All the tramways opened before 1870 predated the Tramways Act of that year. This Act authorised local authorities to grant the rights to operate tramways within the local area to companies for a period of twenty-one years; building of the tramway could either be undertaken by the authority and leased to the operator or by the operator itself. The Act also imposed a duty upon the operator of maintaining the strip of road 18in either side of the outer running rails; in many ways, this was the Achilles' heel of the Act in that at a time when roads were generally badly maintained, this well-managed strip in the middle meant it became available to all road users and the tram was increasingly perceived as a cause of delays to other road users. At the end of the twenty-one-year lease, or periodically thereafter, the local authority was entitled to buy the assets of the company at a written-down value. This further weakness in the Act dissuaded leaseholders from investing in the business as the potential selling price did not reflect the investment undertaken. The 1870 Act was subsequently amended, most notably with the Light Railways Act of 1896, but represented the basis upon which most tramways were built.

The first tramway opened in the region after 1870 was the Southport Tramways Co. Opened on 31 May 1873 and eventually extending over 6¼ route miles, the standard-gauge network was acquired by Southport Corporation and Birkdale UDC (which was absorbed into Southport on 1 January 1916) in 1896 and leased back to the company on 25 March of the same year. From July 1901 the system was converted to electric traction and the last horse tram operated on 26 March 1902. There was also a second horse tramway in the district, the Birkdale & Southport Tramways Co, which operated over a four-mile standard-gauge route from 12 May 1883. Taken over

The Birkdale & Southport Tramways Co introduced horse trams on 12 May 1883. Barry Cross Collection/Online Transport Archive

The route along Eccles Old Road to Patricroft was one of the horse-tram services operated by the Manchester Carriage & Tramways Co. Barry Cross Collection/Online Transport Archive

by the corporation in 1900, the company continued to operate the line while it was electrified. The last horse trams operated on 13 December 1902.

This was followed by the network that was to serve Manchester and Salford. In 1876 the Manchester Suburban Tramways Co was established, with its first standard-gauge route opening on 17 May 1877. This concern was taken over by the Manchester Carriage Co, with the company renamed the Manchester Carriage & Tramways Co. Trading as Manchester & Salford Tramways, the horse network expanded to 78 route miles operated by some 366 trams and included operations in Ashton and Stretford. Operating the system was taken over by Salford and Manchester corporations in 1901 with a view to electrification, with the last horse trams operating in Manchester on 13 April 1904 and Salford on 25 March 1903.

The next horse tramway to open in the north-west was the Preston Tramways Co on 20 March 1879. This was a 3ft 6in

The Preston Tramways Co operated six double-deck horse trams over a single route. Barry Cross Collection/Online Transport Archive

Viewed at Saltney in about 1900, Chester Tramways Co No.4 was one of the second generation of trams operated by the company. Barry Cross Collection/Online Transport Archive

gauge route, almost 2½ route miles in length, linking the centre with Fulwood. Operated by six double-deck cars, the line was transferred to W. Harding & Co on 1 January 1887. The new owner had already started operation, from 14 April 1882, of a second 3ft 6in gauge system extending slightly over 4½ route miles. This traded as Preston Corporation Tramways and was operated by eight double-deck trams. Horse tram operation ceased on 31 December 1901 and was replaced by corporation-owned electric trams.

The Chester Tramways Co introduced horse trams on 10 June 1879. In all, eighteen standard-gauge trams eventually operated over a single 2¼-mile route. In 1886 No.9 was converted unsuccessfully to operate on compressed air. The corporation took over operation on 1 January 1902 and the last horse trams operated on 27 December 1902.

On 2 August 1880 the Wigan Tramways Co introduced 3ft 6in gauge horse trams to

For about a decade, from September 1890 until 1900, horse trams operated in Bolton courtesy of Bolton Suburban. Barry Cross Collection/Online Transport Archive

The town of Stockport had two horse-tram operators: the Manchester Carriage & Tramways Co operated the route linking the two, and the Stockport & Hazel Grove Carriage & Tramway Co operated two routes. The latter's No.2 is shown here. Barry Cross Collection/ Online Transport Archive

the town. Operating some 7¾ route miles with a fleet of twelve trams, the company introduced steam traction two years later when the last horse trams operated.

The first of an extensive network of horse tram routes to serve Bolton opened on 1 September 1880. Bolton Suburban was operated by E. Holden & Co under lease from Bolton Corporation (plus the local boards of Astley Bridge and Farnworth); the standard-gauge network reached eighteen route miles by 1892 with a maximum fleet of forty-eight trams. Following the corporation takeover in 1899, the last horse trams operated in 1900.

Horse trams first appeared in Stockport, courtesy of the Manchester Carriage & Tramways Co, on a route linking Manchester and Stockport via

The St Helens & District Tramways Co fleet comprised of six Eades-patent reversible double-deck cars, such as No.1 illustrated here, built by the Ashbury Railway Carriage & Iron Co of Manchester, along with seven other trams. Barry Cross Collection/Online Transport Archive

The horse trams of the Morecambe Tramways Co began operation on 3 June 1887. Barry Cross Collection/Online Transport Archive

Levenshulme on 7 May 1880. A separate company, the Stockport & Hazel Grove Carriage & Tramway Co, operated two other standard-gauge routes in the town from 1890. The Manchester–Stockport route was electrified in 1902 but horse operation of the latter ended on 24 January 1905.

The Manchester Carriage & Tramways Co also introduced horse trams on the route through Hollinwood to Oldham; operation of service started on 16 September 1880 and survived until 1 November 1901. The same company also operated a horse tramway in Stalybridge between 14 June 1881 and 14 October 1903.

Horse trams operated in St Helens via the St Helens & District Tramways Co. This had been established in 1879 but it was not until 5 November 1881 that services began over the first section to Prescot. Extensions to the standard-gauge system saw the network reach nine miles by the end of 1882. The company was, however, not successful and was taken over on 1 October 1889 by the St Helens & District Tramways Co. The new owners replaced the majority of horse trams with steam on 4 April 1890. The final horse-operated route, to Haydock, is believed to have been converted to steam in May 1890 (although horse operation might have lasted until October 1893).

Courtesy of the Blackburn Corporation Tramways Co, horse trams first operated in the town on 28 May 1887. The company also operated steam trams, with the 4ft 0in gauge fleet comprising nineteen steam-tram trailers alongside eight horse trams. Operation of the 8¾-mile system passed to the corporation on 24 August 1898. All the ex-company vehicles were withdrawn by 9 August 1901.

Less than a week after the first horse

Morecambe Corporation operated horse trams from 20 July 1909 to abandonment on 6 October 1926. Apart from the seventeen cars acquired from the company, a further four new horse trams were acquired from, ironically, EE in 1919 and 1922. Barry Cross Collection/Online Transport Archive

From 2 August 1890 the Lancaster & District Tramways Co operated fourteen locally built double-deck trams. A number were cut down to single deck by lowering the upper-deck seating to waistrail level.
Barry Cross Collection/ Online Transport Archive

trams operated in Blackburn, the Morecambe Tramways Co introduced standard-gauge horse trams to the seaside resort. Opened on 3 June 1887, the company's route extended over 2¾ route miles from Morecambe to Heysham. Eventually the company operated seventeen trams; however, fourteen of these (along with just over 1½ route miles) were transferred to Morecambe Corporation on 30 July 1909; the remaining three trams followed in 1913. The corporation had funded a company-operated extension in 1898, taking the service to Bare. This meant that when taking over operation, the corporation operated over nearly 2½ route miles. From 5 January 1912 the remaining section of the company's route, from Heysham to the borough boundary, was operated by petrol trams. Corporation horse trams operated until 6 October 1926; when replaced by buses, the horse trams in Morecambe represented the last such operation in England.

Another late horse tramway operator was the Lancaster & District Tramways Co. This concern began operating its 4¼-mile route from Morecambe to Lancaster on 2 August 1890. The service was operated by fourteen locally built double-deck trams supplied by the Lancaster Railway Carriage & Wagon Co and survived to be replaced by company-owned buses on 31 December 1921.

The last 'new' horse tram operator in the region was Farnworth UDC. Following the takeover by the local authorities of the routes of the Bolton Suburban Co, the short section of line in Farnworth was operated by the UDC using horse traction between 9 January 1902 and 1 April 1906.

The first steam tramway in the north-

The Blackburn & Over Darwen Tramways Co operated seventeen steam tram engines. The first seven came from Kitson & Co in 1881/82, and the next seven were supplied by Thomas Green & Sons in 1885/86, with three further Kitson-built locomotives following in 1897/98. Here one of the Green-built locomotives is seen hauling one of the company's eight four-wheel double-deck trailers. A further eight bogie trailers were operated, as were, for a short period, four open workmen's cars. Barry Cross Collection/ Online Transport Archive

The second steam tram operation in Blackburn was operated by the Blackburn Corporation Tramways Co and later by Blackburn Corporation itself. A total of twenty-two steam tram engines were used eventually; the first fifteen were built by Thomas Green & Sons and delivered in 1887/88. These were supplemented by seven, one of which is illustrated here, acquired in 1899 from the North Staffordshire Tramways Co. These engines had originally been supplied new by Beyer Peacock Wilkinson in 1894. Barry Cross Collection/ Online Transport Archive

west of England was that owned by the Blackburn & Over Darwen Tramways Co; this 8¾-mile-long 4ft 0in gauge line opened on 16 April 1881. In all, seventeen locomotives and twenty-three trailers were acquired during the company's life; the operation passed to Blackburn and Darwen corporations on 1 January 1899, with the former receiving three and the latter ten of the surviving thirteen locomotives and thirteen trailers respectively. Steam operation of the route ended on 16 October 1900.

There was a second steam tram operation in Blackburn, which was also

Burnley & District Tramways Co steam tram engine No.16 was the penultimate locomotive delivered to the company; it and No.17 were built by the Falcon Engine & Car Works of Loughborough in 1897. It is seen here attached to double-deck trailer No.15; this and trailer No.14 were also acquired from Falcon and were new in 1897. Barry Cross Collection/Online Transport Archive

4ft 0in gauge and was owned by the Blackburn Corporation Tramways Co. It opened on 28 May 1887, with the company operating over some 8¾ route miles with a fleet of twenty-two steam engines, supplied by Thomas Green and Beyer Peacock Wilkinson, allied to nineteen bogie trailers. The company also operated eight horse trams from 1888. The operation passed to Blackburn Corporation on 24 August 1898 and the final steam trams operated on 9 August 1901.

On 17 September 1881, courtesy of the Burnley & District Tramways Co, the first standard-gauge steam trams operated in the north-west. This seven-mile route was originally operated by five Kitson-built locomotives; these were withdrawn on 1 May 1882 and then, until March 1883, the route was operated by horse tram pending delivery of the first of twelve Falcon-built steam locomotives. In all, eighteen trailers were used. The line passed to Burnley Corporation on 1 March 1900 and steam operation ended on 17 November 1901.

The next steam tramway was that of the Wigan Tramways Co. On 8 August 1882 operation passed from horse to steam traction. In total, the company used twelve Wilkinson-built locomotives. The company went into receivership in 1890

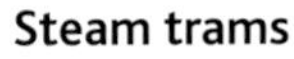

Steam trams were introduced to Wigan by the Wigan Tramways Co but were operated by the Wigan & District Tramways Co from October 1891 until 26 September1904. This view dates to the early 1890s and shows the last of the original steam tram engines, No.12, supplied by Wilkinson in 1887. Barry Cross Collection/Online Transport Archive

With Rochdale Corporation No.27, a Brush-built open-top car of 1905, in the background, one of the MBROT's 3ft 6in gauge steam tram engines and trailers is pictured at the Sudden terminus towards the end of steam tram operation when the service was operated by Heywood Corporation. Barry Cross Collection/Online Transport Archive

and, from October 1891, the tramway was operated by the Wigan & District Tramways Co. Seven of the original twelve locomotives were operated, with a further eleven being acquired between 1893 and 1896. A total of sixteen trailers were operated. Although bought by the corporation on 30 September 1902, the operation was leased back to the company until the final steam trams operated on 26 September 1904.

The largest steam-tram network in the region was operated by the Manchester, Bury, Rochdale & Oldham Tramways (MBROT). This company operated both standard and 3ft 6in gauge steam trams – 9½ and 20¾ route miles respectively – with some ninety-one locomotives (of which twenty-seven were standard gauge) and eighty-one trailers (of which twenty-six were standard gauge). The first operations started in Rochdale on 7 March 1883; those in Oldham began in November 1885; and those in Bury in 1886. Manchester was never actually served by the company and so its name was dropped from the firm's title in 1888. The company's operations were eventually replaced by corporation-operated electric trams; the last steam trams in Oldham operated on 19 November 1901, in Bury during April 1904 and in Rochdale on 8 May 1905.

On 11 July 1885 the Barrow-in-Furness Tramways Co introduced steam trams to the town. A three-route network, extending over 5½ miles, was operated by eight locomotives supplied by Kitson. Following the purchase of the company by British Electric Traction (BET) on 23 December 1899, two locomotives and trailers were acquired from the North Staffordshire Tramways. In June 1902 a depot fire destroyed a number of locomotives and

The Barrow-in-Furness Tramways Co operated ten steam tram engines and ten trailers. Barry Cross Collection/Online Transport Archive

trailers; these were not replaced and steam trams stopped operating on 13 July 1903, being eventually replaced by BET-owned electric trams.

The Accrington Corporation Steam Tramways Co began operating its nine-mile 4ft 0in gauge route linking the town with Haslingden on 5 April 1886. In all, the company employed twenty-three Green-built locomotives, of which four were bought from Blackburn Corporation in 1901. A total of seventeen trailers were acquired new from the Ashbury Railway Carriage & Iron Co of Manchester (fourteen) and from Milnes (three) with further examples being bought from Blackburn and Burnley between 1899 and 1902. Following municipalisation in September 1907, the last steam trams operated in Accrington on 31 December 1907 and in Haslingden on 27 September 1908.

The Rossendale Valley Tramways Co operated, from 31 January 1889, a 4ft 0in gauge steam tramway between Rawtenstall and Bacup. Extending eventually over almost 6½ route miles, the line was operated by twelve Thomas Green-built locomotives and twelve trailers. The line was acquired by BET with a view to possible electrification; however, the corporations involved, Bacup and Rawtenstall, were eager to take over the operation themselves.

The Accrington Street Tramways Co operated twenty-three Thomas Green & Sons steam tram engines. Barry Cross Collection/Online Transport Archive

The Rossendale Valley Tramways Co possessed twelve trailers: the first ten were acquired new from Milnes for the line's opening and two were acquired from Blackburn Corporation in 1901. Barry Cross Collection/ Online Transport Archive

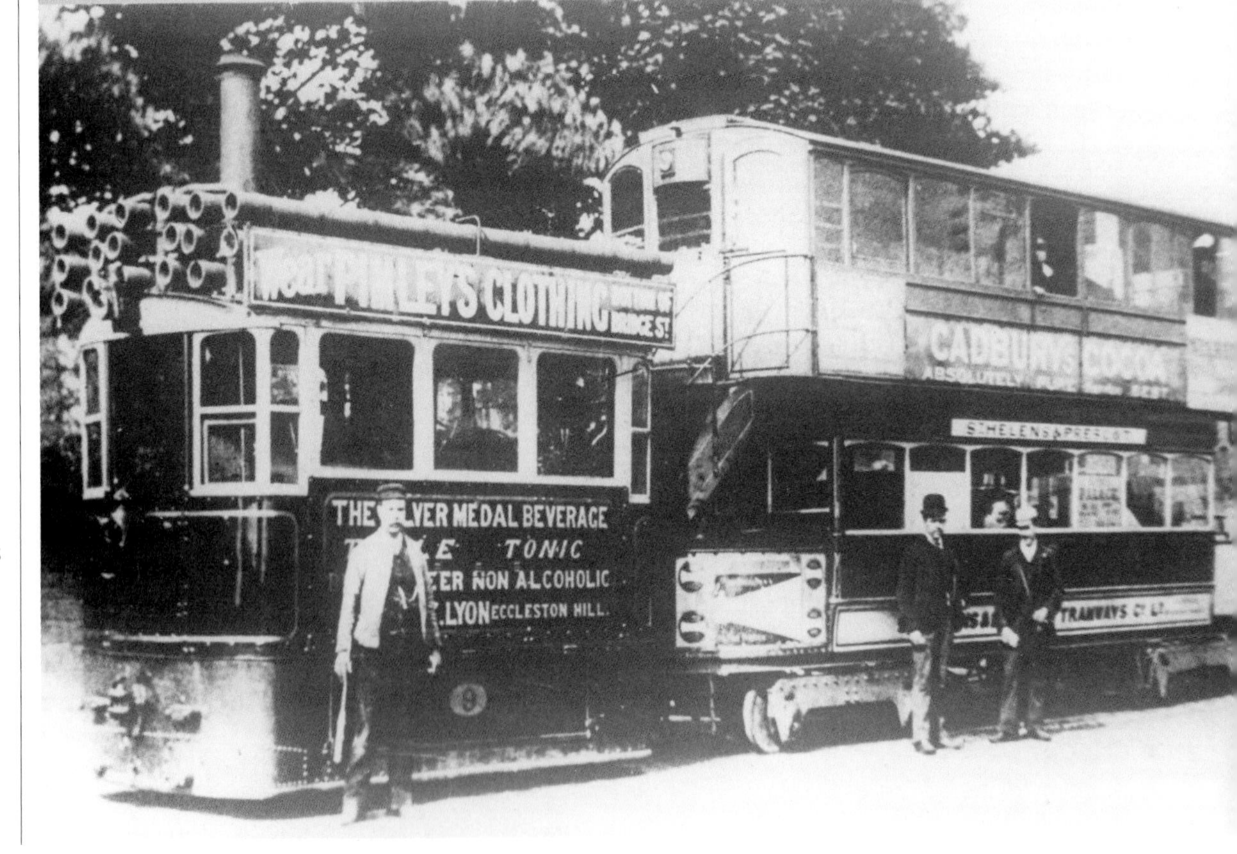

St Helens & District Tramways Co services were provided using nine steam tram engines, the last of which is illustrated here, that were supplied in 1890/91. Barry Cross Collection/ Online Transport Archive

This could not happen until the end of the original twenty-one-year lease and so company operation of steam trams continued until 1 October 1908. Steam operation over the route ended on 22 July 1909 – the last urban steam tram operation in Britain. Rawtenstall kept two of the surviving steam locomotives for use as snowploughs.

The St Helens & District Tramways Co began operating steam trams on 24 May 1890 and operated 10¼ route miles with a fleet of nine Green-built locomotives allied to ten Milnes-built double-deck trailers supplied between 1890 and 1893. To electrify the line, the new twenty-one-year lease on the line, granted by the corporation on 1 October 1898 following its purchase of the track, was transferred on 1 February 1899 to a new company, sharing the same name as the original, with the last steam tram operating on 7 April 1900.

The last steam operation to begin was that of Heywood Corporation. This short-lived system operated from 20 December 1904 to 20 September 1905 following the withdrawal of Rochdale Corporation from the route it had operated from 14 June 1904 in succession to the MBROT. Operation of the route was again taken over by Rochdale Corporation from 20 September 1905.

Alongside horse and steam trams, there were two other forms of propulsion that powered trams in the north-west. On 11 July 1896 the British Gas Traction Co introduced town-gas-powered trams to Lytham St Annes. The standard-gauge route, which was just over 6¼ miles in length and operated by sixteen trams, was sold to the Blackpool, St Annes & Lytham Tramways Co. The gas trams ceased operating on 28 May 1903 with electrification. Gas-powered trams also operated on the 2½-mile-long standard-gauge route operated by the British Gas Traction Co on behalf of the line's owners, Trafford Park Estates, between 23 July 1897 and 1899; gas tram operation continued until 14 July 1903 when the standard-gauge line was electrified.

Further to the north, the surviving 1¼ miles of the Morecambe Tramways

Following the end of steam tram operations of the MBROT, Heywood Corporation took over operating the short section of line within its boundaries in December 1904. Barry Cross Collection/ Online Transport Archive

Following the transfer of the bulk of its route to Morecambe Corporation in 1909, the Morecambe Tramways Co persisted with horse operation of the remaining 1¼-mile section of route. On 5 January 1912, however, it introduced petrol-powered trams to the service. Three trams were delivered in 1911 and a fourth, illustrated here, followed in 1913. Barry Cross Collection/ Online Transport Archive

In 1891 Milnes supplied two open-top trams to the Blackpool Electric Tramway Co to replace two earlier single-deck crossbench cars. Note the conduit rail visible beneath No.10's lifeguard. Barry Cross Collection/ Online Transport Archive

Co's route, following the transfer of the remaining 1½ miles to Morecambe Corporation on 20 July 1909, was operated by petrol-powered trams from 5 January 1912. Four standard-gauge single-deck trams were supplied by United Electric Car Co (UEC) with 55hp Leyland petrol engines. The service survived until 24 October 1924.

Many of the steam trams already outlined began operation after the first electric tramways. Blackpool can lay claim to one of the pioneering electric tramways in the British Isles; indeed, the conduit tramway opened by the Blackpool Electric Tramway Co on 29 September 1885 was the first electric tramway to serve a primarily urban area. Promoted by Michael Holroyd Smith, the standard-gauge route, which extended to almost three miles ultimately, was originally operated by six double-deck and two single-deck crossbench cars with trailers. In operation the conduit proved troublesome, with sand often blocking the conduit. After Blackpool Corporation assumed ownership on 10 September 1892, the route was converted to overhead operation during the second half of 1899. As part of the Promenade route, the line is still in operation and has recently been fully modernised. One of the original open-top cars, No.4, was converted into a works car in 1912 and, on final withdrawal, was preserved and eventually restored to near original condition.

Blackpool also hosted another of the pioneering electric tramways – the Blackpool & Fleetwood Tramroad Co. This standard-gauge line, linking Blackpool with Fleetwood, opened on 14 July 1898. Operated exclusively by single-deck trams, of which forty-one had been obtained between opening and 1914,

The first ten trams acquired by the Blackpool & Fleetwood Tramroad Co were Milnes-built bogie crossbench cars Nos.1-10, similar to No.4 illustrated here in 1898 when new. Fitted with Milnes bogies, the ten cars passed to Blackpool Corporation on 1 January 1920, being renumbered 126-35. Stanley Eades Collection/Online Transport Archive

The first new trams acquired by Blackpool Corporation in 1900 were ten open-top Dreadnought trams. These were Nos.17-26 and the penultimate of the branch is pictured when new. They were built by the Midland Railway-Carriage & Wagon Co and fitted with that company's bogies. The twin stairs allowed rapid boarding and unloading of passengers. Stanley Eades Collection/ Online Transport Archive

the company was acquired by Blackpool Corporation on 1 January 1920. One of the ex-Blackpool & Fleetwood trams was converted into a works car, No.5, in 1942 and, following withdrawal in 1960, was restored as Blackpool & Fleetwood No.40. This was originally a UEC-built single-deck bogie car and now forms part of the National Tramway Museum (NTM) collection.

Following the acquisition of the conduit tramway, the corporation extended the line and further expansion occurred during the first decade of the twentieth century. The pivotal point in the history of Blackpool's trams came with the appointment of Walter Luff as general manager in 1933. With trams in retreat across much of the region, he recognised there was pressure in Blackpool to convert certain routes, and that the lack of recent investment undermined the long-term future of the system. His five-year plan, presented on 20 February 1933, advocated modernising the main route from Starr Gate to Fleetwood and acquiring a fleet of modern trams (developed in conjunction with English Electric (EE) based in Preston) along with basic maintenance of the town services while their future was determined. Adopted by the council, the result was that from June 1933 onwards the fleet received a significant number of new streamlined trams. Although the majority of the town services survived, two sections, to Layton and along Central Drive, were converted to bus operation on 19 October 1936.

Immediately south of Blackpool lie Lytham and St Annes. Courtesy of the British Gas Traction Co gas trams had been introduced in 1896 but the company was acquired by the Blackpool, Lytham & St Annes Tramways Co two years later. The new owners converted the route to electric traction, with the first of the new trams operating on 28 May 1903. Company operation continued until 28 October 1920 when services passed to St Annes UDC (which became Lytham St Annes Corporation two years later). Through services operated through to Blackpool but the entire Lytham system was converted to corporation-owned buses during 1936 and 1937, with the final trams operating on 28 April 1937. This was not, however, the final operation of trams over Lytham-

Following the use of gas trams, the Blackpool, St Annes & Lytham Tramways Co introduced electric trams on 28 May 1903. In all, the company acquired forty trams: thirty from BEC in 1903 and ten, Nos.31-40, from Brush on Brush-built Conaty trucks in 1905. Barry Cross Collection/Online Transport Archive

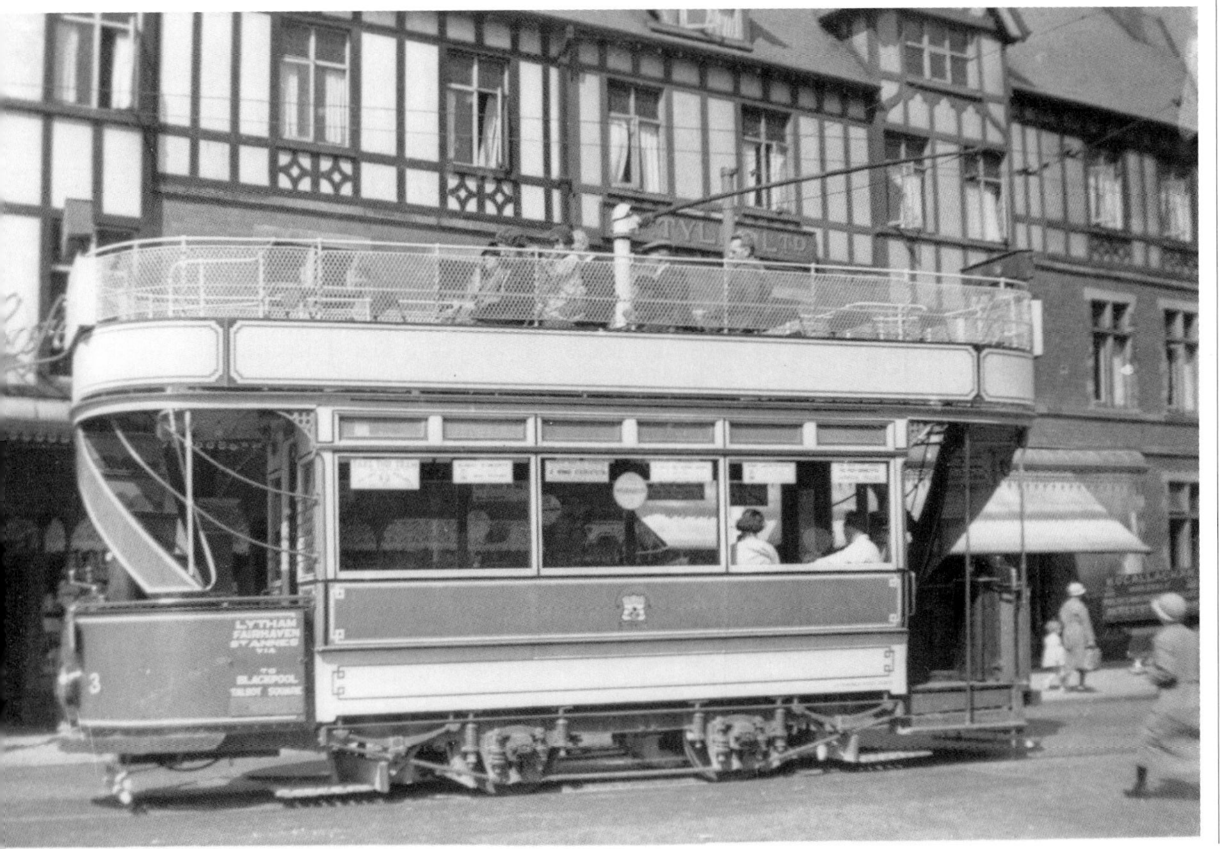

Following the takeover of the company's operations on 28 October 1920, the cars were to appear in the livery of St Annes UDC initially and then Lytham St Annes Corporation. No.3 was one of the original batch of thirty trams in 1903, which were all originally fitted with BEC-built SB40 trucks. Lytham St Annes acquired ten balcony-top cars new in 1924 and four single-deck and two double-deck trams second-hand in 1933 and 1934. Barry Cross Collection/Online Transport Archive

This postcard, postmarked 23 January 1909, shows Liverpool No.146, one of 300 open-top cars, Nos.142-441, built by ERTCW during 1900 and 1901. All were supplied with Brill 21E trucks and had been fitted with top covers by 1905. Barry Cross Collection/Online Transport Archive

owned track, as a 1¼-mile stretch at Squires Gate, alongside which the Lytham depot was situated and which linked the Blackpool routes that terminated at Squires Gate and Starr Gate, was used by Blackpool Corporation trams from 1957 to 1962.

Following the opening of the Blackpool system, the next electric tramway to begin operation was in Liverpool. The corporation had taken over the Liverpool United Tramways & Omnibus Co on 1 January 1897 and had worked on electrifying the system; the first electric trams operated on 16 November 1898. The corporation network eventually extended over more than ninety-four route miles with an additional four route miles operated on behalf of Bootle Corporation. The system continued

To operate the Great Crosby tramway, the Liverpool Overhead Railway acquired sixteen trams between 1899 and 1903. There included eight open-top cars supplied by ERTCW on Brill 21E trucks. At closure No.4 was one of two of the batch that remained in open-top condition. Barry Cross Collection/Online Transport Archive

expanding during the 1930s, with the last pre-war extension – from Garston to Allerton – opening on 4 July 1939 and the very last being at Kirkby on 12 April 1944. More than a quarter of the route network was built on reservations, the first of which, to Bowring Park, had been completed in 1914. At the outbreak of war, the Liverpool fleet comprised almost 750 trams, of which about half were modern cars that had been completed during the 1930s.

To the north of the Liverpool system, there was the Great Crosby Tramway. This was operated by the Liverpool Overhead Railway and extended for just over 2½ route miles from Bootle to Great Crosby. The standard-gauge line began operation on 19 June 1900. Although Liverpool Corporation had plans to take over and modernise the route, these came to nothing and the tramway was replaced by buses. The last day of operation was 31 December 1925.

Further to the north, there were two operators of electric trams in Southport. Following its acquisition of part of the

Southport Corporation No.14 was one of a batch of nine open-top tramcars supplied by ERTCW in 1900. All were supplied with Brill 21E trucks and some were fitted with UEC-built top covers by 1910. Southport originally numbered its double-deck cars with even numbers so this batch were Nos.2, 4, 6 and so on, whereas odd numbers were used for single-deck cars. This only changed post-1918 with the acquisition of a number of the ex-Southport Tramways Co cars, some of which were given odd numbers between 1 and 17. Barry Cross Collection/Online Transport Archive

To operate its new electric service, the Southport Tramways Co acquired twenty open-top double-deck cars from Brush fitted with Brush-built trucks in 1901. Nineteen passed to Southport Corporation when the company's lease expired. The only addition to the company's fleet after 1901 was the purchase of one single-deck demi-car from Brush in 1903; this did not survive to pass to corporation ownership. Barry Cross Collection/Online Transport Archive

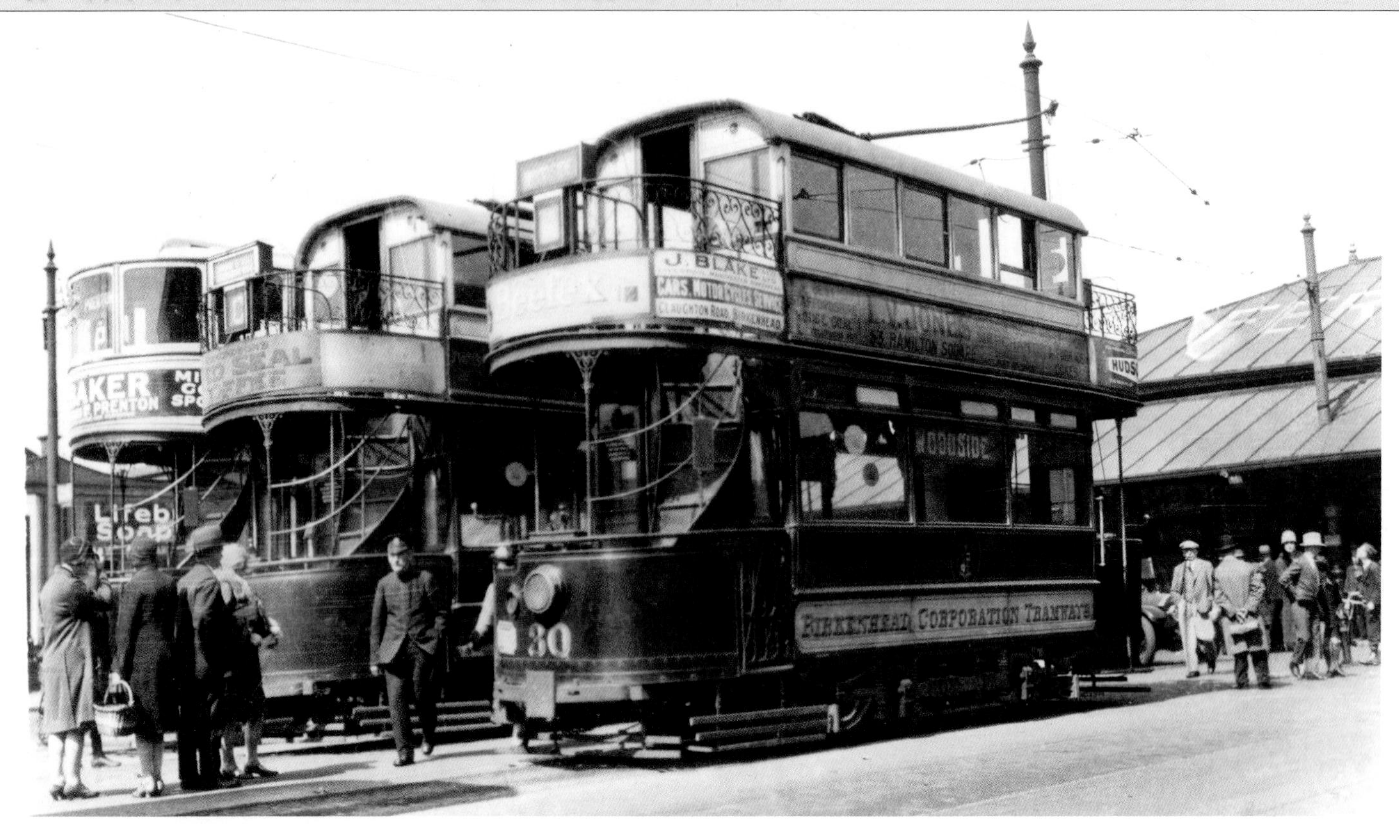

In 1901 Birkenhead Corporation was supplied with forty-four new trams by Milnes; Nos.1-13 were single-deck, whereas Nos.14-44 were open-top double-deckers. The latter were fitted originally with Peckham Cantilever 9A trucks, although a number were fitted with 21E trucks after 1920. Eighteen received some form of top cover between 1903 and 1914, but the remaining thirteen, Nos.24-36, were not so treated until 1922 and 1923. No.30, one of the cars fitted with a 21E truck, is seen at Woodside. Barry Cross Collection/ Online Transport Archive

Numerically the last passenger car in the Wallasey Corporation fleet, No.78 was one of a batch of ten built by Brush and delivered in 1922. Fitted with Peckham P22 trucks, they were supplied with Bellamy-type top covers from new. The car is seen outside the depot at Seaview Road. Barry Cross Collection/ Online Transport Archive

Birkdale company's route, Southport Corporation introduced electric trams on 18 July 1900. The BET-owned Southport Tramways Co, with a lease renewed in 1897, electrified its services, with the first operating on 11 August 1901. The two systems were integrated under corporation control in 1918 on expiry of the company's lease, with the corporation beginning operation of the erstwhile company lines on 28 February 1918. The system reached its final route mileage, of just over 17¼, following the opening of two extensions in 1924. However, conversion to corporation-owned buses began in 1931 and the last trams operated on 31 December 1934.

Across the Mersey, there were two corporation-owned electric tramways. The first to begin operation was Birkenhead, which introduced electric trams on 4 February 1901. These initially served the line inherited from the Hoylake Co to New Ferry. Electrifying the ex-Birkenhead United's routes followed and the Birkenhead system reached its peak route mileage, of just under 13½, in 1909. Conversion to corporation-owned

Following the conversion of the horse tramway to 3ft 6in gauge and its conversion to electric traction, Chester Corporation introduced twelve Milnes-built open-top trams in 1903. The fleet ultimately numbered eighteen cars. The penultimate of the original batch is pictured en route to Saltney. Barry Cross Collection/Online Transport Archive

buses began in 1931, with the last route converted on 17 July 1937. To the north was Wallasey Corporation; here standard-gauge electric trams began operation, following the corporation's takeover and conversion of the lines operated by the Wallasey Tramways Co on 1 April 1901, on 17 March 1902. Eventually the corporation operated some twelve route miles, but these were converted to bus operation between 1929 and 30 November 1933.

To the south, Chester saw the company-owned horse trams taken over by the corporation on 1 January 1902. The company trams had operated over standard gauge but the corporation relaid the track to 3ft 6in to operate electric trams. Services began on 6 April 1903 and the system eventually extended over 3½ route miles. In all, some eighteen trams operated, with the system finally converted to bus operation on 15 February 1930.

Between 1902 and 1919 the Liverpool & Prescot Light Railway operated a line connecting the systems of Liverpool and St Helens. The company owned seven trams in total, but these were numbered 37-43 in the New St Helens & District Tramways Co fleet. Nos.42 and 43 were acquired in 1902 from BEC. Fitted with BEC SB650 trucks, these were originally ordered by Aberdeen Corporation but the order had been cancelled. Fitted with canopies in 1908, both passed to SLT in 1919. Barry Cross Collection/Online Transport Archive

Between 1899 and 1919, the tramways of St Helens were operated by the New St Helens & District Tramways Co. In 1900 Brush supplied twenty open-top bogie cars, Nos.17-36, to the company. All were fitted with Brill 22E bogies. Barry Cross Collection/Online Transport Archive

At Knotty Ash, the electric trams of Liverpool Corporation met those of the Liverpool & Prescot Light Railway. This line, which extended just over three route miles, opened on 25 June 1902 and possessed seven trams. These were owned by the company but formed part of the fleet of St Helens Corporation. On 1 October 1919, Liverpool Corporation took over the light railway, modernised it and extended corporation tram services to Prescot. The seven company-owned trams passed to the South Lancashire Tramways (SLT).

At Prescot, the light railway connected to the electric tramways that served St Helens. On 1 October 1898 the corporation extended the lease to the St Helens & District Tramways Co; to fund converting the existing steam-tram services to electric traction, the company was reconstituted and electric services were introduced on 19 July 1899. St Helens Corporation took over some nineteen route miles of standard-gauge electric tramway on the expiry of the lease, on 30 September 1919. Initially some modernising of track and equipment was undertaken, but trolleybuses were introduced in 1927 and the last trams operated on 23 March 1929.

To the south-east of St Helens was Warrington; here the corporation introduced standard-gauge electric trams on 21 April 1902. In all, the network extended eventually over almost seven route miles with twenty-seven trams being operated, the last six of which were acquired in 1919. As late as 1933 one of the 1919 Brush-built cars was rebuilt but the system did not last much longer, with the last trams operating on 28 August 1935.

At Blackbrook, the trams of St Helens met the company-owned trams of SLT. Ultimately the company operated over almost forty route miles over standard-gauge lines owned by a number of local authorities; one of these was Farnworth UDC, which had independently operated electric trams on its own and later on Kearsley UDC's behalf from 9 January 1902 until the lines were leased to SLT on 1 April 1906. The first section of the SLT system, from Lowton St Mary's to Four Lane Ends, began operation on 20 October 1902. From 1 January 1906 the company was taken over by the Lancashire United Tramways, although the name South Lancashire Tramways/ Transport was retained through the tram and trolleybus era. Although Bolton took over the routes in Farnworth to Walkden and the Black Horse in the late 1920s, the remainder of the SLT system remained

In 1927 St Helens Corporation acquired two single-deck cars from Wigan Corporation; originally numbered Nos.30 and 31, the two were renumbered 13 and 14 in 1929. The two cars had been supplied to Wigan by ERTCW during 1904 and 1905 and were fitted with Brill 22E bogies. Maurice O'Connor/NTM

In 1902 Milnes supplied Warrington with twenty-one open-top double-deck cars; Nos.1-10 were fitted with Brill 21E trucks, whereas Nos.11-21 received Brush A. The latter were probably fitted with replacement 21E trucks by 1920. The majority of the open-top cars, including No.7, received top covers between 1905 and 1907 and a number were further modernised in the late 1920s. Latterly No.7 reverted to open-top condition. Barry Cross Collection/ Online Transport Archive

With the extension to Swinton under way in the background, SLT No.39 stands at the then Boothstown terminus. The line opened to Boothstown on 20 April 1905 and then to Swinton on 27 September 1906. No.39, seen in original condition, was one of forty-five open-top cars supplied to the company by Milnes in 1902. The majority of the cars were subsequently fitted with top covers. Barry Cross Collection/Online Transport Archive

Farnworth UDC briefly operated electric trams. Never a financial success, the operation was subsequently leased to SLT. One of the UDC's fleet of thirteen open-top double-decks cars is seen at the junction of Buckley Lane and Albert Road. The trams were built by Milnes and fitted with Brill 22E bogies. All thirteen passed to SLT on 1 April 1906 and became SLT Nos.46-58. Eleven were fitted with new EE open-balcony bodies between 1923 and 1926, and all received replacement bogies. Six were sold for further service to Bolton Corporation in 1933. Barry Cross Collection/Online Transport Archive

intact until 3 August 1930 when the route from Ashton to Atherton was converted to trolleybus operation. The rest of the network was progressively converted to bus and trolleybus operation, with the final company-owned trams operating over the routes from Bolton to Leigh and from Leigh to Lowton St Mary's on 16 December 1933.

The SLT system connected at Ashton and Hindley to the electric trams operated by Wigan Corporation and the systems came into close proximity at Platt Bridge, but never formed a connection there. Wigan was unusual in operating both 3ft 6in and standard-gauge trams. Initially narrow-gauge trams were introduced by the corporation on 25 January 1901. Although the Wigan Tramways Co planned to convert its network to electric

Pictured at Melverley, Wigan Corporation No.76 was one of a batch of eighteen cars supplied by ERTCW during 1904 and 1905. Fitted with Brill 22E bogies, No.76 was one of at least eight of the type rebuilt between 1921 and 1926. Barry Cross Collection/Online Transport Archive

During 1901 and 1902, Milnes supplied Salford Corporation with 100 open-top trams. These were fitted with Brill 21E trucks. No.42 is illustrated here in original condition. This car was one of fifty-five converted as fully enclosed Box cars between 1926 and 1929. Renumbered 242, it remained in service until the 1937/38 financial year. All 100 had been withdrawn by the middle of 1939. Barry Cross Collection/Online Transport Archive

traction, these were thwarted by the corporation takeover on 1 October 1902. The corporation then converted the standard-gauge steam-operated routes, with the first electric trams operating on 4 October 1905; the first conversion from narrow gauge was completed on 5 July 1905, with standard-gauge trams taking over the Standish route. Following extensions, the Wigan system reached its peak extent in April 1906. At this date it comprised 6½ route miles of 3ft 6in and eighteen miles of 4ft 8 ½in (of which just over six route miles were leased). The corporation continued to operate two gauges to the early 1920s; from 1923 onwards the surviving 3ft 6in gauge routes were either converted to standard gauge or to trolleybus. The last narrow-gauge trams operated in 1926, and the standard-gauge routes were converted to bus operation from 1928 through to abandonment on 28 March 1931.

Further to the east, the SLT system also connected into the corporation-owned tramways of Salford at Swinton, Pendlebury and Worsley. Following the takeover of the horse tramways within its boundaries, Salford Corporation began operating electric trams on 4 October 1901. Apart from those within its borough boundaries, the corporation also operated over track leased from councils in Eccles, Pendlebury, Prestwich, Swinton and Whitefield. Salford's system was interlinked with that of Manchester, although relations with the larger city were not always harmonious. The Salford fleet reached its maximum extent in the 1920s when some 230 standard-gauge trams were operated over a network of forty route miles but, from the early

Two of the seven electric trams operated by the Trafford Park Estates, Nos.5 and 10, are pictured during the company's relatively short history. No.5 was one of five open-top cars fitted with Brill 21E trucks (Nos.5-9), and No.10 was supplied with Brill 27G bogies; both were built by BEC and all seven cars passed to Salford Corporation in 1905. No.10, as Salford No.161, was rebuilt by the corporation in 1924; subsequently renumbered 151 and later 380, it survived until March 1947. Nos.5-9 became Salford Nos.173-177; No.173 was acquired with a top cover and was further rebuilt in the 1920s as fully enclosed. No.173 survived until the 1938/39 financial year, with the other four all withdrawn by 1936. Barry Cross Collection/Online Transport Archive

1930s, the network contracted. If war had not intervened, the corporation had intended to replace the final tram routes during 1940, but war put these plans into abeyance and so some sixty-one trams, most in poor condition, soldiered on until peace was restored.

To the south of Salford was the Trafford Park Estate; this industrial area was a centre of manufacturing with both Manchester and Salford corporations operating into the estate to convey workers to and from the factories.

Linked to the corporation routes was the line inherited by the Trafford Park Estates Co from the British Gas Traction Co, which had operated the route using gas-powered trams, in 1899. In all, the company inherited some 2¼ route miles. Electric trams were first introduced to part of the route on 14 July 1903; the electrified section was taken over by Manchester and Salford corporations on 31 October 1905 and survived until 1946. Gas-powered trams operated over the section from Trafford Park to Barton until 1 May 1908. From then on the company operated a conventional steam-hauled passenger service until final replacement by buses in 1921.

As with Salford, electric tramcars were introduced to Manchester following the corporation's takeover of the horse-tram network within its boundaries. The first electric trams operated on 6 June 1901 and the network eventually expanded to encompass 123 route miles, excluding lines of other operators over which Manchester trams operated on joint services, at its peak with a maximum fleet of 952 passenger cars. As such, Manchester was the third-

Manchester Corporation No.495 was one of numbers of cars – Nos.487-511 – supplied as open-top cars by Milnes in 1902. Fitted with Brill 21E trucks, all bar No.499 were fitted with top covers by April 1914. No.495 was one of the earliest of the type withdrawn, during the 1924/25 financial year, but the last of the type survived until the 1937/38 financial year. Barry Cross Collection/Online Transport Archive

largest system in Britain. Apart from the track in Manchester itself, the network also encompassed track owned by ten UDCs, including Altrincham and Gorton. Modernising and expanding the Manchester system continued until the late 1920s, with the last route completed, to East Didsbury, opening on 13 December 1926.

In 1928 R. Stuart Pilcher was appointed general manager; in Edinburgh he had modernised the trams but, in Manchester, the future of the tramway system was less secure. Although new trams were

Stockport Corporation No.23 was one of a batch of ten open-top cars, Nos.21-30, supplied by ERTCW during 1902 and 1903. Barry Cross Collection/Online Transport Archive

In 1899 Brush supplied twenty-six single-deck trams to the Oldham, Ashton & Hyde Electric Tramway Co. Fitted with Peckham 8A trucks, the cars often operated with one of the twelve single-deck trailer cars also made by Brush. Four of the latter were motorised in 1900, with the remaining eight trailers sold to Middleton Electric Traction Co in 1903. The OA&H also operated twelve open-top double-deck trams. Barry Cross Collection/Online Transport Archive

acquired, the first conversion occurred in March/April 1930 when route 53 was progressively converted to bus operation. Although there was piecemeal conversion during the 1930s, some routes being replaced by trolleybus after 1935 (a policy opposed by Pilcher), it was not until 17 August 1938 that he produced a report outlining the final conversion of the tramways over a three-year period.

SHMD No.12, seen here at Mossley station, was one of ten, Nos.11-20, open-top trams supplied by BEC in 1904. Fitted with McGuire 21EM trucks, the majority received open-balcony top covers from 1912 onwards. Although No.12 was withdrawn before the Second World War, sister car No.18 was one of the fleet that survived post-war. Barry Cross Collection/Online Transport Archive

Seven open-top double-deck cars and two single-deck cars, one of which was acquired from Sheffield Corporation, were operated by the Urban Electric Supply Co in Glossop. No.3, seen here on the opening day, was supplied by Milnes in 1903; like the other six double-deck cars, it was fitted with a Milnes-built truck. Barry Cross Collection/ Online Transport Archive

However, war meant the anticipated conversion date of 1942 was impractical and, apart from one conversion (route 51 Miller Street to Oxford Road on 23 March 1940), the wartime years actually saw services reintroduced. The last was the extension of route 13 from Chorlton to Southern Cemetery on 21 December 1942.

To the south of Manchester, but connected to it through lines at Levenshulme and Reddish Lane, was the system operated by Stockport Corporation. Centred on Mersey Square, Stockport trams operated a network of 14½ route miles. Electric operation began on 26 August 1901. The Stockport system was operated by a fleet of double-deck cars, and its fate was inextricably linked to that of Manchester. Although a short section – from Gatley to Cheadle – was converted to bus on 21 September 1931, the bulk of the system was intact in September 1939.

The tramways of Stockport also connected with those of a further operator; at Gee Cross a link was established with the network operated by Stalybridge, Hyde, Mossley & Dukinfield Tramways & Electricity Board (SHMD). The line from Hyde to Gee Cross was originally part of the BET-owned Oldham, Ashton & Hyde Electric Tramway. This standard-gauge route ran from Gee Cross to Hathershaw, on the boundary with Oldham, via Hyde, Denton and Ashton, a distance of seven miles, and services began on 12 June 1899. In all, the company used some forty-two trams plus twelve trailers, of which four of the former were acquired from Middleton. Company operation ended on 2 July 1921, with the route passing to Ashton, Manchester and SHMD.

Operating the SHMD's own network began on 21 May 1904. In all, the SHMD network extended over twenty-one route miles but, from the late 1920s, conversion to bus began. In 1931 the decision was

Although the majority of the trams operated by Ashton-under-Lyne Corporation were double-deck, there were six single-deckers acquired new in 1905, Nos.13-18 (supplied by ERTCW on Brill 21E trucks), and two acquired from Middleton Electric Traction, Nos.39 and 40, in 1921. Barry Cross Collection/Online Transport Archive

made to convert all the surviving routes and, by 1939, the system had contracted to the routes to Denton, over which the through service to Manchester (operated by Manchester cars only since 1935) ran, and to Gee Cross for the through service to Stockport. To operate the Gee Cross route, SHMD kept a handful of trams. Undoubtedly the outbreak of war prolonged the SHMD operation.

A short distance to the east of the SHMD system and actually situated in Derbyshire, Glossop was home to a small standard-gauge tramway operated by the

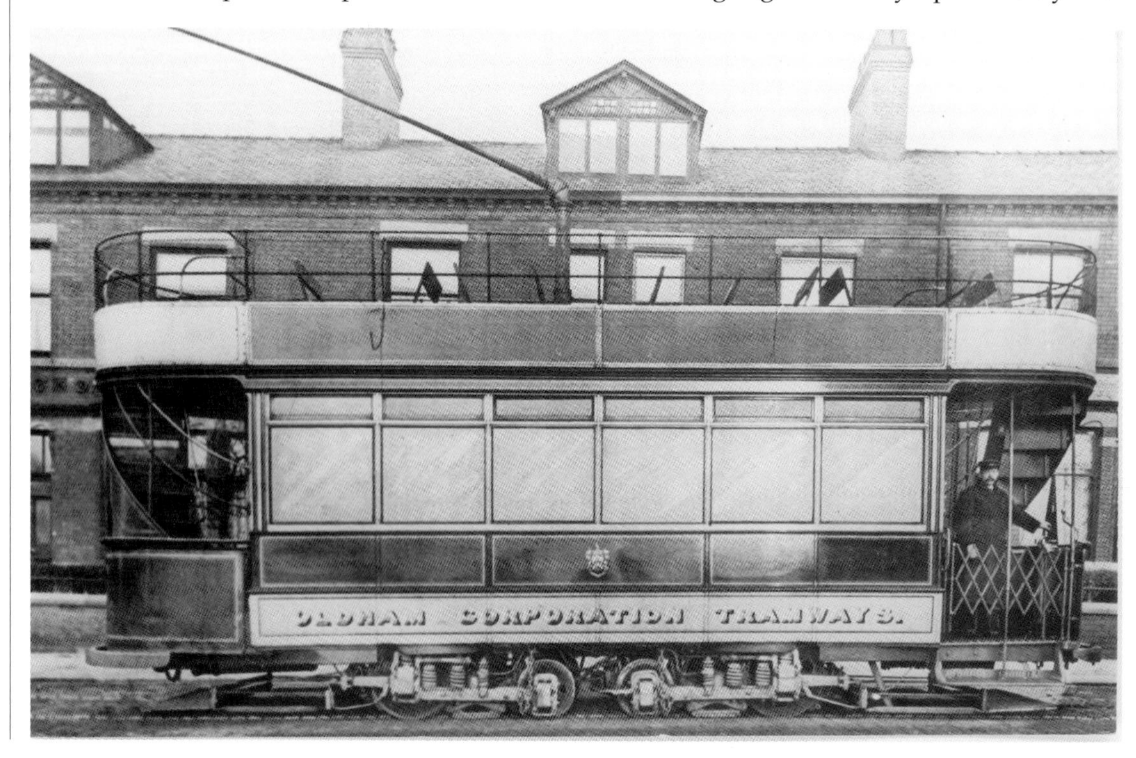

Oldham No.3 was supplied by ERTCW in 1900; its original Brill 22E bogies were replaced by Brill 27G bogies in 1907. It was withdrawn and scrapped, in Manchester, in 1940. Barry Cross Collection/Online Transport Archive

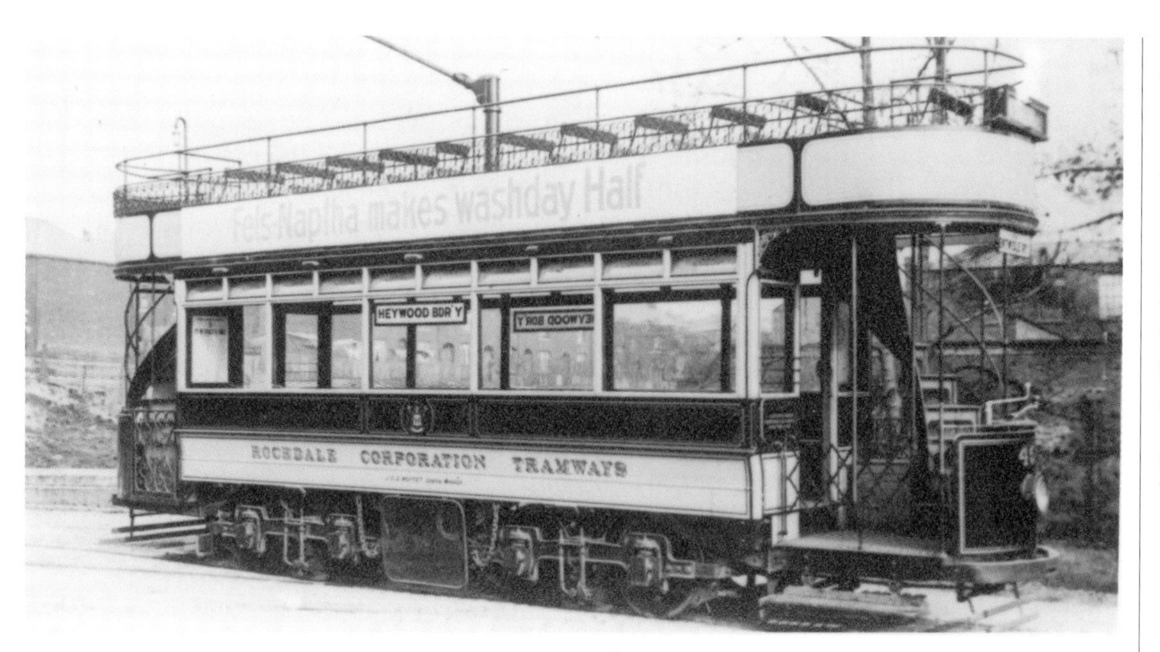

Rochdale No.45 was one of six cars, Nos.44-49, built by Brush in 1905 and fitted with Brush D bogies. In all, Rochdale owned ninety-four passenger trams; the last of these were ten fully enclosed cars delivered between 1925 and 1928. Barry Cross Collection/Online Transport Archive

Urban Electricity Supply Co. Operation began on the two-route system on 21 August 1903 and eventually nine trams were operated, the last of which was acquired from Sheffield Corporation in 1918. The system was replaced by buses operated by the North Western Road Car Co on 24 December 1927.

Reverting to the area of Lancashire to the east of Manchester, Ashton Corporation operated a compact network of routes, with electric services starting on 16 August 1902. In 1921, the year in which the last new trams were acquired, the corporation took over the section of the erstwhile Oldham, Ashton & Hyde Electric Tramway in the town. Through services were operated to Manchester and, following the 1921 takeover, to Oldham via Hathershaw. Converting Ashton's standard-gauge fleet to bus and trolleybus began in 1931 and the last trams operated on 1 March 1938.

To the north of Ashton was

Middleton Electric Traction Co No.25 was the last of four single-deck combination cars supplied to the company by Brush in 1902. Fitted with Brush bogies, the four cars had a short life in Lancashire, being sold to Potteries Motor Traction in 1907. Barry Cross Collection/Online Transport Archive

Oldham; here corporation-owned, standard-gauge electric cars began operation on 15 December 1900 over the Chadderton to Rochdale Road route. The company-operated horse and steam-tram routes passed to Oldham Corporation in 1901 and were converted to electric operation. In all, the network eventually extended to 24½ route miles. The last new extension opened on 4 June 1914 but the system expanded slightly on 9 August 1925 when a section of the Middleton Electric Traction Co, from Chadderton to Mills Hill Bridge, was taken over. Although the first conversions to bus occurred in 1928, despite the purchase of twelve new fully enclosed trams in 1926, the final decision to convert the surviving routes to bus operation was only taken in 1935.

The final two routes were scheduled for closure in September 1939 but war brought a reprieve; however, the section from the town centre to Shaws Wren Nest was converted to bus on 2 December 1939 as a result of the poor condition of the track.

Further to the north, but connected to the Oldham system at the Summit terminus, was the standard-gauge Rochdale system. The steam trams operated by the MBROT in the Rochdale area were taken over by the corporation in 1902. The corporation converted its lines to standard gauge and electrified them, with the first electric trams operating on 22 May 1902. With the final extension, from Royton to Bacup, opening in 1902, the Rochdale system eventually extended over just under twenty-seven route miles. The trams were progressively converted to municipal bus operation from 1930, with the last trams operating on 12 November 1932.

Sandwiched between Rochdale, Manchester to the south and Oldham to the east was Middleton. On 27 March 1902 the BET subsidiary, the Middleton Electric Traction Co, introduced standard-gauge electric trams. The company operated over 8½ route miles of track until 9 August 1925. On this date part of the company's lines passed to Oldham and Rochdale corporations, with Middleton Corporation acquiring the remainder with operation leased to Manchester Corporation. The corporation takeover introduced new through services. The ex-Middleton fleet was split between Manchester, Oldham and Rochdale corporations with SLT taking over one car. The ex-company routes were converted to bus operation between 1932 and 1935; the last to succumb, on 11 June 1935, was the route from Middleton to Oldham.

One of the consequences of the corporation takeover of the Middleton system was the opening, on 19 May 1928, of a connection between the ex-Middleton system and the electric trams serving Heywood at Hopwood along Heywood New Road (Manchester Corporation then operated a through service from Manchester to Heywood having taken over the lease of the Hopwood to Heywood section from Bury Corporation). Although Heywood

To introduce electric trams to Bury, Milnes built fourteen bogie and fourteen four-wheel open-top cars – Nos.1-14 and 15-28 respectively – in 1903. One of the latter is seen at the Jericho terminus. Barry Cross Collection/ Online Transport Archive

In 1899 ERTCW supplied forty open-top cars to Bolton, which were all fitted with Brill 21E trucks; heavily rebuilt, no fewer than eighteen of the type – but not No.26 illustrated here – were still in service in 1945. Barry Cross Collection/Online Transport Archive

Corporation had operated steam trams in succession to the MBROT, it leased operating its 3½ route miles to Bury and Rochdale corporations. Also leased to Bury Corporation were the eight route miles situated in Radcliffe UDC. Bury Corporation began operating standard-gauge electric trams on 3 June 1903 and in Radcliffe on 4 January 1905. The bulk of the Bury system, including its operations in Heywood and Radcliffe, were converted to bus between 1933

Seen in original condition in Darwen, Blackburn No.29 was one of eight open-top cars supplied by Milnes, on Brill 22E bogies, in 1899. Barry Cross Collection/Online Transport Archive

A Darwen tram pictured at the Hoddlesden terminus. The lightly trafficked route was finally converted on 13 October 1937, having been largely bus operated since 1930. Barry Cross Collection/ Online Transport Archive

Accrington No.16 was one of a batch of fourteen, Nos.5-18, open-balcony trams built by Brush and delivered in 1907. Originally fitted with Brush Conaty trucks, these were eventually replaced by Brush flexible trucks. Barry Cross Collection/ Online Transport Archive

and 1938. However, one through route, from Tottington to Walmersley, was still operational at the outbreak of war and this was supplemented by reintroducing the service to Starkies, along Manchester Road, on 20 September 1939. The fleet then comprised some twenty cars, but this was reduced in 1943 by the sale of four trams to Bolton.

In June 1899 the existing horse-tram operator in Bolton, E. Holden & Co, sold out to the corporation. On 9 December 1899 the first corporation electric trams

operated on routes to Great Lever, Tonge Moor and Toothill Bridge. The last wholly new extension, from Smithills to Westhoughton, opened on 19 December 1924, taking the corporation's network to more than 32¼ route miles, but the Bolton system expanded further through operating the Walkden and Farnworth sections under SLT's lease from Farnworth UDC after 1927. Although there had been a minor abandonment in Horwich before the First World War, with the closure of the Victoria Road loop, the process of tramway abandonment began in 1928 with the conversion of the short Darcy Lever route. During the 1930s, conversion to corporation-owned buses claimed more than half of the system with only some seventy-eight trams in service by the outbreak of war. The final peacetime conversion was the route to Halliwell, which was converted to bus on 13 August 1939; however, this was reversed on 1 April 1940 when the trams were restored to save fuel. Towards the end of the war, with the track condition giving serious concern, permission was granted by the Ministry of War Transport to convert the Farnworth and Walkden routes on 12 November 1944.

Although the trams of the Liverpool to Manchester corridor were predominantly standard gauge, there was a second

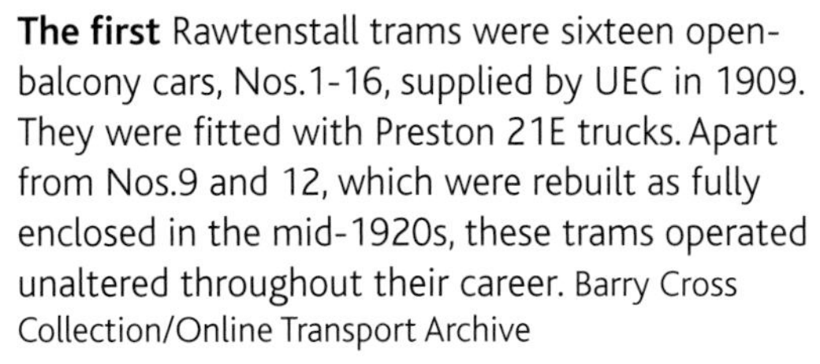

The first Rawtenstall trams were sixteen open-balcony cars, Nos.1-16, supplied by UEC in 1909. They were fitted with Preston 21E trucks. Apart from Nos.9 and 12, which were rebuilt as fully enclosed in the mid-1920s, these trams operated unaltered throughout their career. Barry Cross Collection/Online Transport Archive

network of electric tramways serving the area, from Blackburn to Colne, that were all 4ft 0in gauge. The first of these systems to begin electric operation was Blackburn Corporation on 20 March 1899 in place of the steam trams of the Blackburn Corporation Tramways Co. Following the conversion of the separate Blackburn & Over Darwen route, over which steam trams last operated on 16 October 1900, on 1 December 1900, the Blackburn system reached a peak extent of 14¾ route miles following the opening of extensions to Audley and Cherry Tree in 1903. Although no new trams were acquired after 1908, the system remained intact until the 1930s when both the Audley (on 13 February 1935) and Cherry Tree (on 31 March 1939) were converted to bus. These conversions saw the fleet's thirteen single-deck cars withdrawn.

The assets of the Blackburn & Over Darwen company were split with Darwen Corporation. Electric operation of the section in Darwen began on 16 October 1900, with powers to convert the existing steam line from Whitehall, south of the town, to the boundary with Blackburn having been obtained on 9 August 1900. The final extension, the steeply graded route to Hoddlesden, opened on 11 October 1901. This took the Darwen network to 4½ route miles. Despite powers being obtained in 1926 to operate buses, Darwen's system remained intact until the late 1930s.

To the east of Blackburn is Accrington. Electric operation by the corporation began on 1 January 1908 and the network, which included the routes taken over from the steam trams of the Accrington Corporation Steam Tramways Co in September 1907, as well as extensions to Oswaldtwistle and the cemetery, eventually extended to just over seven route miles. Although new trams were acquired as late as 1926, the entire system was converted to bus, with the last trams operating on 9 January 1932. Accrington owned forty-three passenger cars, all supplied by Brush; five were sold to the Llandudno & Colwyn Bay Electric Railway, one to Lytham St Annes Corporation, three to Southend-on-Sea Corporation and two to Sunderland Corporation.

Between 1901 and 1903 Milnes supplied thirty-eight open-top trams, Nos.1-38, to Burnley. Fitted originally with Brill 22E bogies, all received replacement Burnley bogies in 1914 and were fitted with open-balcony top covers (Nos.9-11 in 1910 and the remainder between 1911 and 1920). In all, Burnley operated seventy-two passenger trams, with the last new cars being five single-deckers supplied in 1921. Barry Cross Collection/Online Transport Archive

The last new trams acquired by Nelson were three lowbridge open-balcony double-deckers supplied by EE in 1925. These were acquired to replace three single-deck combination cars. Nelson owned twenty passenger cars during its thirty-year existence. Barry Cross Collection/Online Transport Archive

To the south, Haslingden also took over part of the assets of the Accrington Corporation Steam Tramways Co in September 1907. The steam trams lasted longer in Haslingden, not being withdrawn until 27 September 1908, with electric operation having started on 5 September of the same year. Electric tram operation over the three-mile route continued until replacement by buses on 30 April 1930. Accrington Corporation operated the route, although the replacement buses were provided by Haslingden Corporation.

The southern terminus of Haslingden's one route connected with the tramways of Rawtenstall Corporation. Following the 1908 purchase of the steam Rossendale Valley Tramways Co by Rawtenstall and Bacup corporations, electric trams began operation on 15 May 1909. In all, Rawtenstall operated, on behalf of itself and of Bacup Corporation (which owned no trams), some thirty-two trams, with the last new cars delivered in 1921. In all, the Rawtenstall network extended over some 11¾ route miles and the last electric trams operated on 31 March 1932, with an official ceremony a week later.

To the north of Rawtenstall and Bacup and to the east of Accrington (but physically separated from all three) is

The third constituent in the Burnley, Colne & Nelson Joint Committee was Colne Corporation following its takeover of the Colne & Trawden Light Railway Co. The company possessed twelve open-top double-deck cars. The first six, Nos.1-6, were supplied by Milnes in 1903 and were fitted with Milnes-built trucks. As No.6 is seen in open-top condition, the photograph must predate 1911 as all six of the batch received Milnes Voss-built open-balcony top covers that year. Barry Cross Collection/Online Transport Archive

In 1904, for the opening of Preston Corporation's electric services, ERTCW supplied thirty open-top trams: Nos.1-26 were fitted with Brill 21E trucks, and Nos.27-30 had Brill 22E bogies. One of the former is seen in original condition. Of the former, eighteen received short-top covers between 1907 and 1913. A number, probably nine in all, were fully enclosed between 1924 and 1928. Preston's last new trams were three built in the corporation's own workshops during 1928 and 1929 plus three acquired from Lincoln in 1929. Barry Cross Collection/Online Transport Archive

Burnley. Although the steam trams of the Burnley & District Tramways Co had been standard gauge, when the corporation took over and electrified the route, it selected 4ft 0in. The first section of the Burnley network began operation on 16 December 1901 and eventually the system extended over some thirteen route miles.

To the north of Burnley lies Nelson; here the corporation inaugurated its electric tramway on 23 February 1903. Part of the 3½ route miles owned by Nelson Corporation was leased to Burnley Corporation, and a short section of the route between the two towns was actually owned by Reedley Hallows Parish Council – the only parish council in Britain to own a stretch of tramway.

Beyond Nelson is Colne; the electric tramways that served the town began operation on 30 November 1903 under the ownership of the Colne & Trawden Light Railway Co. The corporation took over on 25 March 1914. The system extended over 5¼ route miles and the company possessed thirteen trams; the corporation invested in new trams after the takeover, with the last to enter service being three fully enclosed cars delivered in 1926.

The surviving tramways of Burnley, Colne and Nelson corporations merged to form part of the Burnley, Colne & Nelson Joint Transport Committee on 1 April 1933, but by this date the trams were

The first ten trams acquired by Lancaster Corporation in late 1902, Nos.1-10, were built locally by the Lancaster Railway Carriage & Wagon Co. A further two cars, Nos.11 and 12, were acquired from Milnes Voss in 1905. The trams were fitted with Brill 21E (Nos.1-10) and M&G 21EM (Nos.11 and 12) trucks. Of the twelve, six received open-balcony top covers between 1911 and 1913. The remaining six, including Nos.1, 10, 11 and 12, were converted to one-man-operated single-deck cars between 1917 and 1923; this condition is illustrated here. Barry Cross Collection/Online Transport Archive

in decline. Much of the Colne network, save for the through route towards Nelson, had been converted to bus in the late 1920s and two routes had closed in Burnley in 1932. Trams stopped operating in Colne and Nelson on 6 January 1934 and in Burnley on 7 May 1935.

To the east of the Fylde coast, Preston Corporation built a 10½-route mile standard-gauge network to replace the earlier two 3ft 6in gauge horse tramways. The first electric trams operated on 7 June 1904. Preston was also home to one of Britain's most important tramcar manufacturers – EE (from 1918) and its predecessors (Electric Railway & Tramway Carriage Works [ERTCW] and UEC). In all, some 8,350 tramcars were made in the town. Inevitably the corporation supported its home business and, between 1904 and 1914, thirty-nine trams were acquired from ERTCW and UEC. The Preston system closed on 15 December 1935.

The single-deck combination car was a feature of a number of tramway operators in north-west England. In 1903, BET acquired five of the type, Nos.8-12, for operation in Barrow. BET owned twenty-eight trams during its sixteen-year operation at Barrow, and the corporation acquired twenty-two more – including a further four combination cars acquired from Southport in 1920. Barry Cross Collection/Online Transport Archive

In 1912 the City of Carlisle Electric Tramways Co acquired twelve trams from UEC on Brill 21E trucks to replace the trams supplied by ERTCW in 1900. Nos.1-8 were double-deck and 9-12 were single-deck. These were the last wholly new trams acquired by the company. Barry Cross Collection/ Online Transport Archive

Further to the north, apart from the horse tramway of the Lancaster & District Tramways Co, which was never electrified, Lancaster Corporation operated a three route mile system of electric trams from 14 January 1903 to 31 March 1930. In all, the corporation bought twelve standard-gauge cars.

Historically there was a part of Lancashire detached from the remainder of the county. This was centred on Barrow-in-Furness. On 23 December 1899 BET acquired the steam-town operations of the 4ft 0in gauge Barrow-in-Furness Tramways Co. The 5½-mile network was converted to electric traction, with the first trams operating on 6 February 1904. Unusually operated directly by BET rather than by a subsidiary between then and 1 January 1920, when the corporation took over, the final trams operated on 5 April 1932.

The northernmost tramway in the region, as well as the only one to serve Cumberland, was the City of Carlisle Electric Tramways Co. Operation of the 3ft 6in gauge system began on 30 June 1900. Initially fifteen electric trams operated over a network of 5¾ route miles. The bulk of the fleet was renewed in 1912 but three cars – one from Ilkeston Corporation and the other two believed to have been based around trucks acquired from Ilkeston fitted with new EE bodies – entered service between 1920 and 1925. The system was converted to bus on 21 November 1931.

BLACKBURN

The onset of war in September 1939 suspended the tramway abandonment programme; a five-year plan had been agreed in 1938. Four routes – to Wilpshire (which had been scheduled for conversion in March 1940), Church, Preston New Road and the joint service to Darwen – remained, operated by forty-eight double-deck trams. The city centre, with its one-way system, resulted in a complex network of lines.

The Blackburn trams suffered damage during the war. The most serious incident occurred on 31 August 1940 when tram No.52 was damaged during a German raid; the driver was killed and the conductor died later in hospital. Although there was maintenance of track during the war years, including buying new track, certain sections were in poor condition. Part of the Wilpshire route was replaced by buses for a brief period during summer 1944 to permit the repair of the track.

In August 1944 the general manager, A. Potts, who had been appointed in 1938, issued a report recommending converting the Preston New Road route to bus. Although not progressed immediately, the corporation reiterated its policy of abandonment. Converting the Preston New Road route, which had originally been slated for autumn 1945 – it was announced as 'imminent' in September 1945 but reported as delayed in the *Northern Daily Telegraph* in October 1945 – finally took place on 5 January 1946. The last car from the Preston New Road terminus was No.42, which departed at 10pm. Although the route itself was closed, football specials continued to operate to Ewood Park until 19 April 1946, when Blackburn Rovers played their last home game of the season.

On 4 September 1946, No.39 and No.57 were involved in a collision slightly west of the Church terminus; although no passengers were injured, both cars sustained damage. Later in the year, as spare parts became problematic, a number of cars were cannibalised to supply parts for the remainder of the fleet.

On 5 October 1946 Darwen converted

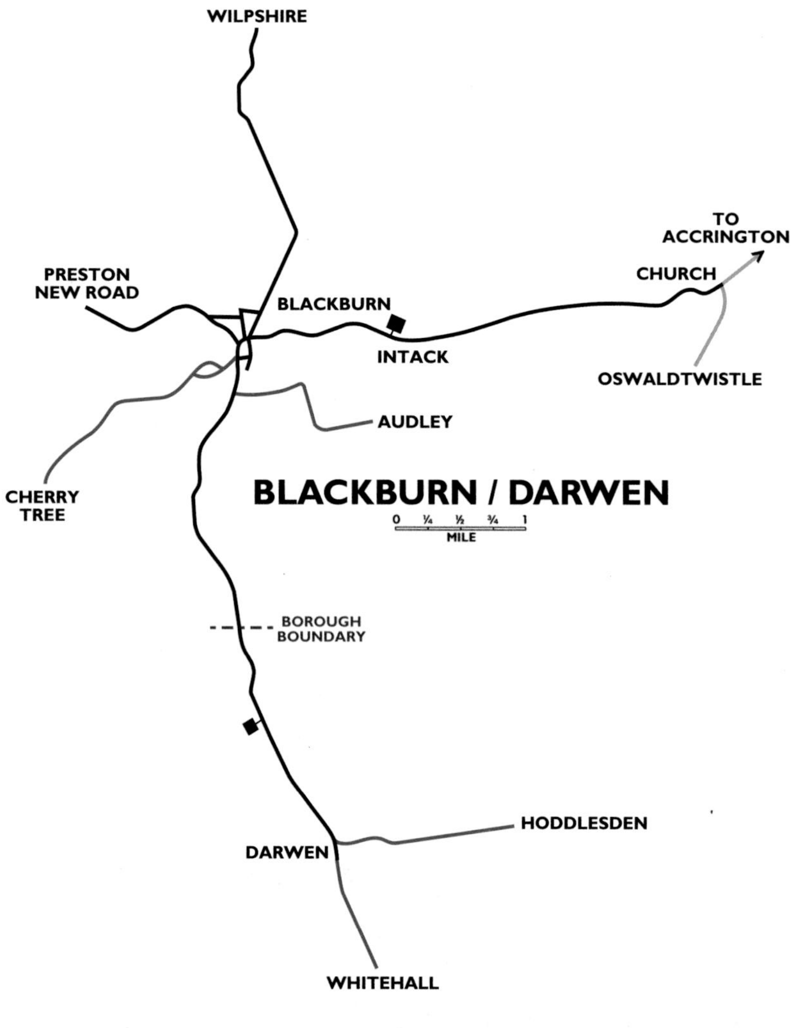

On 18 April 1949 members of the LRTL undertook a tour of the system. Here tour car No.41 is pictured on the original crossover at the boundary with Darwen. When the Darwen system closed in October 1946, a new crossover was installed slightly to the south of this location. John Meredith/Online Transport Archive

During the LRTL tour of the system on 18 April 1949, No.53, one of the last of the open-top cars to remain in service, was brought out of Intack depot, in a partly dismantled state, for the party to photograph. John Meredith/Online Transport Archive

One of the eight 'Siemens' cars, No.34, is seen at Intack. The last of these cars survived until October 1945. Maurice O'Connor/ NTM

its section of the through route to bus; Blackburn trams, however, continued to operate to the borough boundary. From 2 to 5 November 1946, Blackburn staff took industrial action over the schedule for the replacement buses on the Preston New Road, which temporarily ended all operations.

Although conversion remained the official policy, it was not until August 1947 that an application was made to the Ministry of War Transport to convert the system. New buses were ordered later in the year. An indication that the trams were now living on borrowed time was the withdrawal of No.43 following an accident on 6 November 1947.

The next closure was the route to Wilpshire; this last operated on 21 December 1947. At the same time the corporation announced that delays in the delivery of new buses would result in the remaining routes surviving longer than anticipated. By the end of the year, the operational fleet had been reduced to some thirty cars. The delay meant limited track repairs were undertaken during 1948, although elsewhere preparations for the final conversion were in hand. Another tram to succumb following accident damage was No.67, withdrawn on 25 September 1948. By the end of 1948 the fleet was further reduced – to twenty-five cars – and the General Manager expressed concern over the state of certain sections of track.

Following Potts' recommendation at the end of 1948, the rural section between Intack and Church was converted to bus on 16 January 1949. This closure saw seven cars withdrawn, reducing the fleet to eighteen.

The next section to succumb was that to the Darwen boundary, which last operated on 2 July 1949. Final abandonment occurred on 3 September 1949 with the conversion of the line to Intack. The official last car, suitably decorated, was No.74. No Blackburn tram survived into preservation, with the majority of the fleet dismantled at Intack depot. This closure marked the end of the last part of the one-time 4ft 0in gauge network of east Lancashire tramways.

Depots

Blackburn had two depots during the electric era, although the one at Simmons Street was closed before 1902. The main depot and workshop was located at Intack, dating originally to 28 May 1887. The existing tram depot was extended to the west in 1926 to provide accommodation for buses. The depot and works survived until final closure of the system on 3 September 1949.

Closures

5 January 1946	Blackburn to Preston New Road
21 December 1947	Blackburn to Wilpshire
16 January 1949	Intack to Church
2 July 1949	Blackburn to Darwen boundary
3 September 1949	Blackburn to Intack

Blackburn Fleet

28-35

These eight cars, known as the 'Siemens' cars after the supplier of their electrical equipment, were the first electric tramcars supplied to Blackburn Corporation. Built in 1899 by Milnes with Brill 22E bogies, the cars were open top and unvestibuled when new. They were rebuilt between 1914 and 1921 when they were fitted with extended lower-deck canopies and vestibules, but remained open top until withdrawal. The original Siemens equipment was also replaced. Latterly, they served as extras or football specials. Five were withdrawn towards the end of the war, with the remaining three taken out of service by October 1945. Their early demise was because they were the last cars to retain maximum-traction bogies and thus incurred higher maintenance costs.

36-75

In 1901 Milnes delivered a further batch of forty cars, this time on Peckham 14B equal wheel bogies. Delivered as open-top cars, Nos.45, 49 and 61 received fully enclosed top covers in 1907, followed by No.62 in 1912. The remainder of the type were fully enclosed between 1923 and 1935 with the exception of Nos.36, 47, 51, 53-55, 59 and 66. These eight remained open top until withdrawal; Nos.53 and 59, which succumbed in January 1949, were the last to remain in service. All were withdrawn between late 1946 (when a number succumbed to provide spare parts) and the closure of the system on 3 September 1949.

Pictured on Blackburn Road, on the long Church route, No.46 was one of forty cars supplied by Milnes that formed the core of the fleet from 1901 until closure, some having received new or second-hand motors.
F.E.J. Ward/Online Transport Archive

Standard No.28 pictured in inclement weather on South Promenade on 16 April 1949. This was one of the last open-balcony 'Standards' to survive, not being scrapped until April 1958. John Meredith/Online Transport Archive

BLACKPOOL

Although two short sections of route had been converted to bus operation before the war, Blackpool emerged post-war with a fleet of some 200 cars, the bulk of which had been delivered during the 1930s, operating over 18 route miles. Its manager, Walter Luff, believed the tramcar had a future. There remained doubts about the future of the town routes but the authorisation to relay the Marton route, finally given in January 1947 with work starting in June 1949, was a good sign.

Luff's positive views were quoted in *Transport World* during summer 1945: 'Blackpool's trams have been operating extremely satisfactorily during the war years, and it is by no means certain that the change to trolleybuses at one time suggested for the Marton route will take place.' In fact, Luff was keener to experiment with more modern tram equipment, and he ordered a set of equipment from Maley & Taunton (M&T). The possibility of converting the Marton route, however, rumbled on; in early 1946 it was again under active consideration but it was noted that the cost of tramway renewal was £12,000 less than the cost of the replacement trolleybuses and offered a fifteen rather than a ten-year life. Nos.208 and 303 were experimentally fitted with variable automatic multinotch brakes and acceleration control (VAMBAC) with resilient wheel trucks during 1946/47 to test the new equipment; the conversion was made permanent in 1953.

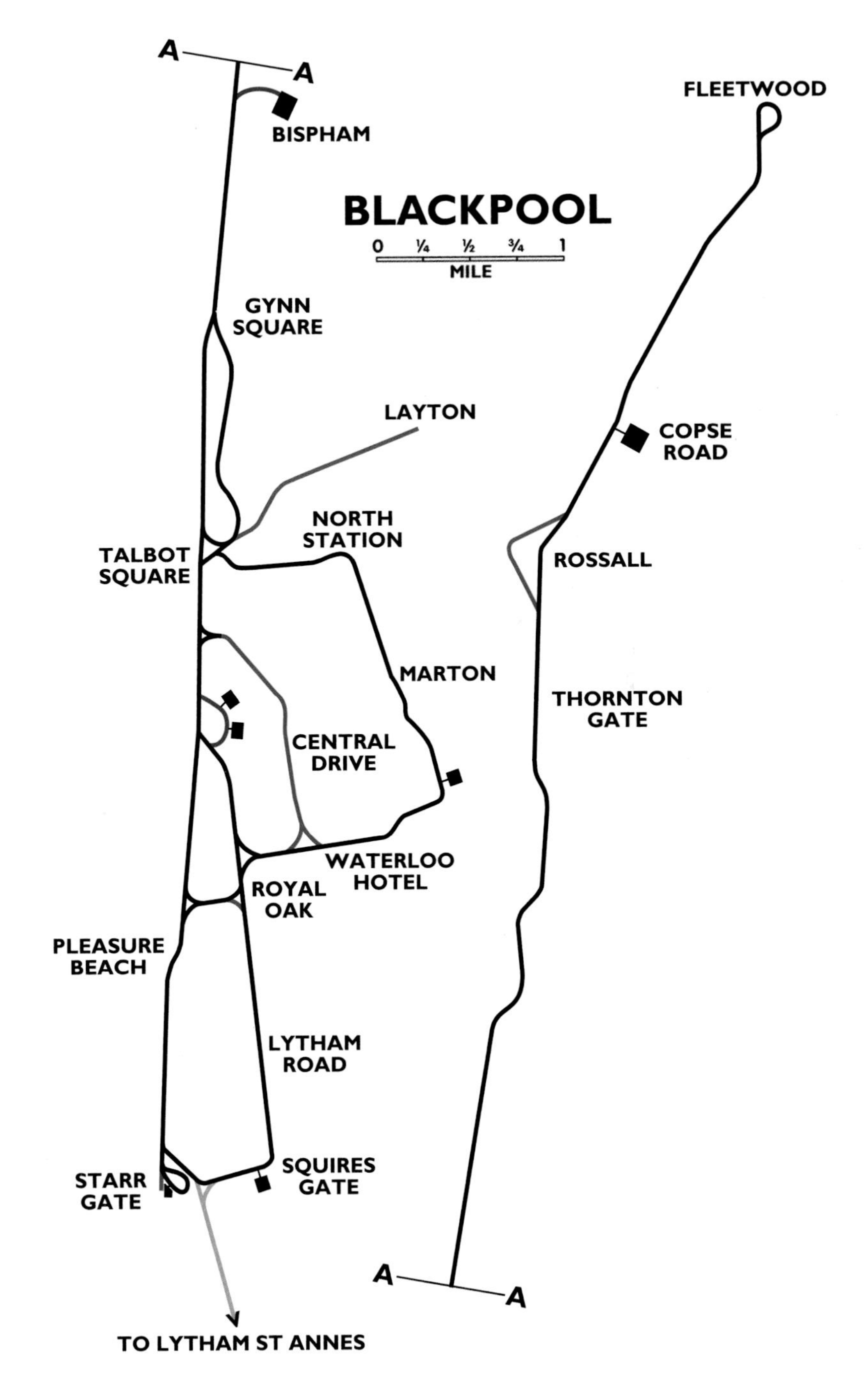

Two railcoaches, Nos.208 and 303, were fitted experimentally with VAMBAC to test the equipment for use on the Marton route. Here the former emerges from Rigby Road depot on 17 April 1949 before operating an LRTL tour. John Meredith/ Online Transport Archive

In early 1949 there were proposals – never progressed – to extend the Fleetwood line to Lancaster. On 1 May 1949 the coal sidings at Thornton Gate were closed. The sidings became the location of the new permanent way yard in early 1963, allowing Copse Road depot to be closed and sold. On 17 June 1949 the remaining section of the abandoned Layton route, in Talbot Road beyond North Station, was covered over; this had been retained latterly to provide an emergency connection between the Promenade route and the North Station terminus of services from Fleetwood along Dickson Road. More positive news, however, was an order for twenty new trams; this was eventually increased to twenty-five single-deck 50ft-long cars with tenders due to be received no later than 15 February 1950 (it was subsequently reported that ten tenders had been received). The first of the 10-21 batch of trams due to receive VAMBAC control, No.21, was so equipped in late summer 1949.

The Coronation class was delivered during 1952 and 1953. When new, as illustrated here, the cars were fitted with M&T HS44 bogies and Crompton Parkinson VAMBAC. Unfortunately the type never proved wholly successful. Phil Tatt/Online Transport Archive

By spring 1951 progress in converting the twelve 'Sun Saloons' of 1939 to VAMBAC with resilient wheel trucks was progressing; alongside experimental No.208, Nos.17-21 had been completed. This process continued until late spring 1952 when the last two, Nos.11 and 13, were completed. Nos.10-21 were based at Marton depot, where they were joined by No.208 in early 1952 for operation over the Marton route.

Summer 1952 witnessed the turning circle at Starr Gate being slightly enlarged; this had been one of three introduced in 1937, the other two being sited at the Pleasure Beach and Little Bispham. On 7 August 1952 a test was held to prove that modern trams could safely negotiate the curve at Whitegate Drive on the Marton route; there was concern that the length and width of the new cars being delivered were too great. The new Roberts-built trams, with No.304 the first delivered, were the first 8ft-wide trams operated by Blackpool; previously the maximum width had been 7ft 6in. The extra six inches needed a greater separation between the running lines but Blackpool had been progressively undertaking this as the lines were relaid from 1933 onwards. The process was completed on the Promenade route in 1948.

By autumn 1952, the new Coronation cars were entering service. No.308 was delivered on 17 October with Nos.304-07 operational. On the Marton route, the VAMBAC-equipped cars were supplemented by Nos.212/19/222/69/72/83, all of which had been fitted with swivelling trolleyheads; in contrast, No.208 had reverted to a fixed trolleyhead and so was no longer compatible with the Marton route. The delivery of the Coronation cars allowed older cars to be withdrawn and stored in Blundell Street, including some of the surviving 'Standards'. It was not until 25 July that the first Standard operation of 1953 was noted when No.41 was in use on the Marton route. During summer 1953, six of the type, Nos.35, 41, 153/47/52/59, were recorded in passenger service.

The new year heralded the dawn of a new era with the retirement, on 20 June, of Walter Luff; he was succeeded by Joseph Franklin. Just before Luff's retirement, however, the Promenade route suffered damage on 7 March when

Towards the end of 1957 a number of 'Standards' were offered for sale as scrap; they were moved to the sidings at Thornton Gate on 29 January 1958. Here the trams await their fate. R.L. Wilson Collection/Online Transport Archive

the highest tide ever recorded, 32ft 4in, damaged the tramway. Franklin inherited nineteen Standard cars, Nos.28, 40-42, 48, 49, 99, 100/43-45/47/51-53/55/58-60/77, with a number having been scrapped over the previous few years. During the summer, the numbers of passengers carried saw the surviving cars pressed into service; on 31 July 1954, for example, Nos.41, 48, 49, 143/47/58/59 all operated on the Promenade and Lytham Road services.

The first car to carry Franklin's name as general manager was Balloon No.259; it also appeared in a new livery. The single-deck cars had been gradually repainted in a new livery for a couple of years and, by summer 1954, only Nos.167-75, 206/13/74/90 were in the old predominantly green livery. No.207 emerged later in 1954 in a further revised singe-deck livery, similar to that adopted on No.259. It was decided to scrap thirteen double and five single-deck cars that had been out of use for some time, although not all succumbed; those that were scrapped as a result included 'Standards' Nos.36, 45, 51, 99, 100/48-51/55/56 and Pantograph car No.176 (which had been used for passenger flow experiments). No.167 was converted to a works car at the same time, and Standard No.144 escaped scrapping, being preserved in the US.

A further threat to the town services was defeated on 30 March 1955 when, following a two-hour debate, the town council agreed to keep the Lytham Road service. Later in 1955 double-deck cars appeared in Fleetwood for the first time; to counter concerns about capacity, a shuttle service using two double-deck cars launched on 5 July 1955 from Fleetwood Ferry to Broadwater. The new service operated on Fleetwood market days – Tuesdays and Fridays – during the morning and evening peak and at lunchtime. Less positive news was that the track in Squires Gate, used for the circular tour until the outbreak of war and by Lytham St Annes cars to access their depot, was covered over.

During 1956, some Balloon double-deck cars emerged with modified front indicators; the first so treated were Nos.240/45/50/52/53/55-57. The annual illuminations saw, for the first time, the use of double-deckers on illumination tours. 'Standards' Nos.41, 42, 48, 143/47/58 were among the cars used; in 1959 Nos.158 and 159 were fitted with permanent illuminations, keeping them until withdrawal in 1966.

On 22 February 1957 the council approved expenditure of £2,500 to fund an experiment in trailer operation; work was undertaken on Nos.275/76 to convert them into a twin-car set. It was also decided to reintroduce a circular tour for the first time since 1939; this involved uncovering the eastbound track in Squires Gate Lane (covered over in 1955). Four types of tram were tested over the uncovered section during May. The new service was launched on 9 July and, between then and 19 September (when the service ended for the year), 1,019 trips were made with a total of 50,296 passengers carried. The end of the year saw the number of 'Standards' further reduced with Nos.28, 42, 145/52/53/77 offered for scrap. The six were moved from Marton depot to Thornton Gate on 29 January 1958; all were scrapped by the end of April.

More positive was the first operation, late on 18 January 1958, of the test twin-car set between Starr Gate and Fleetwood. Summer 1958 needed continued use of 'Standards' with Nos.41, 48, 49, 147/58/59 noted in service. One of the other nine survivors, No.143, was rebuilt as works car No.3 during the summer; it was fitted with a diesel engine to permit independent operation. In theory, the new works car was to replace existing works car No.4, but this car was kept at Rigby Road, for operation on the section south to Starr Gate. Another works car, weedkiller No.7, was withdrawn and scrapped at Thornton Gate (in early 1960); one of its tanks was retained and, placed on a truck, formed a trailer that could be towed by the corporation's electric locomotive.

Although the twin-car set was stored over the winter, having last operated in mid-October 1958, such was its success

In 1959 two of the surviving 'standard' cars, Nos.158 and 159, were fitted permanently with lights for use during the annual Blackpool illuminations. In this guise they survived until 1966. Harry Luff/Online Transport Archive

Following the experimental conversion of Nos.275/76 into a motor and trailer set, Blackpool bought a batch of trailers to operate with modified railcoaches. No.T5 is pictured at Fleetwood following conversion into a permanently coupled bidirectional set with power car No.275. J. Joyce/Online Transport Archive

that, on 7 January 1959, it was decided to seek tenders for supplying ten trailers. During 1958, the set had carried more than 96,000 passengers. Later in the year tenders from Metropolitan-Cammell-Weymann (MCW) (at £4,833 per trailer body) and M&T (at £2,797 per pair of bogies) were accepted while powers to borrow the £76,000 needed to fund the purchases were sought.

In early 1959 it was agreed to permit external advertising on double-deck trams and buses; No.256 was the first tram to receive adverts. The summer witnessed the operation of six of the surviving 'Standards'; the first new converted illuminated car – the *Blackpool Belle* – since the war emerged on 27 August for the first time. On 13 November, recognising that September 1960 would mark the seventy-fifth anniversary of the first electric trams, the Transport Committee sanctioned the expenditure of £700 to restore three historic trams; these included the last surviving conduit car and one of the original Blackpool & Fleetwood crossbench cars. The first of these entered Rigby Road for repairs in February 1960.

Although 1960 was a year of celebration, it was also a year in which the non-Promenade routes began being eliminated. In early 1960 the Highways Committee suggested removing trams from the North Station/Dickson Road section to improve traffic flows at Gynn Square; the Transport Department countered this by arguing the existing track had a life of up to twelve years.

The section was reprieved later in the year – the cost of replacement buses at £52,000 being far in excess of the scrap value of the eight trams that would have been withdrawn – but a new threat to the Lytham Road route emerged instead. Here the track was largely some 25 years old and needed replacing; the Transport Committee recommended conversion on 7 October 1960 on the grounds that the cost of replacement buses, at £52,000, was less than the cost of relaying the track (£140,000). The committee also

The first of the town routes to succumb was Lytham Road to Squires Gate on 29 October 1961. Here a VAMBAC car makes its way northwards along Lytham Road towards the town centre. R. Stephens/Online Transport Archive

With Marton depot in the background, one of the VAMBAC-fitted 'Sun saloons' heads south towards Royal Oak. The Marton route was the last all-street track route in the UK. The VAMBAC cars had provided a high-quality service but the two-man 48-seat trams were now considered no longer financially viable. R.W.A. Jones/Online Transport Archive

recommended revising the terminal arrangements at North Station – this was completed in early 1961 and when the line was cut back a few yards and a trolley reverser installed. This was first used on 10 March 1961. Plans to extend the Marton route to St John's Church were abandoned as a result of a 1927 agreement that stopped the installation of a tram stop outside the church. The Town Council approved converting the Lytham Road route on 19 October. The number of 'Standards' was further reduced by the dismantling of No.41 following damage sustained in a derailment on 26 July 1960.

Whereas the town routes were under threat, there was happier news with the introduction to service of the first three trailers on 19 July (No.T1), 13 August (No. T2) and 10 September (No.T3). There was also the celebration, on 29 September, of seventy-five years of electric tram operation. A procession, formed of conduit car No.1, Blackpool & Fleetwood crossbench No.2, Dreadnought No.59, 'Standard' No.40, Blackpool & Fleetwood No.40, Pantograph No.170, streamlined cars Nos.217, 239, 249, Coronation No.321 and twin-set Nos.276 plus T3, was the highlight of the day.

The final trailer, No.T10, was delivered on 23 January 1961; in all, ten power cars were converted, including No.275, which entered Rigby Road to have its motors reinstated on 3 November 1961. Initially the power cars and trailers were interchangeable but gradually they operated in set formations. Less positive, however, was the Transport Committee deciding on 7 April 1961 to convert the Marton route ; this was approved by the full council on 5 June. It was also agreed to bring forward, to the end of October, the conversion of the Lytham Road route. This service last operated on 29 October 1961; the final car from Cabin to Squires Gate was No.268, which was preceded by No.218, and the last car from South Pier was No.222 at 11.19pm. The final car from Squires Gate to Rigby Road, at 11.45pm, was also No.268. South Pier was served by Marton cars during the season beyond Royal Oak. The Lytham Road closure also involved the end of the recently reintroduced 'circular tour', which used the reopened tracks along Squires Gate Lane.

Early 1962 witnessed the long-planned track realignment in front of the

Metropole Hotel to the north of Talbot Square. The summer saw the scrapping of a number of the Pantograph cars: Nos.169/71/73 were all disposed of, and No.167 was preserved and replaced as a permanent way gang car by No.170. The choice of No.167 was due to retention of its original trucks; the remainder had been retrucked in the early 1950s by equipment reused from Nos.10-21. On 27 July the Transport Committee recommended converting the Dickson Road route at the end of October 1963. Before this, however, 28 October 1962 witnessed the conversion of the Marton route, resulting in some thirty trams deemed surplus to requirements; the cars threatened with scrapping included all the VAMBAC-fitted cars converted for use on the route – the remaining examples of the 10-21 batch plus Nos.208 and 303. Also potential victims were Nos.160/72/75. A total of seventeen trams were sold to a Chorley-based company for dismantling at Marton depot; these were Nos.12-20, 175, 200/07/08/10/14/23 and 303. During February 1963, Nos.18, 175, 210 and 223 succumbed and an illuminated car, the *Lifeboat*, was dismantled at Crich for spares.

The ghost life of the Marton route continued briefly into 1963; at the route's closure a number of operational – but stored – trams remained in the depot. Once Blundell Street was cleared, these went there for further storage. A total of twenty-three trams moved between 28 February and 2 March; conversely, one tram, No.303, made its way in the reverse direction to Marton depot on 28 February for scrapping. The final cars to leave Marton for Rigby Road, Nos.48 and 251 plus the cut-down *Gondola*, departed in a convoy from Marton depot on 11 March. Thereafter the overhead over the remaining section to the depot was disconnected.

The final closure of the town routes came on 27 October when the service 1 from Fleetwood to North Station via Dickson Road was abandoned. This was the only Blackpool tram route to have a route number. The last car was No.290, which left North Station for Fleetwood at 10.53pm; the official last car was No.256. Contemporaneously with this came the closure of Bispham depot as an operating base. The depot continued as a store for withdrawn trams, most notably the earliest of the railcoaches (Nos.200-24). The last survivors of these, Nos.211-13/16/17, were sold for scrap to J. Robinson of Chorley in late 1965. Bispham depot was finally emptied on 7 January 1966 when Coronation No.313 was towed away by permanent way No.5. Copse Road depot was also closed and the site sold.

During summer 1964, one of the Coronation cars, No.323, saw its VAMBAC equipment replaced with conventional and more reliable Z4 control equipment salvaged from withdrawn railcoaches; the next to undergo the treatment later in the year was No.328. A number were similarly treated over the next few years. On 27 May 1964 the Town Council agreed to expenditure of £4,000 to build a short section of track linking Blundell Street depot with Rigby Road; this was to reduce use of the Princess Street track, believed to be the world's oldest extant electric street tramway, which had been largely unused since the war and use of which was annoying local residents. Due to the concentration of the operating fleet and all maintenance on the Rigby Road depot, the track layout at the depot and the facilities had undergone considerable alteration. This work was largely completed during 1964. In late 1964 railcoach No.224 replaced No.170 as the permanent way gang car; the Pantograph formed the basis of a new illuminated tram – *HMS Blackpool*. No.224 was itself replaced as No.5 in the works fleet by No.221 in late 1965. The works fleet was further altered by the withdrawal of the electric locomotive, preserved at Crich, and of rail grinder No.2; equipment from the latter was used to restore Manchester single-deck car No.765.

On 27 October 1963 the final significant section of street tramway in Britain to close operated for the last time. The first of the Brush-built railcoaches, No.284, is pictured at North Station on 13 October 1963. Examination of the overhead shows part of the trolley reverser introduced at the terminus in 1961. R.L. Wilson/Online Transport Archive

In 1969 railcoach No.618 was rebuilt with tapered ends and an increased seating capacity. It operated in this rebuilt form until it was further rebuilt, emerging as the last of the OMO cars in 1976. It is pictured at the Fleetwood terminus in August 1969 when newly rebuilt. Harry Luff/ Online Transport Archive

To improve flexibility, a number of the twin-sets were converted to bidirectional operation through being permanently coupled and with control equipment installed on the trailer cars; Nos.271-275 plus Nos.T1-T5 were converted during 1965. Another car modified during the year was No.264, which was rebuilt using the glass-fibre cab-ends originally bought to convert two additional power cars for the twin sets that were never produced. The summer saw the withdrawal of No.160, which was cannibalised for spares. No.160 moved to the scrapline on 1 July 1966 and was broken up early in 1967. No.147, also slated for withdrawal, was temporarily reprieved. At the end of July the tram fleet stood at 117 passenger cars, six works cars and six illuminated cars. However, this number shrank

further when the last three 'Standards', Nos.147/58/59, were withdrawn following a farewell tour on 29 October 1966. Of these, No.147 sailed to the US on board the *Manchester Commerce* on 9 September 1967, No.158 went to Crich where it was broken up for spares and No.159 was preserved at Carlton Colville; it departed for East Anglia on 17 April 1967.

The following year saw the fleet further reduced so that by summer the number of passenger cars stood at 108. Among the casualties were Coronation No.313, which was scrapped for spares in March, and four of the 'Boats', Nos.229/31/32/34, all of which had been unused for some time. The summer also witnessed a fleet renumbering, with the single-deck cars being renumbered in the 6xx series and the 'Balloons' being renumbered 700-726. The service fleet was reduced to five in the autumn with the scrapping of television car No.16 (ex-toastrack No.165); this left sister car No.17 still in service. Later in the year, No.618 was rebuilt; the car emerged in its new guise in January 1969. A further casualty later in the year was Coronation No.647, which was scrapped following a collision with the *Santa Fe* locomotive during the 1968 illuminations. The Z4 controllers from No.647 were salvaged and used to convert No.656 from VAMBAC.

Towards the end of 1968 proposals emerged for abandoning the Promenade tramway and its alignment used for building a dual carriageway; this was comprehensively rejected by the Transport Committee on 17 January 1969 but it was evident that funds for fleet replacement would not be available and that modernisation could only be achieved by rebuilding the existing fleet. Summer 1969 saw the final operation of the bulk of the VAMBAC-fitted Coronation cars; only three, Nos.641/42/44, survived

Following the test conversion of one of the railcoaches to operate as an OMO car, it was decided to convert six cars for OMO use. No.3, seen here at Fleetwood on 26 April 1975, was converted from No.610 and entered service as an OMO car in 1972. Operation of the OMO trams probably contributed to the survival of the system, particularly during the winter months. Michael H. Waller

to operate in 1970 and the last public operation of a VAMBAC car was No.641 on 10 October 1970. Three of the Z4-fitted 'Coronations' were also withdrawn in late 1970 (Nos.643/58/59). The redundant Coronation cars found their way to Thornton Gate for scrap: Nos.646/51 in April/May 1970, for example, and No.645/48/50/53 in June and July the same year.

Elsewhere during 1970 the fleet saw No.638 modified as a test for one-man operation (OMO) duties; however, due to problems agreeing terms with the unions for OMO the car was underused in this form (indeed, it was often pressed into service following completion as a two-man car at busy periods). Two more of the twin-car sets, Nos.676/677+686/87, were modified for bidirectional operation; until modified, No.677 was occasionally operated as a single car (as were Nos.678-80, which were never converted). In early 1971 No.601 was fitted experimentally with a pantograph loaned from Crich; it operated with this for the summer before having is trolleypole reinstated and being shipped across the Atlantic for display at a trade fair and preservation. Four further Z4-fitted Coronations were withdrawn in late 1971: Nos.654/56/57/64; this left only four of the type still in service: Nos.655/60-63.

Authorisation was given to build six OMO trams based upon Nos.610/16/17/20 along with works car No.5 (which had been withdrawn earlier in the year due to the poor condition of its bodywork) and un-renumbered No.220. The first of the rebuilt cars, No.1, was unveiled on 7 March 1972 in a new sunshine yellow and crimson livery; this was used on all the OMO cars until No.10, which emerged in a new red and cream livery (the original livery lacked visibility in poor weather). The OMO cars needed longer than usual trolleypoles; these were sourced either from Walsall trolleybuses or from withdrawn Coronation cars. Following the introduction of the first OMO cars, authorisation was given later in the year to build a further seventeen; in reality, only thirteen in all were completed. The first of the type formally entered service on 30 October 1972.

The works fleet was renumbered Nos.751-57 to accommodate the numbering of the OMO cars. No.757, originally toastrack No.166, was withdrawn in early 1972 and transferred to Crich for restoration. No.751, converted from railcoach No.628, was a new works car under construction; it entered service in March 1973. To complete the renumbering of the works fleet, the unnumbered ex-Blackpool & Fleetwood wire trailer was made No.750 and the railmounted tower wagon became No.749.

With the authorisation for additional OMO cars, work went ahead on converting the trams. No.5 was completed in October 1972 and spring 1973 saw work on Nos.6, 7 (ex-619) and 8 (ex-612) in progress. By summer 1973 work on a further five cars, Nos.9-13, was in hand, although other calls on the staff in the workshops delayed completion of the cars with the final example not being delivered until 1976. Late 1973 saw No.624 become the permanent way gang car; since No.5's withdrawal in the spring the permanent way gang had used any available passenger car.

The new year, 1974, saw a change of general manager, with Joseph Franklin retiring and replaced by Derek Hyde. Work continued on the new OMO cars with No.8 completed towards the end of the year. By early 1975 No.9 was completed with work in hand on Nos.10 and 11. These were the first cars delivered in the new red and cream livery and fitted with Metalastik suspension; the improved running saw the earlier OMO cars retro-fitted with it. On 15 July 1975 No.641, the last of the VAMBAC-fitted Coronation cars, departed Blackpool for storage at Clay Cross; the lorry that delivered No.641 returned with Dreadnought No.59, which was returning to Blackpool

Blackpool has had a long tradition of operating historic and preserved trams over its system. With the approach of the centenary in 1985, the then chairman of the Transport Committee suggested the system host a number of preserved trams from other systems. The first to arrive, on 23 June 1981, was Bolton No.66. This car had originally been withdrawn in 1946 but its lower deck was rescued in 1964 and its restoration was completed shortly before its transfer to Blackpool. It is seen here at Talbot Square on 18 July 1981. Michael H. Waller

having been loaned to the town's Civic Trust.

With a view to the future, the overhead along the section from Starr Gate to Thornton Gate was realigned for pantograph use and No.678 was experimentally fitted with a Brecknell Willis pantograph; before this was removed in May 1976 No.678 completed some 5,000 miles in service with no problems. As a result of the experiment additional pantographs were ordered with one being fitted in early 1976 to OMO No.5. Nos.4 and 13 were subsequently fitted with pantographs but No.5 reverted to a trolleypole later in 1976 as a result of damage to its pantograph, as did No.13 in early 1977. No.4 lost its pantograph following damage on 7 November 1977.

By the end of 1975 the operational fleet of Coronations had been reduced to three, with Nos.663 and 665 out of service but the decision was taken in early 1976 to withdraw all as spares became difficult to obtain. Nos.655/61/62/64 were sold for scrap, and Nos.660/63 were secured for preservation. Other changes in 1976 saw No.603 leave on 6 February on a visit to Philadelphia to help mark the bicentenary of US independence (it returned on 12 July 1977), and No.635 (ex-298) passed into preservation. Summer 1977 saw No.717 emerge with the now standard single indicator blind; this left No.714, which was out of service, as the last of the double-deck cars fitted with the original twin destination boxes. The summer also witnessed two collisions: on 26 June Nos.7 and 637 collided at Derby Baths, and on 22 July, Nos.705 and 706 met. No.705 was seriously damaged and never re-entered service. It was scrapped in late 1982 with its bogies transferred to Liverpool to help in restoring Liverpool No.762.

With work on the OMO cars completed, Rigby Road turned its attention to converting No.725 into the first of the double-deck OMO cars, No.761. This was first tested on 27 April 1979 along Blundell Street, where the overhead was adjusted to allow pantograph operation, before the car entered service on 2 July 1979. OMO No.3 was also fitted with a pantograph but reportedly shortage of funds was preventing the purchase of further pantographs. Work started in early 1980 on converting long-stored No.714 into the second OMO double-deck car.

On 22 November 1980, with Blackpool drawn away at Fleetwood Town in the first round of the FA Cup, the transport department operated a series of football specials; as was commented at the time, this was probably the first time that trams had been used on such a service for many years and special tickets were issued to mark it.

Starting a trend that was – and remains – a feature of Blackpool's more recent operations, preserved Bolton No.66 made its first run in service in Blackpool on 5 July 1981. For computing reasons, the car was given the notional number 666. Elsewhere work was in progress on No.762; it was formally inspected by the Department of Transport on 27 May 1982 shortly after its designer, Stuart Pillar (the department's chief engineer), retired on 31 March. It was fitted with the small pantograph that became the Blackpool standard.

During summer 1983, an order was placed with East Lancs for a new single-deck tram body at a price of £95,000; once completed it was estimated the new tram would cost £138,000. A further preserved tram, Edinburgh No.35, arrived in November 1983 – it was first used in public on 21 April 1984 – and early in 1984 No.638 was sold to W. North for scrap. With a view to sourcing historic trams on loan to mark the centenary of the tramway during 1985, Blackpool No.710 was loaned to Crich in exchange for Glasgow Coronation No.1297, which arrived in Blackpool on 5 April 1984. The Glasgow car was initially fitted with a pantograph in place of its more usual bow collector; this was soon replaced by a conventional trolleypole.

On 17 April 1984 the bodyshell of No.641 arrived from Blackburn and was united with its bogies the following day. Other fleet developments this year saw the decision made to restore No.706, which had been out of service since its collision with No.705 and which had faced being scrapped, to its original open-top condition. During summer 1984, OMO No.1 emerged in a new dark green and cream livery having been fitted with a pantograph; the next so fitted was No.712. The service fleet was reduced on 17 July 1984 by the transfer of No.754 to Beamish for restoration. In January 1985 No.600 went to Heaton Park, and sister car No.601 was restored to original condition and numbered 226. A third, No.603, was preserved in the US, leaving for the last time on 19 February 1985. A fourth example, No.607, was loaned to Crich in exchange for 'Standard' No.40. Less fortunate was OMO No.13, which was scrapped on 23 March 1985. This loss was offset by the arrival of the General Electric Co (GEC)-funded experimental single-deck car, No.651, which arrived on 22 April 1985.

Much of 1985 was spent gearing up for events to mark the centenary of electric tramcar operation in the town. The culmination was a memorable cavalcade of trams on 29 September. The event featured Glasgow No.1297, alongside both modern and historic Blackpool trams, such as 'Standard' No.40 from Crich and the sole surviving ex-conduit car, No.4, which had been converted to operate on batteries so as to recreate its original look. After the events, many of the historic cars ran in public service before returining to the museums from which they had been borrowed, resulting in the return of Nos.607 and 710 from Crich in December 1985.

The end of the year saw two further OMO cars, Nos.2 and 4, withdrawn, with the remaining ten cars all now fitted with pantographs. These were soon replaced by the delivery of the next three cars in the Centenary class, Nos.642-44, from East Lancs; these were delivered in late 1986, by which date ownership of the tramway had changed. As a result of the Transport Act 1985, Blackpool's trams and buses passed to a new company, Blackpool Transport Services, with Anthony Depledge as the Managing Director. The new company formally took over on 20 October 1986. The remaining three Centenary cars, Nos.645-47, were delivered in autumn 1987.

A fourth OMO, No.7, was withdrawn in early 1987; rather than being scrapped, however, it was used as the basis of a new crossbench car, No.619, with work carried out by the team that had restored Bolton No.66. The 'new' car arrived back in Blackpool on 29 July 1987 and entered service, following minor modifications, on 14 September 1987. By this date the fleet of OMO cars had been reduced to eight, with Nos.1, 5, 8, 10 and 11 in service and Nos.6, 9 and 12 in reserve. The arrival of Nos.645-47 allowed the withdrawal of Nos.6 and 9, leaving No.12 as the last of the OMO cars still in the red and white livery; the rest were in green and cream. During 1988, No.606 was loaned to the Glasgow Garden Festival and returned on 25 October. In late 1988 GEC accepted an offer for the body of car No.651 at the end of its trial. Work began during 1989 on its conversion into a further Centenary car, which included replacing the HS44 bogies with Blackpool-built bogies. As No.648, it re-entered public service on 4 January 1990. Summer 1989 saw trailers Nos.689/90 scrapped. These had been sold to GEC some years earlier but had passed to the West Yorkshire Transport Museum project where, as part of the project's rationalisation, they were dismantled. On 30 September 1989 services were suspended from Ash Street to Fleetwood Ferry to allow the rebuilding of the terminus; this work was expected to last six months and services were restored on 6 March 1991, although only one line at the Ferry was available initially while work was completed. During summer 1990, two further OMOs, Nos.1 and 12, were withdrawn, leaving only four in service. Later in the year, works car No.753 was slightly damaged by fire while Dreadnought No.59, which had originally returned to Blackpool in 1975, returned to Crich after operating a farewell special on 11 November 1990. By summer 1991, the gradual conversion of the fleet to pantograph operation was well advanced with forty-three cars now so equipped.

During summer 1992, a pantograph was fitted to No.604; this was the first Boat so fitted and was followed by No.602 (which was also fitted with replacement Z6 controllers at the same time and first operated in this guise on 19 July 1992). The use of pantographs with these cars was not successful as, despite modifications, grease could fall and hit passengers. A similar problem affected open-top double-deck car No.706. All three were subsequently refitted with traditional trolleypoles.

During 1992, three new trams arrived on the system. Two were to be used on the new tramway at Birkenhead and had been built in Hong Kong; numbered Birkenhead Nos.69 and 70, the duo arrived in Blackpool for test on 1 October. However, following inspection by the Railway Inspectorate on 20 October, both failed and needed modification before trials could begin. In August, the body for new double-deck works car

In August 1992 the service fleet was strengthened with the addition of a new double-deck car, East Lancs-built No.754, seen here inside Rigby Road depot on 30 July 1993. R.L. Wilson/Online Transport Archive

No.754 arrived from East Lancs; this was united with ex-railcoach trucks and ex-Boat motors. The new tram was fully commissioned by the summer; the works fleet now comprised Nos.259, 260 and 752 plus the new car with Nos.749 and fire-damaged No.753 in store. Conversely, OMO No.8 was withdrawn, leaving only Nos.5 and 11 available for service.

By summer 1993, operation of the OMO fleet had ended, with Nos.5, 10 and 11 in store with Nos.1, 8 and 12 withdrawn and waiting their fate. No.11 departed from Blackpool on 7 July 1993 for Carnforth; it became a test car, returning to Blackpool for experimental operation during summer 1994. It saw periodic use thereafter until scrapped in September 2000.

Following modification, Birkenhead No.70 was cleared for limited use on 7 June 1993 with No.69 coming slightly later. No.70 first carried passengers, VIPs from Birkenhead, on 14 July and fare-paying passengers four days later. However, following a derailment on the loop at Starr Gate later in the month, operation of the type was limited. Latterly the two were restricted to operation between Little Bispham and Pleasure Beach, using the crossovers as their long wheelbase was deemed unsuitable for the loops at Starr Gate and Little Bispham. No.70 moved to the Wirral in 1994, and No.69 followed on 13 March 1995 after the completion of driver training.

It was not only the two Birkenhead cars with problems. An inspection in August 1993 found bogie faults on Nos.602/04/06 and they were temporarily withdrawn. No.607 had had repairs earlier in the month, and No.605 received replacement bogies from withdrawn OMO cars. Work on replacing the bogies on the 'Boats' was completed during summer 1995. Of the surviving OMOs, No.12 was scrapped in October 1993 and No.1 the following month. The body of No.10 was sold in 1996 to a restaurant owner and moved to a site near Reading for conversion

Between 1998 and 2004, four of the Balloon cars were rebuilt with substantially altered front ends; No.724 was the last completed. All four remain extant, although all have been in store since 2013. It is seen in the new Coastliner livery that launched in 2004. Alan Donaldson/ Online Transport Archive

into a coffee shop. It was subsequently scrapped. No.5 was transferred to the NTM for preservation, and No.8 was eventually preserved locally.

During early 1995, engineers designed a revised front for the Balloon cars, which included a single windscreen and no cab doors. The redesigned front was initially unveiled on one end of No.707. Work was completed in 1998, with the rebuilt car becoming the forerunner of the Millennium type. In all, four of the cars were so modified: following No.707 were Nos.709 (in 2000), No.718 (in 2002) and No.724 (in 2004).

In Easter 1997, No.700 was unveiled followings its restoration to 1942 condition after an extensive refurbishment. As well as keeping its contemporary number at either end, its original fleet number (237) was reinstated over the entrances. On 23 July 1997 the first new tram built in Britain since the Centenary class was delivered to Blackpool for final assembly; this was the RoadLiner, an experimental single-deck car built for Pullman TPL in Cardiff. Given fleet number 611 for its period in Blackpool, the tram, first tested on 1 June 1998, saw limited use until leaving on 17 August 2000.

In spring 1998 work started on the mid-life refurbishment of the Centenary type. The first treated was No.642; its return to traffic was delayed until 4 November 1999 due to braking problems. Following completion of work on 642, attention turned to No.641, which returned to service on 22 August 1999. The third car treated was No.646, which re-emerged with a slightly modified front end in late 2000.

The number of 'Boats' was reduced on 14 September 2000 when No.606 headed to the US; is journey westwards was in exchange for 'Standard' No.147, which was to be repatriated. Restoring No.147 took place during 2001 with certain parts salvaged from the fire-damaged No.143;

the restored car was formally launched at a civic event on 3 April 2002. No.633, which had been stored since January 1999, became the first new illuminated car built for almost forty years as a replacement for the *Rocket* and *Western Train*, which were both due for withdrawal. No.633 emerged as the *Fisherman's Friend Trawler* in late 2001, being renumbered 737 in 2008.

By 2000, the long-term future of the tramway was under consideration and, in early 2002, Blackpool Council and Lancashire County Council submitted a joint bid for £102 million of government funding to modernise fully the tramway and acquire a new fleet of trams.

The first decade of the twenty-first century was marked by increasing uncertainty over the tramway's future as funding for its modernisation was initially rejected by the government in 2004. Limited expenditure was authorised to make sure the system could continue. In late 2004 £3 million was approved for emergency track repairs over the next three years. At the end of 2005 a new bid of £88 million (£22 million from the local councils and £66 million from the government) was submitted. In summer 2006 a further £11.8 million of emergency funding was granted. Work started in early 2007 and included building a new substation at Copse Road and replacing

Two generations of historic Blackpool tram stand alongside each other during the celebrations for the system's 125th anniversary in September 2010. On the left is Balloon No.717, and on the right is 'Standard' No.147. The former had been taken out of service in 2003 suffering from underframe defects; however, following a substantial bequest, the car was restored to near-original condition and restored to service in 2008. The Standard was repatriated from the US in 2000 and returned to public service two years later. The seating capacity of the 'Balloons' was 90 (Nos.250-63) or 94 (Nos.237-49); a number of those with the lower capacity were revised to the higher figure from 1961 onwards. Operation of the cars required the use of two conductors. Philip Hanson/Online Transport Archive

life-expired traction columns. Finally, on 1 February 2008, the funding package was agreed: £60.3 million from the government and £12.5 million each from Blackpool Council and Lancashire County Council; tenders for supplying sixteen 30m low-floor articulated trams plus the new depot at Starr Gate and other infrastructure work were sought with all work to be completed by April 2012.

With Blackpool Tower in the background, one of the operator's new Bombardier Flexicity 2 articulated trams heads south in August 2012, shortly after the introduction of the type to public service. Philip Hanson/Online Transport Archive

Away from the urgent need to invest in infrastructure, the increasingly aged fleet had to soldier on. Giving the Centenary cars their mid-life refurbishment continued until No.648 was completed in summer 2006. By that time more than twenty operational cars had either been fully or partially refurbished since 2000. Among the historic cars, Coronation No.304 was finally restored to its original condition in late 2002, aided by the television programme *Salvage Squad*. On 7 December 2005 the experimental articulated No.611, still privately owned, returned to Blackpool for further trials. Never licensed to carry fare-paying passengers, the car did undergo considerable testing. However, on 30 May 2006 it derailed at Starr Gate – an incident caused by the poor track condition – and on 24 January 2007 it suffered fire damage while operating along the Promenade. Later in 2007 the car was sent for repair; its owners are now based in Preston.

Modernising the tramway resulted in dislocation. From 2009 until the introducing of the new trams, no services operated south of Pleasure Beach as the track was replaced and the new depot built. The last day of the traditional tramway was 6 November 2011; the new modernised system launched on 4 April 2012. Alongside the new trams, some of the existing fleet supplement the service, and a significant number of the traditional fleet were kept to form a heritage fleet based at Rigby Road.

With the modernised tramway a success, the long-mooted extension to North Station has been approved with work expected to start in 2018. A further extension, to Lytham St Annes, is also under consideration.

With part of the system incorporating the world's oldest extant electric street tramway and now more than 130 years old, Blackpool's tramway has a bright future – not something that was likely at various dates in its recent history.

Depots

The corporation has used a number of depots over the years. Three were inherited from the Blackpool & Fleetwood Tramroad Co. Bispham and Copse Road both opened on 14 July 1898 and survived until closure on 27 October 1963; the former was then used until January 1966 as a store and the latter, largely used for the works fleet, was finally demolished during 2016. The third, Bold Street, opened in 1899 and closed in 1920. In Blackpool itself there were two main depots. The main depot and workshop was located at Blundell Street and Rigby Road. Blundell Street was originally opened by the Blackpool Electric Tramways Co and acquired by the corporation on 10 September 1892.

The depot was rebuilt and enlarged in 1898 and served as the main depot and workshop until 1920 when Rigby Road was opened as a workshop. This was extended by adding a new running shed for buses and trams in 1934, after which date Blundell Street gradually stopped being used other than as a store. It was revived in March 1963 following the closure of Marton depot and a new entrance created the following year. Blundell Street closed finally in the early 1980s with demolition begining on 4 November 1982. The track that accessed the depot and gave an alternative route to Rigby Road was severed in April 2013, although it had not been used for a number of years before that date. In 1901 the corporation opened a depot at Marton, which closed on 28 October 1962, although was used for a brief period thereafter for scrapping redundant trams. For the second-generation fleet, a new depot/workshop opened at Starr Gate at Easter 2012, although Rigby Road remains to service the historic cars.

Closures

29 October 1961	Station Road/ Lytham Road
28 October 1962	Marton
27 October 1963	North Station/ Dickson Road

Blackpool Fleet

10-21

The last new trams delivered before the Second World War were twelve Sun Saloons built by EE on EE 4ft 0in bogies.

The last new trams delivered before the war were the twelve Sun Saloons, Nos.10-21. All were rebuilt in 1942. In 1949-51 they were modified to operate with VAMBAC equipment for the Marton route and received replacement M&T HS44 resilient wheel bogies. Here No.12 is pictured passing the depot at Marton on 17 April 1949. John Meredith/Online Transport Archive

Designed for use on summer services along the promenade, the cars had half-size doors and windows and a retractable tarpaulin roof. With the onset of war in 1939, the cars lost their summer trade and were initially used for moving troops to and from rifle ranges. Nicknamed 'cattle trucks' by troops due to the draughts, all were refurbished with proper roofs and full-height windows and doors. After the war, the cars were converted to operate with VAMBAC and were fitted with M&T HS44 resilient wheel bogies between 1949 and 1951. The first withdrawn was No.10 following an accident in January 1959; it was dismantled in 1961, with No.21 following the next year. The remainder survived until the Marton route closed, although No.14 was latterly used as a training car based at Bispham. All were eventually scrapped except preserved No.11.

28, 34-43/45/47-49, 51/53, 99, 100/42-60/77

The early origins of the Standard class are complex. Between 1923 and 1929, a total of forty-two open-balcony cars, Nos.28, 33-43, 45-51/53, 99, 100/42-60/77, were built at Rigby Road (except Nos.146-52 that were built by Hurst Nelson). All were originally built with open lower-deck vestibules, except the last two completed, Nos.51 and 177, which had lower-deck vestibules from new; the remainder had lower-deck vestibules added by 1935. Two of the cars, Nos.100/59, received enclosed upper-deck vestibules when the lower-deck vestibules were added in 1930. Nos.38/39, 41, 143/55/58 also received enclosed upper-deck vestibules in 1930. Nos.42/48-50 were similarly treated in 1938 and Nos.147/49/50/60/77 in 1940. The remaining cars retained their open balconies throughout their operational

Blackpool No.143 was one of 39 Standard cars in service at the end of the war. Withdrawn in 1957, the car became Works Car No.3 in July 1958, being renumbered 753 in 1972. It survived in this role until the early 1990s when, after fire damage, it was withdrawn and replaced. Now restored to passenger operation, it is one of two Standards that form part of the heritage fleet. Stanley Eades Collection/Online Transport Archive

career. All were fitted with Preston McGuire-type bogies except Nos.33/34, 43/46, 53, 99, 100 that had similar bogies supplied by Hurst Nelson. Of these, Nos.43/46 and 53 received Preston bogies in November 1924, December 1927 and February 1928 respectively. Three cars, Nos.33, 46 and 50, were withdrawn and scrapped in 1940, leaving thirty-nine in service at the end of the war. One, No.39, was withdrawn in 1945 but not scrapped until 1951. The next casualties were in 1947 but the final withdrawals occurred as late as 1966 with the demise of Nos.158-160. Nos.158/59 owed their survival to having been converted into illuminated cars in 1959. No.158 was acquired by the Tramway Museum Society and was scrapped in 1978. Of the original cars built, seven survive in preservation: five in the UK and two in the US. Of these, four are fully enclosed – Nos.49 at the NTM, 144 in the US, 147 at Blackpool and 159 at Carlton Colville – with three in open balcony form: Nos.40 at Crich, 48 in the US and 143 at Blackpool.

161-66

These six single-deck toastrack cars were built by the corporation in 1927 on Preston McGuire bogies. Last used in 1939, the cars were effectively withdrawn in 1941 and never re-entered public service after the war, although were still extant. No.161 was converted for works duties, as No.7, in 1944 as a saltwater spray; it became a trailer four years later and was scrapped in 1960. Nos.162/4 were scrapped in 1954. No.163 became the basis of the illuminated *Blackpool Belle* in 1963 and, renumbered 731 in 1968, was preserved following withdrawal. Nos.165/66 were converted to carry

In 1927 Blackpool acquired six single-deck toastrack cars, Nos.161-66, that were built at Rigby Road on Preston McGuire bogies. No.162, pictured here, was one of two scrapped in 1954; the other was No.164. R.W.A. Jones/Online Transport Archive

television equipment for recording broadcasts of the illuminations in 1951; No.166 was preserved following withdrawal and is now fully restored at the NTM. No.165 was scrapped.

167-76
During 1928 and 1929, EE supplied ten single-deck cars with EE McGuire-type equal-wheel bogies. Originally fitted with pantographs, and thus known as 'Pantograph' or 'Pullman' cars, all received conventional trolleypoles in 1933. In 1950 No.176 was modified with an experimental passenger flow; this was unsuccessful and the tram was scrapped in 1954. No.167 was converted for works duties in 1952. The remaining cars, No.168-175, received EE bogies from Nos.10-21 between 1950 and 1953 as the latter were converted for VAMBAC operation. In 1962 No.167 was preserved and now forms part of the NTM collection; it was replaced as a works car by No.170 during summer 1962. All the class was withdrawn by Easter 1961 with the demise of the last two: Nos.172/75. Following withdrawal, Nos.168/74 were rebuilt as illuminated cars: the *Rocket* and *Western Train* carriage respectively. No.170 became the illuminated *HMS Blackpool* when it was withdrawn from works duties in 1965. The remaining cars were all scrapped.

200-24
Following Walter Luff's appointment in 1933, he produced a five-year plan for keeping and modernising the tramway system. Working closely with EE at Preston, he designed new single, and double-deck trams. No.200 was the prototype of the EE-built railcoaches; it was delivered in 1933 and was followed by a further twenty-four during 1933 and 1934. The production cars were two feet longer than the prototype. All this batch were originally fitted with EE bogies, although No.208 was tested with M&T 6ft 0in bogies during 1946 and 1947. All the type, except No.224 (which had been rebuilt in 1961), were withdrawn between 1961 and 1965 and were scrapped except for the following. The underframes of No.209 were used in building the illuminated *Santa Fe* locomotive in 1962, which became No.733 in 1968. No.220 was rebuilt as OMO car No.4 in 1972. No.221 was transferred to works duties as No.PW5; it was rebuilt as OMO car No.5 in 1972. The underframes of No.222 were used in building the illuminated *Hovertram* in 1963, which was renumbered 735 in 1968. No.224 became No.610 in 1968 and was rebuilt as OMO No.3. None survived into preservation in original condition.

225-36
Built by EE on EE 4ft 0in bogies, these twelve modern single-deck 'toastrack' trams were delivered in 1934. The first, No.225, arrived early in the year as the prototype, with the remainder following in July and August. Nicknamed 'Boats', the trams were designed to replace the older toastrack cars on the coastal and circular tours. Stored during the war due to lack of work, they returned to service in 1946. Four of the cars, Nos.229/31/32/34, were withdrawn in the early 1960s following the conversion of the town routes and were scrapped in 1968. The remaining eight were renumbered 600-07. Of these, No.601 was withdrawn and went to California in 1971 for preservation; No.603 was loaned to Philadelphia in 1976 for the US bicentenary celebrations and, following its return to Blackpool, was preserved in San Francisco in 1984; No.605 followed No.603 to San Francisco in 2013; No.606 went to a museum in Ohio in 2000 in exchange for Standard No.147 and is now preserved in Maryland; and No.607 went to the NTM in 2012. The three remaining cars, 600/02/04, form part of the heritage fleet.

In 1927 EE supplied a batch of ten trams, Nos.167-76, that were fitted with pantographs when new. No.170, seen here in Fleetwood, was converted to works duties in 1962 and, three years later, was used as the basis of *HMS Blackpool*. R.W.A. Jones/Online Transport Archive

Blackpool No.218 was one of twenty-five streamlined railcoaches supplied by EE between June 1933 and May 1934. It was delivered in February 1934 and was scrapped in September 1963. Harry Luff/Online Transport Archive

On 16 April 1948 Boat No.235 heads north towards Cabin at Claremont Park, on the North Promenade. A total of twelve of this design were supplied by EE between February and August 1934. No.235 became No.606 in 1968. Withdrawn in the late 1990s, the car was exported to the US in 2000 in exchange for Standard No.147. John Meredith/Online Transport Archive

237-49

Originally delivered from EE as open-top cars fitted with EE 4ft 9in bogies, these thirteen cars were known as 'Luxury Dreadnoughts'. The first delivered, in 1934, was No.226, which was renumbered 237 the same year. Nos.238-49 were all delivered during 1934 and early 1935. All were fitted with top covers during 1941 and 1942. The cars were renumbered 700-12 in 1968 and all remained in service until 1982 when No.705 was scrapped following a collision with No.706 in 1980. The latter was converted back to open-top condition three years later. Of the tweleve survivors at the time of writing, Nos.700/07/09/11 have been refurbished in various guises – Nos.707/09 as 'Millennium' cars – to form part of the operational fleet on the modernised tramway. A further three, Nos.701/04/06, remain in Blackpool. The others are at

Originally numbered 226, No.237, seen here at Lytham Road terminus in October 1950 in the older style livery, was the first of the Luxury Dreadnought open-top double-deckers supplied by EE between February and October 1934. The thirteen cars received fully enclosed top decks during the Second World War and became Nos.700-12 in 1968. Peter N. Williams/Online Transport Archive

Heaton Park (No.702), Beamish (No.703), Sunderland (No.708), Fleetwood (No.710) and the NTM (No.712).

250-63

Alongside the 'Luxury Dreadnoughts', EE also supplied a batch of similar, but fully enclosed, bogie cars. Nos.250-63 were again fitted with EE 4ft 9in bogies and were known as 'Balloons'. Renumbered 713-26 in 1968, all remained in service until the late 1970s. Nos.714/725 were used as the base for the rebuilt Nos.762/61 in 1982 and 1979 respectively, having been withdrawn originally in 1971. The next withdrawn were No.716, which succumbed in 2003 and was eventually scrapped in 2010, and

Following on from the thirteen 'Luxury Dreadnoughts', EE supplied a further fourteen fully enclosed double-deckers, Nos.250-63. No.256 was originally new in February 1935 and became No.719 in 1968. Phil Tatt/Online Transport Archive

A further twenty railcoaches, Nos.264-83, were supplied by EE between June and September 1935. No.275 is pictured at the Pleasure Beach loop on 16 April 1949. John Meredith/ Online Transport Archive

No.722, which was scrapped in 2009. Of the remaining cars, Nos.713/18-20/24 have been refurbished – Nos.718/24 as Millennium cars – to operate over the modernised system, and Nos.715/17/23 remain in Blackpool, No.721 is in Sunderland and No.726 is stored in Fleetwood.

264-83

In 1935 EE supplied a further batch of twenty 'Series 2' railcoaches fitted with 4ft 0in bogies. In 1958 Nos.275/76 were rebuilt as the first twin-car set, with No.275 demotored for the purpose. Following the decision to acquire ten trailer cars, Nos.272-74/77-84 were rebuilt to operate with trailers by 1961. The remaining ten cars, Nos.264-71/82/83, were renumbered 611-20 in 1968; in the same year No.618 was rebuilt with tapered ends. The ten cars were rebuilt as OMO cars Nos.12, 8-11, 1, 6, 13, 7 and 2 respectively between 1972 and 1976.

284-303

For its next batch of trams, the corporation went to Brush. Nos.284-303 were built with EMB Hornless 4ft 3in bogies and were delivered in 1937. Very similar to the EE-built cars, there were slight detail differences to avoid copyright issues. These were the last trams manufactured by Brush. The first withdrawals occurred in 1962 and 1966 when Nos.303 (fitted with the VAMBAC equipment) and 301 (following a serious accident) were taken out of service; the remaining eighteen cars were renumbered 621-38 in 1968. In 1969 No.628 was withdrawn again after an accident – it collided with a Balloon – and was rebuilt to form works car No.260, which is still in service. In 1971 No.624 was also withdrawn and converted for works use (as No.259); this was withdrawn in 2004 and is currently based at Rigby Road for restoration. This was followed in 1972 by the withdrawal for scrap of No.629 and, in 1975, by No.635, which was preserved by the NTM. In 1980, OMO testbed No.638 was withdrawn, and was scrapped in 1984. The last of the type in regular service, Nos.631/32, were withdrawn on 6 November 2011. Of those in service in 1980, four (Nos.621/23/26/30) are preserved, three (Nos.631/32/34) form part of the heritage fleet, No.633 was used as the basis of a new illuminated tram (the *Trawler*) in 2001, three (Nos.625/27/37) are stored locally, No.622 is in use as a classroom at Anchorsholme primary school and No.636 was sold to a Derby-based company as a testbed.

Very similar in style to the EE railcoaches was the batch of twenty streamlined trams, Nos.284-303, supplied by Brush between July and October 1937. Here No.292 is seen at Claremont Park on 16 April 1949. Renumbered 629 in 1968, this tram was scrapped in November 1972. John Meredith/Online Transport Archive

After the war, the first new trams were the twenty-five Coronation cars, Nos.304-28. No.312, pictured here when relatively new, was one of the cars that retained VAMBAC throughout its operational life, being renumbered 649 in 1968. J. Joyce/Online Transport Archive

304-28

In 1950 approval was given to build a batch of new single-deck trams, which became known as the Coronation class. Following the tender process, Charles Roberts & Co was given the contract for making the bodies with M&T that for supplying HS44 bogies. The first of the type, No.304, was delivered on 5 June 1952 and, by December, Nos.305-11 had been received. The remaining seventeen cars were all delivered in 1953 with the last entering service on 7 January 1954. The class was fitted with VAMBAC; however, this proved problematic and, in 1964, No.323 became the first fitted with conventional Z4 controllers from a withdrawn railcoach. Subsequently Nos.306/10/18-22/24-28 were fitted with Z4 controllers. The first withdrawal occurred with the scrapping of No.313 in March 1968, with the remaining twenty-four cars subsequently renumbered 641-64. Those cars that retained VAMBAC were all withdrawn by October 1970; those fitted with Z4 controllers were taken out of service in September 1968 (No.647; ex-No.310 due to an accident with its Z4 controllers transferred to No.656 [ex-320]) and between October 1970 and October 1975 (the remainder). Three of the type – Nos.604 (restored as No.304 and fitted with VAMBAC), 660/663 – survive in preservation in Blackpool.

275/76

In 1958 two of the Brush-built railcoaches of 1937 were rebuilt to form a twin-set: No.276 kept its motors but No.275 was demotored. With the decision to acquire ten trailers No.275 was re-equipped with motors. Nos.275/76 were attached to trailers Nos.T5/T6. When new, the twin-sets only had controls on the power car, which meant operation was effectively limited to those duties that needed the use of loops; in 1965 and 1969 Nos.275/T5 and 276/T6 were permanently coupled with control equipment installed in the trailers. The quartet became Nos.675/85 and 676/86 in 1968. The two twin-sets remain part of the heritage fleet.

No.275 is pictured again, this time shortly after it had been converted in April 1958 as an unpowered trailer to operate alongside No.276 as the pioneer twin-car set. It was restored as a power car in 1961. The twin-sets operated in a predominantly cream livery and were originally designed for limited stop services with stopping places displayed either side of the centre doors. J. Joyce/Online Transport Archive

One of the twin sets, headed by No.671, stands at Fleetwood in July 1981. This car had originally been numbered 271 and was one of seven of the power cars modified when permanently coupled to the unpowered trailer. Michael H. Waller

T1-T10

Following the operation of the experimental twin-car set, ten new unpowered trailer cars were ordered. These were delivered from MCW in 1960 (Nos.T1-T8) and 1961 (Nos.T9 and T10), and renumbered 681-90 in 1968. They were all fitted with M&T 5ft 6in bogies. As delivered, the cars were not fitted with control equipment, which meant the twin-car sets could only operate those duties that used turning loops. As a result, seven, Nos.681-87, were permanently coupled to Nos.671-77 respectively, and had control equipment installed. Nos.688-90 were never permanently coupled and were withdrawn in 1972. The remaining seven trailers continued in use until the new generation of articulated cars arrived. Of the surviving trailers, Nos.682/85/86 form part of the corporation's heritage fleet, No.681 is stored in Merseyside, Nos.683/87 are stored in Fleetwood and No.685 in Sunderland.

271-74/77-81

Following the conversion of Nos.275/76 in 1958, a further eight of the 'Series 2' railcoaches were rebuilt during 1960 and 1961 for use with the new trailers. These cars were renumbered 671-74/77-80 in 1968. Nos.671-4/77 were permanently coupled to Nos.681-4/87, being modified with control equipment installed in the trailer unit. Nos.678-80 were never permanently coupled to Nos.688-90 respectively and these three trailers were withdrawn in 1972 and subsequently scrapped. The remaining seven twin-car sets plus Nos.678-80 remained in service until the twenty-first century, the last being withdrawn from the main fleet with the introduction of the Flexicity trams. Of the eight, Nos.671/72 are part of the corporation's heritage fleet, Nos.673/78 are stored in Fleetwood, No.674 in Sunderland, No.677 was scrapped in June 2007 with parts reused to restore the illuminated *Western* train, No.679 is preserved and is being restored to original condition, and No.680 is part of the Heaton Park collection.

1-13

To reduce operational costs thirteen of the EE railcoaches were rebuilt with extended platforms to permit one-person operation. Built between 1972 and 1976, Nos.1-13 were originally Nos.616/20/10, 220/21, 617/19/12-15/11/18 respectively. The lengthened bodies resulted in problems, most notably a pronounced droop, and withdrawals began in 1984. All were taken out of service by 1993 following the introduction of the Centenary class, although problems with the latter resulted in some OMO cars surviving longer than anticipated. Of the thirteen, all were scrapped except Nos.5, 7 and 8. Unrestored No.5 is preserved by the NTM; No.7, heavily rebuilt as a replica toastrack tram, is based at Heaton Park; and No.8 is preserved at Rigby Road.

761

Following the building of the thirteen OMO cars, attention turned to converting two of the Balloon cars that had been stored since 1971. No.725 was rebuilt as double-deck OMO Jubilee No.761; following substantial bodywork replacement in Rigby Road with the help of Metal Sections and the fitting of corporation-built 5ft 6in bogies, No.761 was formally launched on 4 July 1979. It was withdrawn in 2011 and preserved; it is stored at Rigby Road.

762

Three years after completing No.761, the second of the Jubilee cars, No.762, emerged from Rigby Road Works. Again heavily rebuilt from a Balloon car (No.714) with help from Metal Sections, No.762 was also fitted with corporation-built 5ft 6in bogies but differed from the first in keeping its central doors to

The first of two rebuilt Balloon cars to emerge, 98-seat No.761 was converted from No.725 in 1979. Michael H. Waller

improve passenger flow. The car was tested during April 1982 and formally inspected by the Department of Transport inspectors on 27 May 1982. It was withdrawn in 2011 and now forms part of the NTM collection.

The second Jubilee car, 90-seat No.762 (pictured here in December 1983) was originally No.714. Harry Luff/Online Transport Archive

The first of the Centenary class recorded in March 1985. All the type survived until 2011, when No.641 was the first withdrawn. Harry Luff/Online Transport Archive

641-47

By the 1980s it became evident the OMO cars needed replacement for the winter service and an order was placed with East Lancashire Coachbuilders for ten new single-deck cars. However, this was eventually reduced to seven, the first of which, No.641, being delivered in 1985. Nos.642-44 were supplied in 1986 with the remaining three following in 1987. As 1985 marked the centenary of the opening of the original conduit tramway, the cars became known as the Centenary class. The trams were fitted with bogies built at Rigby Road. Not wholly reliable in service, the cars were progressively modernised in a programme beginning in 1999. The first withdrawn, in mid-2011, was No.641, followed by No.643 in October 2011. The remaining five were withdrawn in November 2011 when the traditional fleet was withdrawn pending the introduction of the replacement Flexicity cars. Although all survived closure, No.646 was scrapped in 2012 following vandalism. No.641 is preserved and on display, and No.642 forms part of the heritage fleet. No.647 is preserved in Sunderland. The remaining three cars, Nos.643-45, were all based initially in the Blackpool area, but their long-term future is uncertain.

651

No.651 was an experimental tram constructed for GEC in 1985 with a body built by East Lancs, similar to that given to Nos.641-47, fitted to modified M&T HS44 bogies reused from a withdrawn Coronation. It was tested by the Railway Inspectorate on 21 June 1985 and entered service on 16 July 1985. It was fitted with experimental switched reluctance traction motors, a technology dating back in principle to the mid-nineteenth century but which had not proved practical until suitable control equipment was developed. No.651 was renumbered 648 in 1990, following modification to make it compatible with Nos.641-47, and was the last of the Centenary class modernised following the programme that started in 1999. No.648 survived until 6 November 2011. Originally intended for preservation at the NTM, No.648 was kept as part of the heritage fleet when this fell through.

Recorded in early 1985, when virtually brand new, No.651 was fitted with modified M&T bogies recovered from a withdrawn Coronation car. Following modification to make it compatible with Nos.641-47, No.651 was renumbered 648 in 1990. Harry Luff/Online Transport Archive

One of the features of the Blackpool system is the operation of illuminated cars during the autumn. Recorded in September 1971 is the *Western* train. Philip Hanson/Online Transport Archive

Illuminated trams

One of the features of the Blackpool system, linked to the annual illuminations, was the operation of illuminated trams. Some were simply existing passenger cars that had undergone little or no modification, but others saw the vehicles radically transformed. In 1945 there were three extant. The oldest was the *Lifeboat*, which had been converted in 1926 from 1901-built No.40 and fitted with a Brush flexible truck. Seating twenty, *Lifeboat* was last used during the 1961 season. In 1927, another of the 1901 batch, No.28, was converted into the single-deck *Gondola*; seating twenty, the tram was withdrawn in 1961 following a collision. The third of the pre-war illuminated cars was that converted in 1937 from an 1899-built single-deck crossbench car, No.141 (ex-Blackpool & Fleetwood Tramway Co No.27), called the *Bandwagon*. This was again rebuilt in 1949 as the *Progress* car; operated without passengers, it survived until 1958. In 1959 two Standard cars, Nos.158 and 159, were fitted with permanent illuminations; the two were last used in 1966.

Between 1959 and 1965 a number of new illuminated cars were added to the fleet. The first, the *Blackpool Belle*, was completed in 1959; this was a conversion of No.163. This was followed in 1961 by the *Rocket*, which was converted from No.168. Nos.209 and 174 were converted in 1962 to form the *Western Train* locomotive and coach respectively. No.222 was used in 1963 as the basis of the *Hovertram*, and in 1965 No.170 was converted into *HMS Blackpool*.

With the fleet renumbering, the six surviving illuminated cars were renumbered 731-36 in the order of construction. No.731, the *Blackpool Belle*, was withdrawn in 1978 and was preserved in the US. In 2001 a further illuminated car was added, No.737; this was the *Trawler*, which was converted from No.633.

Of Nos.732-37, No.735 previously preserved in Sunderland returned to Blackpool in September 2016, Nos.733/34/36/37 were kept and No.732, the *Rocket* (unused since 1999 and cosmetically restored in 2012), joined the heritage fleet in 2014.

Works trams

Aside from the illuminated trams, over the years Blackpool has operated a considerable number of works cars. Some were converted from older passenger cars and their survival in this form allowed for restoration at a later date to original condition, whereas others were purpose-built. Among the former were one of the original conduit cars of 1885, No.4, which was converted to works use in 1912 and restored to passenger condition in 1960; it was later converted for the 1985 centenary to operate on battery power to recreate its original appearance. Three of the Blackpool & Fleetwood crossbench cars (Nos.126, 127 and 132) were converted to works use during the Second World War; No.127, converted to a snowplough, was restored for the seventy-fifth anniversary celebrations in 1960 as Blackpool & Fleetwood No.2. Another Blackpool & Fleetwood survivor was No.40, which became corporation No.114 and was converted to a works car, as No.5, in 1942. It was also restored for the seventy-fifth anniversary in 1960.

Ex-corporation cars converted to works use included ex-Marton Box No.31, which became works car No.4 in 1934; latterly operating as No.754, it remained in service until 1983 and was then preserved. Three of the 1927-built open toastrack cars, Nos.161 (as salt car No.7) and 165/66 (as television cars), were added to the works fleet in 1944, 1951 and 1953 respectively; No.166 was preserved on withdrawal in 1972. No.167 was converted to works use in 1954 and was preserved on withdrawal in 1961. No.143 was converted into a mobile generator following withdrawal in 1957; it emerged as works car No.3 in July 1958 having been fitted with an overhead inspection platform and 8.6 litre diesel engine from a withdrawn Leyland TD5. It was withdrawn, having previously been renumbered 753, in 1990 following fire damage. Although initially threatened with scrapping, the car was eventually preserved and restored to open-balcony condition.

The most significant recent addition to the works fleet is No.754; the body of this double-deck works car was built by East Lancs and operational from August 1992. At the time of writing, the works fleet comprises five vehicles: No.260 (a towed crane converted from No.628), No.750 (a towed reel wagon built in 1907), No.754, No.939 (a road / rail vehicle supplied in 2003) and an unnumbered battery-powered shunter based at the new depot to move the new fleet.

001-016

In July 2009 sixteen new trams for the route were ordered from Bombardier. The Flexicity 2 trams were built between 2011 and 2012 at factories in Germany and Austria, with the first officially unveiled in Blackpool on 8 September 2011. All sixteen of the five-section trams entered service in 2012, with the last, No.016, appearing on 3 July. A further two have been ordered with delivery scheduled for late 2017. This will give the fleet increased capacity to deal with the extension to North station.

Pictured outside Copse Road depot are two of the work trams converted from cars inherited from the Blackpool & Fleetwood Tramway Co. Nearest the camera is crossbench No.6, and in the background is No.5. The latter was restored as Blackpool & Fleetwood No.40 for the seventy-fifth celebrations in 1960. Milnes-built No.6 was originally Blackpool & Fleetwood No.1 and dated from 1898.
Phil Tatt/Online Transport Archive

BOLTON

During the 1930s, Bolton Corporation had seen much of its tramway system converted to bus operation. Early casualties included the route to Smithills in 1933 and the through route to Bury the following year. In 1936 the corporation decided upon the complete conversion of the system. The final pre-war conversion, to Halliwell, took place on 13 August 1939. With war preventing the anticipated final conversion of the system, the Halliwell service was restored on 1 April 1940.

In early 1943 the fleet was increased by four cars by acquiring Bury Nos.21, 55, 56 and 58, which became Nos.331 and 451-53 respectively. However, lack of wartime maintenance saw the condemnation of the track inherited from SLT on the routes to Farnworth and Walkden, F and G respectively, on 3 October 1944. This resulted in their withdrawal on 11 November 1944, although the corporation-owned track to Moses Gate was retained and used for services to the football ground at Burnden Park and on Sunday mornings.

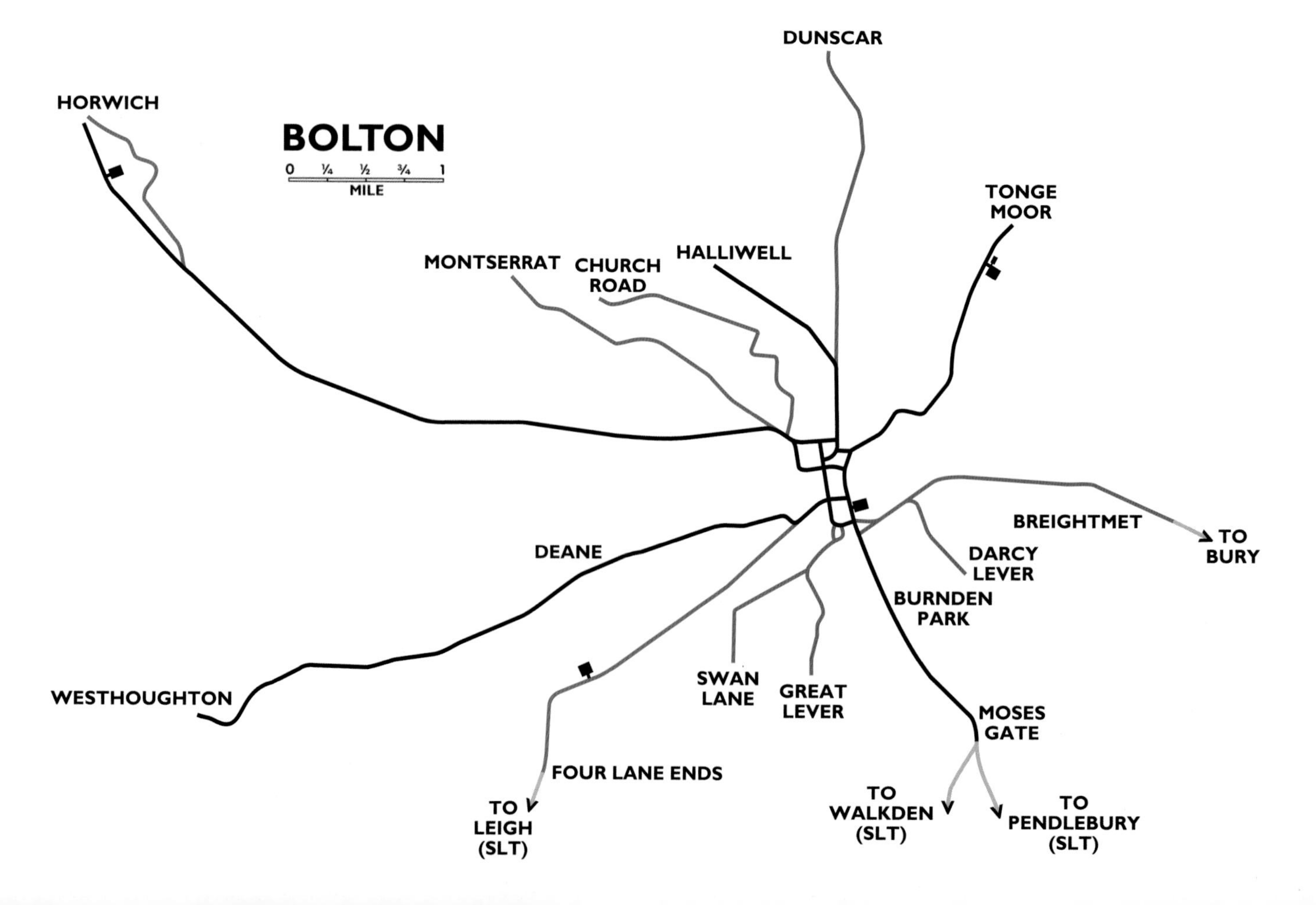

One of eight cars supplied by EE in 1921, No.417 is seen showing the 'T' destination allocated to the Tonge Moor service. Barry Cross Collection/Online Transport Archive

Post-war, Bolton quickly restarted its tramway conversion programme. It was announced in June 1945 that sixty-seven new buses were to be ordered to facilitate the conversion. The first post-war casualty was route H to Halliwell, which last operated on 5 August 1945. Moses Gate lost its Sunday morning services probably in late 1945 but the football specials operated until the end of the 1945/46 season. The last match to which trams operated was probably that on 27 April 1946. Initially it seemed as though the corporation would reinstate the football specials for the 1946/47 season; however, it was discovered that a short section of track had been lifted in Manchester Road and so the specials were not reintroduced.

On 6 October 1946 the next conversion took place with the withdrawal of trams from service N to Horwich, plus the associated short workings; the last car from Horwich was No.422. Following this conversion, twelve of the newest trams were transferred to the Tonge Moor route. This was followed on 3 November 1946 by the withdrawal of trams from the outer section of the Westhoughton route beyond Deane. Pending converting the remainder of the route, a shuttle bus replacement service operated. This continued until 8 December 1946 when the service to Deane was converted.

In December 1946 officials from the transport committee investigated trolleybus operation; having visited seven systems, they recommended the

Pictured on route H, No.421 was one of ten cars supplied by EE in 1923. Bolton was one of a number of north-west operators to use route letters rather than numbers. Barry Cross Collection/ Online Transport Archive

trolleybus as a suitable vehicle for Bolton. Bolton already owned four trolleybuses, albeit liveried and numbered as part of the SLT fleet, and there was trolleybus overhead in the town courtesy of the SLT route from Leigh to Bolton. However, it was decided that the final conversion would be to the motorbus.

The end of the Bolton system came on 29 March 1947 when the service to Tonge Moor operated for the last time. The official last car, suitably decorated, was No.440. Although no Bolton tram was preserved when the system closed, the body of No.66 was subsequently acquired for preservation and fully restored.

Depots

During the electric tramcar era, Bolton possessed five depots; however, three closed before the Second World War: Tonge Moor (in 1911), Dabhill (28 March 1936) and Bridgeman Street (17 August 1936). This meant only the main depot and workshop, at Bradshawgate, and a smaller depot at Horwich remained operational. The former had originally opened in September 1880 and was extended in 1913. It continued to accommodate trams until final closure on 29 March 1947. The depot at Horwich opened originally on 19 May 1900 and survived until 6 October 1946.

Closures

5 August 1945	Halliwell
Late 1945	Moses Gate
27 April 1946	Burnden Park
6 October 1946	Horwich
3 November 1946	Deane-Westhoughton
8 December 1946	Deane
29 March 1947	Tonge Moor

Bolton No.320 was one of twelve cars that survived post-war from the first batch of forty open-top cars originally supplied by ERTCW in 1899.
Barry Cross Collection/Online Transport Archive

Pictured as Bury No.21 before its move to Bolton, No.331 was acquired in 1943. W.A. Camwell/NTM

Bolton Fleet
308-10/12/13/15/19/20/23/24/27/30
The Bolton system opened with a batch of forty open-top trams, Nos.1-40, that had been supplied by ERTCW on Brill 21E trucks. Nos.15 and 23 received open-balcony top covers by 1914. Nos.8-10 were rebuilt with new EE bodies in 1926, and Nos.12/14/19, 20/24/27 and 30 received enclosed top covers between 1924 and 1927. Nos.33-40 were withdrawn before 1933, replaced by eight cars acquired from SLT. Further cars from the original batch were all withdrawn before the Second World War. The surviving cars were renumbered 308 and so on in 1940 and were withdrawn for scrap between 1945 and 1947.

331
This car was bought from Bury in 1943. Originally one of a batch of fourteen, Nos.15-28, acquired from Milnes in 1903, No.21 was built as an open-top car fitted with an M&G truck. It, and three other cars, were rebuilt by Bury as fully enclosed in the mid-1920s. In 1944 the car's existing M&G 21EM truck was replaced by a Bolton 21E truck. No.331 was withdrawn after the war.

One of the eight cars acquired from SLT, No.339 is seen on route F. Barry Cross Collection/Online Transport Archive

334-37/39/40

In 1933 Bolton Corporation acquired eight trams from SLT; Nos.33-40 had originally been SLT Nos.44, 45, 47, 48, 50, 54, 55 and 58 respectively. These were all open-balcony cars fitted with EMB Burnley-type bogies. Nos.44 and 45 had been built by EE in 1927, and the remaining six had been rebuilt by SLT between 1923 and 1925 from Milnes trams delivered as open-top cars to Farnworth UDC during 1901 and 1902. Originally numbered 33-40 when acquired, the cars became Nos.333-40 in 1940. No.338 was withdrawn during the war, with the remaining seven scrapped between 1945 and 1947.

Two of the batch of eight open-top cars supplied by ERTCW to Bolton in 1901, by now renumbered Nos.341/45, remained in service post-war. Barry Cross Collection/Online Transport Archive

During 1901 and 1902, ERTCW supplied Bolton with a batch of twenty-two open-top cars, Nos.60-81. All were fitted with open-balcony top covers before the First World War; eleven of the type, including No.368 pictured here, survived post-war. Barry Cross Collection/ Online Transport Archive

No.401 was one of seven balcony-top bogie cars supplied by UEC in 1910. All survived post-war. Barry Cross Collection/ Online Transport Archive

341/45
These two cars were the survivors of a batch of eight, Nos.41-48, built as open-top cars by ERTCW in 1900. Fitted with Brill 21E trucks, the cars were fitted with balcony tops between 1903 and 1914. Nos.40/42-44/46-48 were all withdrawn before 1940 when Nos.41 and 45 became Nos.341 and 345 respectively. The last two were scrapped by 1947.

360/65-68/74/76-80
During 1901 and 1902, ERTCW supplied a batch of twenty-two cars, Nos.60-81, that were fitted with Brill 22E bogies. Fitted with open-balcony tops before 1914, all were rebuilt during 1929 and 1930 with fully enclosed top decks. Nos.61-64, 69-73, 75 and 81 were withdrawn before 1940 when the remainder were renumbered 360 and so on. The surviving cars were all taken out of service between 1945 and 1947; although not preserved at the time, No.366 was subsequently rescued and fully restored as No.66.

397-403
These seven cars were supplied as Nos.97-103 by UEC on Brill 22E bogies in 1910. Fitted with open-balcony tops from new, all were rebuilt with fully enclosed upper decks during 1929 and 1930. Renumbered Nos.397-403 in 1940, all survived through the war, being scrapped between 1945 and 1947.

No.405 was one of a trio of cars supplied by EE in 1928; these were the last new trams bought by Bolton. Maurice O'Connor/NTM

404-06

In 1928 EE supplied three fully enclosed cars, Nos.104-06, on Brill 22E bogie; these were the last new tramcars acquired by the corporation. Renumbered 404-06 in 1940, the trio survived to be withdrawn between 1945 and 1947.

407-12

A further batch of UEC-built open-balcony cars, Nos.107-12, was supplied in 1912. Again fitted with Brill 22E bogies, all received fully enclosed top decks during 1929 and 1930. Renumbered 407-12 in 1940, all were withdrawn by 1947.

Originally delivered as an open-balcony car in 1912, No.407 was one of six cars built by UEC. All were rebuilt as fully enclosed during 1929 and 1930. Barry Cross Collection/Online Transport Archive

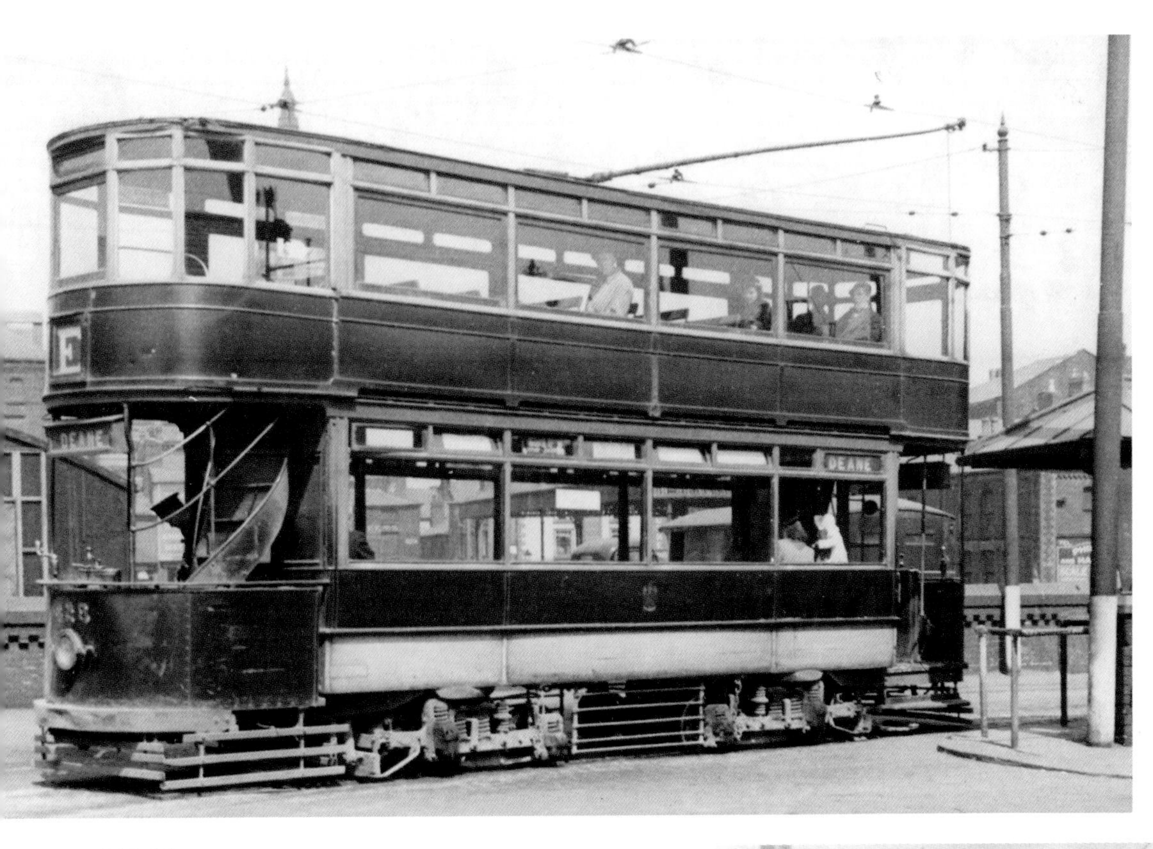

No.425, pictured on route E to Deane (a short working on the route to Westhoughton), was one of eighteen bogie trams supplied by EE in 1920 and 1923. Barry Cross Collection/ Online Transport Archive

No.450 was one of twelve fully enclosed double-deckers supplied by EE in 1927. F.N.T. Lloyd-Jones/ Online Transport Archive

In addition to four-wheel car No.331, Bolton also acquired three bogie cars from Bury in 1943. The first of the three is seen on route O to Albert Road; this was a short working on the long route west to Horwich. Maurice O'Connor/ NTM

413-30
In 1920 EE supplied eight open-balcony cars, Nos.113-20, which were followed three years later by a further ten, Nos.121-30. All were fitted with Brill 22E bogies and were rebuilt as fully enclosed during 1929 and 1930. Renumbered 413-30 in 1940, all were withdrawn between 1945 and 1947.

439-50
Bolton received twelve fully enclosed bogie cars built by EE on Brill 22E bogies in 1927; all were withdrawn between 1945 and 1947.

451-53
In 1943 the corporation acquired three bogie trams from neighbouring Bury. Originally Bury Nos.55/56/58 respectively, the three trams had been delivered in 1925 and were fully enclosed from new. Built by EE, the three were fitted with that company's Burnley-type bogies. They were all withdrawn between 1945 and 1947.

BURY

Before the Second World War Bury had pursued a programme of tramway conversion; by September 1939 only two routes, to Tottington and Walmersley, remained operational, with a fleet of some twenty-three trams. On 30 September 1939 the section of line from the town centre to Gigg Lane, adjacent to the football ground at Starkies, was reintroduced. This was a short section of the route that had once operated southwards to provide a link with Manchester. In 1943 the Bury fleet was reduced by the sale of four cars, Nos.21, 55, 56 and 58, to Bolton, leaving the fleet at nineteen. Of these, the bogies cars, Nos.1-14 plus Nos.57, 59 and 60, were generally used on the services to Tottington and Walmersley, and the two surviving four-wheel cars, Nos.30 and 38, operated the shuttle to Starkies. In March 1943 R. Le Fevre took over as general manager in place of C.P. Paige, who had taken over as general manager of neighbouring Oldham.

Although a relatively small system, Bury had unusual facets. One of these, a consequence of the number of narrow streets in the town, was the considerable use of interlaced track, in one section of which there was an unusual slip crossover.

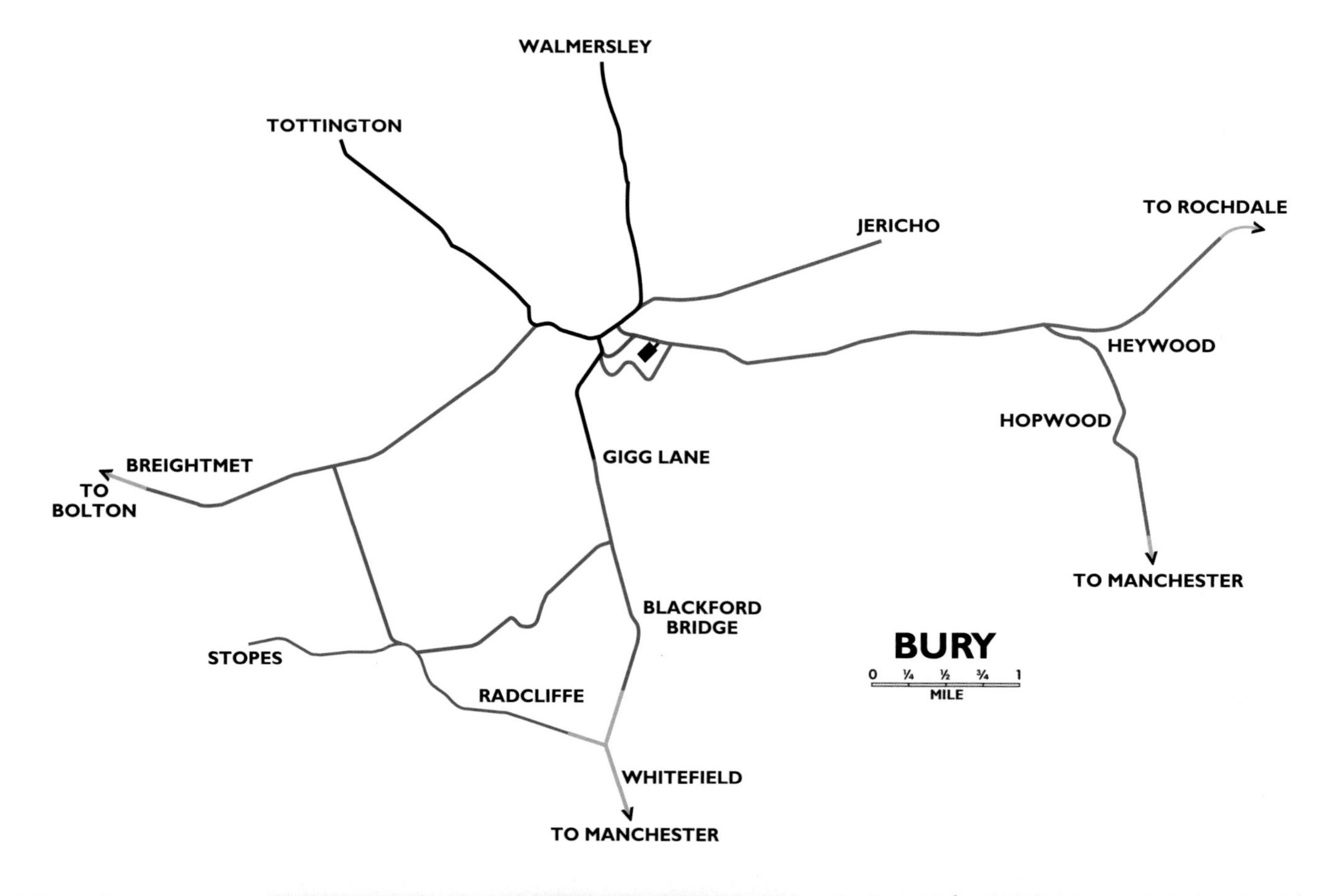

Standing in front of the Derby Hall, in the town centre, on 17 August 1947 is No.11. Given the state of the car, there is a certain irony in the statement promoting 'For inner cleanliness'. Barry Cross Collection/Online Transport Archive

The first post-war conversion in Bury occurred on 6 July 1946; this was the service operating from Gigg Lane at Starkies that was latterly operated on Saturday mornings only by a single car. During 1946, it was announced that the last two routes would be converted to bus within two years. In the event, this proved optimistic. The first conversion took place on 15 February 1948 with buses taking over the Tottington service. This allowed the sale of fully enclosed four-wheel car No.30 to Sunderland.

The final tramway operation in Bury occurred on 13 February 1949 with the conversion of the route to Walmersley. The official last car was No.13. No Bury car survived into preservation.

The final route to serve Bury was that to Walmersley; this was converted on 13 February 1949. Recorded at the Walmersley terminus on 18 July 1947 is No.5. Barry Cross Collection/Online Transport Archive

The service to Tottington last operated on 15 February 1948; here another of the bogie cars, No.8, stands at the Tottington terminus. W.A. Camwell/NTM

Depots

During electric trams era, Bury possessed only one depot, Rochdale Road, which opened on 3 June 1903 and closed with the tramway system on 13 February 1949.

Closures

6 July 1946	Starkies
15 February 1948	Tottington
13 February 1949	Walmersley

Bury Fleet

1-14

Delivered originally by Milnes in 1903 as open-top bogie cars fitted with McGuire No.3 maximum-traction bogies, Nos.1-14 were rebuilt as fully enclosed during 1925 and 1926 when all were fitted with EE Burnley-type bogies. All were withdrawn with the final closure.

No.30, seen here at the terminus at Starkies, was one of a number of trams in the fleet rebuilt as fully enclosed during the 1920s. Fitted with air brakes, it was sold to Sunderland in 1947. Maurice O'Connor/NTM

30 (ii) and 38 (ii)
These two trams, along with Nos.15 (withdrawn before the war) and 21 (sold to Bolton in 1943), were rebuilt as fully enclosed trams by Bury during the mid-1920s; they were originally part of a Milnes-built batch, Nos.15-28, delivered in 1903. The original numbers of Nos.30 and 38 are uncertain; they were renumbered when rebuilt. No.30 was fitted with a replacement EMB truck and air brakes in 1930; it was sold to Sunderland in 1947, where it survived until 1954. No.38 kept its original M&G 21EM truck until withdrawal.

57/59, 60
The last new trams acquired by Bury were a batch of six fully enclosed cars, Nos.55-60, built by EE on EE Burnley-type bogies. Three of the batch, Nos.55/56/58, were sold to Bolton in 1943. The remaining three cars were all withdrawn at closure in 1949.

The last new trams acquired were six fully enclosed cars supplied by EE in 1925. Three were sold to Bolton in 1943 but the remaining three, including No.60, remained in service until final closure. F.N.T. Lloyd-Jones/Online Transport Archive

DARWEN

Although Darwen had acquired two streamlined double-deckers from EE as late as 1936, much of the network had been converted to bus before the war. The route to Hoddlesden, which had been largely bus operated since 1930, was finally converted on 13 October 1937, and the line south to Whitehall succumbed in January 1939. The latter route was reinstated in September 1939 but finally closed on 31 March 1940.

The corporation, despite the pressures of war, was keen to convert the sole surviving service. In April 1940 an application to convert the Blackburn route was rejected by the Ministry of War Transport, as was a further attempt on 30 September 1941.

That conversion was still the aim was confirmed in early 1945, by which stage the state of the track was poor and the operational fleet was reduced to only five vehicles. In February 1945 Darwen indicated to Blackburn that it intended to withdraw its trams from October 1945. The Blackburn Transport Committee commented that it hoped to keep the trams running 'for a few more years yet'.

The next possible date proposed

The second Darwen No.17 was one of two fully enclosed cars supplied by Brush in 1924. It was seriously damaged and withdrawn during the war. Maurice O'Connor/NTM

Delivered in 1936 the two handsome streamlined cars, known as 'The Queens' or 'The Queen Marys' (Queen Mary and Queen Elizabeth), were the most modern 4ft 0in gauge trams operated in Britain. No 24 is pictured pre-war. The two cars were acquired primarily for use on the jointly operated route between the town and Blackburn. Darwen possessed the smallest municipal tram fleet after the war. Maurice O'Connor/NTM

for closure of the Darwen system was 31 March 1946; when this was not undertaken Blackburn offered additional trams to continue operating the through route until final closure could be achieved. At the time, although Darwen was desperate to close, the Blackburn section of the through route was not immediately scheduled for closure. On 9 April 1946 two Darwen cars, including one of the two streamlined cars (which was not seriously damaged), were involved in an accident. Fortunately there were no casualties. The small Darwen fleet was further reduced during summer 1946 with the sale of the two streamlined cars to the Llandudno & Colwyn Bay.

The end of the Darwen system was not long in coming; the final tram, No.3 with suitable decorations, operated on Saturday, 5 October 1946. The three surviving trams were all withdrawn for scrap; Blackburn's trams continued to operate the northern section of the through route until 2 July 1949.

Depot

The small fleet was accommodated in a single depot on Lorne Street that had originally been opened by the Blackburn & Over Darwen Tramways Co. It closed to trams with the abandonment of the system on 5 October 1946.

With the statue to the Victorian prime minister William Gladstone in the background, No.3, one of five cars that Darwen rebuilt during the 1920s, stands in Blackburn centre. Barry Cross Collection/ Online Transport Archive

Closure

5 October 1946	Circus to Blackburn boundary

3/7

Nos.3 and 7 were two of five cars (the others being 5, 8 and 15) built by Darwen itself using reconstructed lower decks between 1925 and 1929. These were fitted with Burnley bogies and newly built fully enclosed top decks. The two survivors were withdrawn in 1946.

10

During the war, Darwen's small fleet of trams suffered damage. No.17, which had originally been supplied by Brush as a fully enclosed double-decker on Burnley bogies, overturned and was seriously damaged, and Nos.8 and 10 had been withdrawn. No.8 was one of the five cars rebuilt between 1925 and 1929, and No.10 dated from 1933 and was a further fully enclosed car converted by the corporation; this was again based upon a rebuilt lower deck and Burnley bogies but, this time, was fitted with the top deck from a tram acquired from Rawtenstall. There were also two other cars acquired from Rawtenstall that entered service with Darwen – Nos.9 and 11 (the latter on the truck from Darwen's original No.11) – but neither survived into 1945. To supplement a fleet that had been reduced to four cars, Nos.3, 7, 23 and 24, a 'new' No.10 was built by the corporation in 1941. This comprised the lower deck and bogies from the damaged No.17 and No.8's top deck. No.10 survived until the closure of the system.

23/24

In 1936 the corporation acquired two double-deck streamlined trams from EE on EE maximum-traction bogies. No.23 and 24 were sold to the Llandudno & Colwyn Bay Electric Railway in mid-1946; regauged to 3ft 6in and renumbered 24 and 23 respectively, they survived until scrapped after that line closed in 1956.

As a result of accident damage and other withdrawals, the fleet was reduced to four cars early in the war. To supplement this meagre number a 'new' No.10 was built using parts salvaged from withdrawn trams. Maurice O'Connor/NTM

The last new trams acquired were two streamlined cars built by EE in 1936. One is pictured shortly before withdrawal. J.H. Roberts/Online Transport Archive

LIVERPOOL

Under Walter Grey Marks, manager from 1934, the tramways of Liverpool underwent major expansion and ongoing modernisation during the rest of the 1930s. All boded well for the future as the majority of the new routes were built on reserved track and more than 300 new trams were constructed between 1933 and 1942. Although Marks had overseen the conversion from tram to trolleybus in Nottingham, he recognised that modern trams had a pivotal role to play in the future of Liverpool, which was reflected in his presidency of the campaigning group the Light Railway Transport League.

Throughout the war Liverpool was a major target for the Luftwaffe, but this did not stop the tramway from

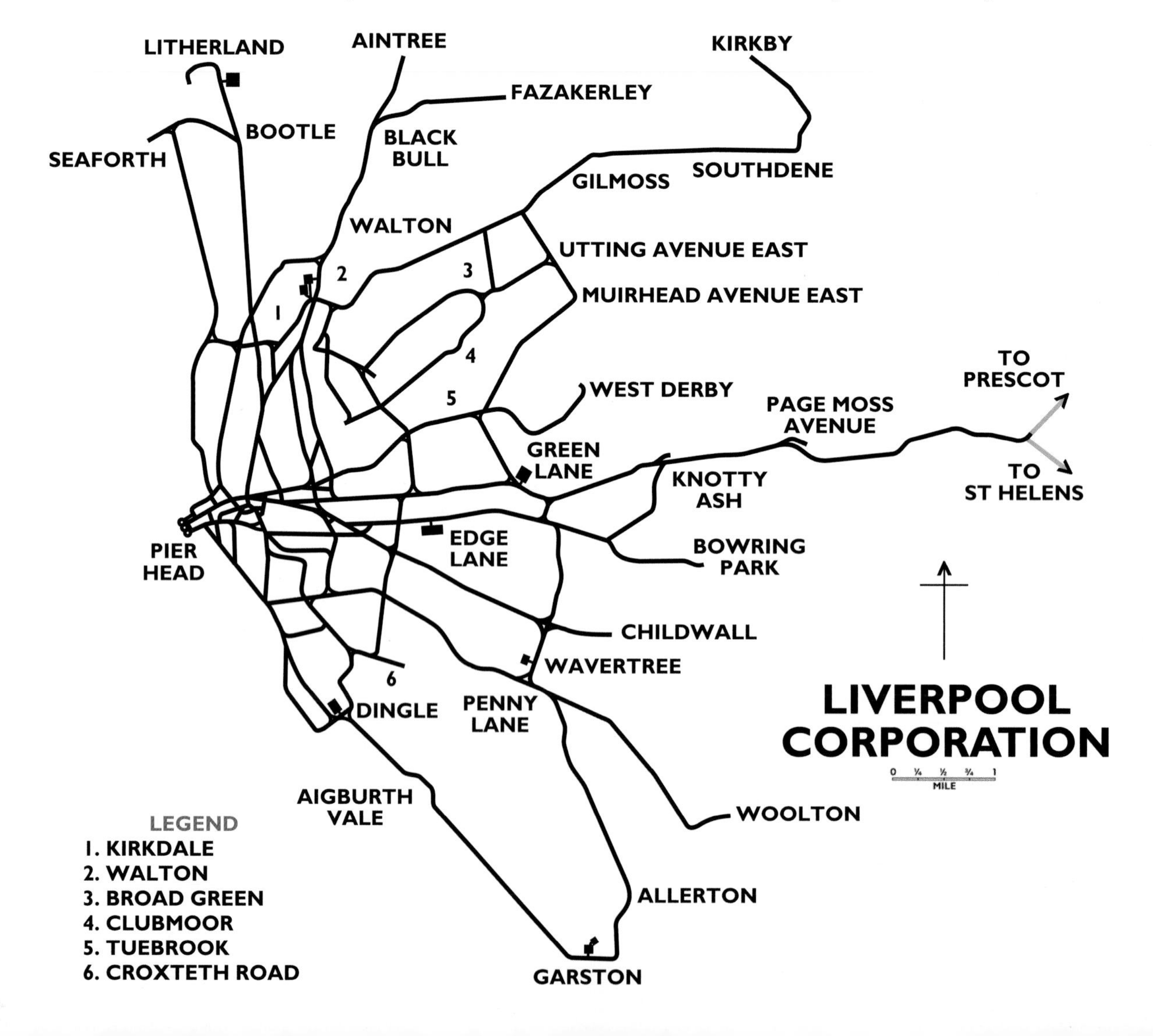

expanding eastwards to serve a massive Royal Ordnance Factory at Kirkby (the very last section of new reserved track opening for peak-hour use on 12 April 1944), giving an overall total of ninety-seven route miles. Building new trams continued at Edge Lane until 1942. During the war, the whole of Merseyside suffered heavy damage and increasing numbers of trams were put out of action often due to mechanical and structural problems. Some were eventually repaired but others never returned to service. As the war progressed, the number of trams withdrawn due to electrical and mechanical failures increased.

As the end of the war approached, Liverpool, as elsewhere, looked to the future of public transport. In a series of reports produced during 1944 and 1945, Marks acknowledged that growing traffic congestion was one of the major issues; he believed reserved tracks offered an alternative to the bus. Indeed, with just over twenty-seven miles of segregated 'grass tracks', Liverpool was ideal for a modern tramway system. He also explored the revolutionary idea of tram subways and high-speed single-deckers. However, on 16 October 1945 the Transport Committee opted to support his cheapest option – conversion to buses. It was reckoned that 900 buses would replace the 744 trams (many of which were laid up awaiting repair) over a ten-year period. Despite a local pressure group forming, the Liverpool Tramway Passengers' Association, which campaigned for retaining the system, the full council voted to accept the recommendation in November 1945.

However, during the course of 1945 it was very much business as usual as work was undertaken to reverse years of wartime neglect. For example, in early 1945 the reserved track at Aigburth was relaid and a new roundabout at Page Moss involved a revised track arrangement to cater for the heavy volume of traffic. Later the same year, the track along Mather Avenue was relaid. This was a high-speed section where the powerful streamliners with their four 40hp motors often exceeded 45mph. However, not all was positive. For example, on 25 January 1945 bogie

One of the features of the Liverpool system was the extensive use of reserved track sections outside the city centre; here one of the modern cars heads along the Prescot light railway in April 1949. Liverpool was the only major system still totally intact in 1945.
J.H. Roberts/Online Transport Archive

car No.910 ran away in the city centre and collided with No.850, killing one person and injuring seventy-nine. Both cars were write-offs.

Although the actual abandonment programme was not yet published, there was increased opposition including from within the council. In mid-1946, the *Liverpool Daily Post* reported that a petition against conversion had been signed by some 1,500. In 1946 cars appeared in a new, brighter – malachite rather than olive green – livery. Two routes withdrawn during the war – No.30 Walton (Spellow Lane) to Pier Head and No.31 Walton (Spellow Lane to Pier Head via Netherfield Road and Heyworth Street respectively) – were reintroduced on 20 May 1946 on half-hourly schedules but the 43A Pier Head to Utting Avenue via Robson Street was withdrawn without replacement in October. Expenditure on trackwork costing £5,399 was approved and in early 1947 part of the reserved track along Muirhead Avenue was relaid; to alleviate overcrowding on the Pier Head's south loop a new siding was laid. On 6 January 1947, route 16 (Pier Head to Litherland via Vauxhall Road), which had been temporarily withdrawn during the war, was reinstated following repairs to a bridge in Bankhall; and the temporary short working, route 16A (Pier Head to Kirkdale station via Vauxhall Road), made its final runs in August 1947.

On 7 November 1947 a serious fire at Green Lane depot destroyed sixty-six trams and damaged several others. Apart from the passenger cars destroyed, two works cars also went up in smoke. Some

The first significant routes converted to bus operation were the circle routes on 12 June 1948. Here Baby Grand No.216 on route 27 passes a car on route 26 at South Castle Street. E.A. Gahan/Online Transport Archive

fourteen trams were driven or pushed out of the depot by crews risking their lives, but a derailment at the depot entrance stopped more cars from escaping. In all, almost ten per cent of the operable fleet was lost including many of the streamlined cars. Although replacements were offered by other operators, these were declined; in place, it was announced buses would be drafted in and reduced frequencies introduced on tram routes. The fire had started on board No.295 and quickly spread through the timber-roofed building. An earlier fire at Green Lane in February 1942 had seen five cars destroyed.

The trams destroyed in November 1947 were: handbrake 'Standards' Nos.13, 52, 74, 78, 139, 640/41/49/55/57/65/70/86/91/92, 711/13/17; air braked 'Standards' Nos.126, 316-18/29/34/36/40/67/82/85/86/91, 407/20/45, 728; streamlined four-wheel cars Nos.233/34/56/82/90-92/94/95, 300; streamlined bogie cars Nos.159/63/73, 876/82/88/92/94-96/98, 908/12/15/59/60/80/87/91; snowploughs Nos.506/97; and two salt cars. Nos.41, 157, 328 and 887 were damaged but restored to service and four sets of trucks were salvaged and reused under Nos.879/81, 957/92. Other salvaged equipment was sold to Leeds and Glasgow.

Following council approval of the conversion programme in 1947, the first two routes were abandoned on 12 June 1948. These were the heavily used 'Belt routes' with their sections of narrow single track and loops: 26/26A the Outer Circular from South Castle Street (via Everton Valley and Oakfield Road) and the 27/27A Outer Circular from South Castle Street (via Park Lane and Lodge Lane). The short working numbers 26A and 27A were rarely shown on the indicator blinds. The use of red on white route numbers to indicate cars terminating mostly at South Castle Street ended in 1947, although this colour combination could still be seen for some time afterwards.

In July 1948 Marks was succeeded by his deputy, W.M. Hall, whose job included overseeing the tram to bus conversion. The next routes to go survived longer than planned until approval was eventually obtained from the traffic commissioners and the busy cross-city route 3 – Walton to Dingle (via Cazneau Street, Lime Street and Park Road) – was converted as from 12 December 1948 and the 43/43B (Pier Head to Utting Avenue [via Dale Street and Everton Valley]) as from 16 January 1949. Converting route 3 marked the abandonment of the track in Norton Street, St Anne's Street and Cazneau Street and the diversion of routes 23, 24 and 28 to terminate at South Castle Street.

Despite the conversion programme, in early 1949 the Ministry of Transport approved expenditure of £675,00 for track renewal over a two-year period. Two more routes were replaced in May 1949: the 15 (Pier Head to Croxteth Road via Church Street and Princes Road) and the 12 (South Castle Street to West Derby via Church Street) operating for the last time on the 14 May and 21 May respectively. Closed before the war, the 15 had been quickly reinstated with the outbreak of hostilities. Paralleled by various bus routes, it involved less than a mile of track and needed only four cars to maintain the off-peak timetable. The replacement of the 12 involved full closure of the first section of reserved track. Shortly after, the long route 10 (South Castle Street to Prescot via Prescot Road) was replaced as from 26 June 1949 together with short workings 9 and 9A, although these numbers continued to be used for a while by cars working to and from Green Lane depot. This conversion had originally been scheduled for April but was deferred due to local opposition. South-end routes 1,

The next route converted was the 3, from Walton to Dingle. This route survived until 11 December 1948. M. J. O'Connor/NTM

1A and 1B (Pier Head to Dingle, Aigburth or Garston) were discontinued as from 13 August 1949 together with cross-city route 20 (Aigburth Vale to Aintree via Park Road, Whitechapel and Scotland Road). As a result of these abandonments, Park Road and Whitechapel were closed to trams and routes 8, 21, 33 and 45 were revised. The next conversion, took place on 14/15 October 1949 and involved the peak-hour-only 5A (Pier Head to Penny Lane) as well as routes 4 (Pier Head to Penny Lane via Wavertree Road) and 5 (Pier Head to Penny Lane via Smithdown Road), which operated as circles with a change of number at Penny Lane. Also replaced were the routes serving Woolton: the 4W (Castle Street via Dale Street and Wavertree Road); the 5W (Castle Street via Church Street, Myrtle Street and Smithdown Road); and the unnumbered, long peak-hour cross-city route from Woolton to Gillmoss and Kirkby, in reality an extension of the 48. At the same time, routes 8 and 8A were diverted to operate via Myrtle Street to allow the abandonment of the worn track in

May 1949 witnessed the conversion of two routes: the 15 on 14 May and the 12 on 21 May. Here No.316 is pictured on South Castle Street while operating on the latter. No.316 was destroyed in the Green Lane depot fire of November 1947. W. J. Haynes

The last route converted to bus in 1949 was the former route 4A from Pier Head to Childwall. Seen here while the service retained a route number is No.601. C. A. Noon/ Online Transport Archive

Mount Pleasant and Oxford Street and all outbound cars formerly using Ranelagh Street were rerouted via Parker Street and Eliot Street.

Three further conversions occurred during 1949. On 5 November two peak-hour-only routes – the 7 (Old Haymarket to Penny Lane via London Road and Smithdown Road) and the 32 (South Castle Street to Penny Lane via Park Lane and Upper Parliament Street) – operated for the last time. And as from 12 December, the former route 4A (Pier Head to Childwall Five Ways via Wavertree Road), unnumbered since the conversions in October, was replaced by buses. This group of south-end abandonments led to Prince Alfred Road depot closing. Other work saw the reserved track along Utting Avenue reduced to a single line used each morning and evening by a handful of cars on industrial route 37 (Seaforth to Utting Avenue East). This probably also marked the end of football cars bringing Liverpool FC supporters from the city to Anfield. To improve services on the trunk line to Aintree, routes 30 and 31 were extended from Walton in November 1949. In the meantime, nearly 150 cars were refurbished between 1950 and 1953 and a new simplified livery was introduced.

It is hard to believe but nearly 100 of the city's modern trams were off the road with faults until the middle of 1950. However, as tracks were relaid and cars overhauled and repainted, opposition to the replacement programme increased. In early 1950 the *Liverpool Daily Post* commented: 'There is evidence of growing dissatisfaction among people using passenger transport routes affected by the gradual turnover from trams to buses. There was perhaps bound to be an unsettling transitory period, but on some routes where the change has been in operation for two or three months the present bus services are proving quite inadequate.'

The first curtailment of 1950 involved relocating the terminus at Bowring

Park to the end of the reserved track in February. This meant cars no longer had to cross the busy road to reach the former roadside terminus among the trees. The next routes to go were the 30 (Pier Head and Aintree) and the cross-city 46 (Penny Lane to Walton via Netherfield Road) as from 3 September 1950. At the same time, route 25 was rerouted to allow for closure of the worn single track and loops section along Netherfield Road, and the 31 was truncated to terminate once again at Walton and rerouted via Dale Street. Industrial services 34 (Seaforth to Longview) and 38 (Seaforth to Penny Lane) were also replaced as from 2 September 1950.

In summer 1950 it had been announced that all the routes serving the Borough of Bootle (which owned the track, some of which was in lamentable condition) were to be replaced and Litherland depot converted into a bus garage. This was accomplished in stages. Five routes operated for the last time on 2/3 December 1950: the 16 (Pier Head to Litherland via Vauxhall Road and Bridge Road), peak-hour 22A (Pier Head to Fazakerley via Hale Road), 23 (South Castle Street to Seaforth via Stanley Road and Rimrose Road), 24 (South Castle Street to Seaforth via Stanley Road and Knowsley Road) and 28 (South Castle Street to Litherland via Stanley Road and Bridge Road). Next came route 17 (Pier Head to Seaforth via Great Howard Street and Rimrose Road), which operated for the last time on 30 December. As a result of the closure of Tithebarne Street, route 22 was diverted along Dale Street, although Great Crosshall Street was retained as a peak-hour boarding point.

In February 1951, the Bootle conversion programme was completed. Four routes ran for the last time on 10 February, three of which only ran at peak times mostly carrying workers to and from the labour-intensive north-end docks and none penetrated the central area. These were all-day route 18 (Seaforth to Breck Road via Sandhill Lane and Breckfield Road North) and industrial services 18A (Seaforth to Grant Gardens via Sandhills Lane and St Domingo Road), the 36 (Seaforth to Lower Lane or Gilmoss via Melrose Road and Walton Hall Avenue) and 37 (Seaforth to Utting Avenue East via Everton Valley). The final Bootle route replaced was the peak hour only 35 (Seaforth to Fazakerley via Melrose Road), which operated for the last time on 15 February 1951. Freshly painted No.990 was specially driven over to make the final ceremonial run. Carrying various civic dignitaries, it left the once bustling terminus at Seaforth at 6.30pm.

Although some of the newer cars were still being rebuilt at Edge Lane, each conversion led to the withdrawal of older cars, some of which were still in the former red livery including Nos.137 and 577. Major track renewal continued on routes that were scheduled to survive for some time and in a few places disused junctions were replaced by plain track. The building of new roundabouts led to various track modifications, for example at the junction of Princes Road and Croxteth Road and on Walton Hall Avenue at Stopgate Lane where the tracks were laid through the centre of the roundabout (in contrast to the revised junction at Edge Lane and St Oswald's Street where the tracks circumnavigated the new roundabout opened in June 1951).

Rationalising the terminal arrangements at the Pier Head led to the north loop closing in January 1951 and the rerouting (in some cases) and redistribution of services 2, 13, 14, 19, 22, 31 and 44 to the surviving centre and south loops.

On 4 August 1951 two more routes were converted: the cross-city 21 (Aigburth Vale to Aintree via Mill Street and Scotland Road) and the 22 (Pier Head to Fazakerley via Scotland Road). To

Four routes were converted to bus on 3 December 1950. Here No.91 awaits departure from Pier Head north loop with a service to Litherland. Note the air raid shelter on the left. R.G. Hemsall

Route 18 from Breck Road to Seaforth was one of four services operated by tram for the last time on 10 February 1951. Here No.305 is seen awaiting departure. M. J. O'Connor/NTM

offset partially these closures two new, shortlived services were introduced: route 2 (Pier Head to Aintree via Scotland Road) and route 45A (South Castle Street to Aigburth via Mill Street). The latter only survived until 8 September 1951 when it was abandoned together with the 45 (Pier Head to Garston via Mill Street). At Garston, cars on the 45 returned to the city via route 8 and cars on the 8 returned to the city as 45s. To create a new 'circle', routes 8 and 33 were now linked numbers being changed en route usually at Aigburth, Garston or Penny Lane. The 45 conversion also marked the end of operation along Castle Street with all trams using Church Street now accessing the Pier Head by way of James Street. South Castle Street also stopped being a regular terminus, although one track around the Victoria Monument was kept for use in emergencies and for one scheduled journey per week. Dingle depot was closed as a running depot but remained accessible to trams until early January 1952.

There was one final conversion in 1951 – the recently introduced route 2 (Pier Head to Black Bull or Aintree via Scotland Road and Rice Lane) was replaced as from 10 November. This was the last route serving Aintree, which had once seen streams of trams on racedays, with some showing 'Races' on the indicator. Other sporting references included 'Football', 'Football Ground' and 'Cricket Ground'. Many of these sporting extras had loaded in Victoria Street, which had no regular service. The very last football extras ran in late October 1956 carrying Everton supporters.

By the end of 1951, the system had contracted to some sixty route miles, including twenty-five miles on reserved track worked by fifteen basic services from four depots. It was operated by approximately 350 trams, including a few remaining variants of the Priestly 'Standards', some of which, like No.701, had been repainted, possibly by mistake, into the new 'Hall' green and cream livery.

On 3 November 1951 No.852 is seen on route 25 at the Dingle turning onto Aigburth Road. John Meredith/Online Transport Archive

No.925 pictured at Penny Lane on route 49 on 12 October 1947; this was one of three routes converted on 5/6 September 1952. No.925 was sold for further service to Glasgow. R.B. Parr/NTM

On 5 January 1952 the cross-city 25 (Aigburth Vale to Walton via Princes Road and Heyworth Street) and the 31 (Pier Head to Walton via Heyworth Street) were converted. The previous day, the handful of daily journeys on the lengthy unnumbered industrial service that linked Dingle to Kirkby by way of routes 25 and 29 was operated for the last time. This closure led to most of the surviving Priestly 'Standards' being withdrawn, although four were converted into snowploughs and painted into overall green. This left just a few of the modernised and newer 'Standards', mostly used as peak-hour extras from Edge Lane depot, although occasionally appearing on all-day duties.

With this closure, Walton depot (usually referred to as 'Spellow Lane' on destination blinds) was isolated from the operational network, cars having to work in and out over tracks with no regular service. These included a lengthy section along St Domingo Road and Heyworth Street as far as Grant Gardens, which was kept for depot workings, diversions and football extras and featured short lengths of single and interlaced track.

The next conversion occurred on 21 June 1952 and marked the end of the frequent 10C (Pierhead to Longview via Dale Street) as well as the unnumbered peak-hour service from Edge Lane (Southbank Road) to Longview. Only a short section of reserved track was actually abandoned and the 10B continued to operate as far as Page Moss on a reduced twenty-minute off-peak headway but supplemented by many peak-hour extras. However, there was now no Sunday service. Route 39 was also discontinued. This number had been displayed for short workings on the 40 as well as for cars returning to Edge Lane depot, a practice that continued unofficially for several more months.

By the end of August 1952 the last 'Standards' had been withdrawn so that by the end of the year the non-streamlined fleet consisted of nine EE bogie cars, six Priestly bogie cars, and a mix of fifty-two 'Cabin cars' and 'Marks bogies'.

At this stage, the remaining system

was in reasonably good shape with miles of segregated reservation, recently relaid track and many rebuilt or refurbished cars ranging in age from 10 to 21 years old. This could still have formed the basis for a modern light rail system, but it was not to be. From Friday 5 September 1952 two industrial services were converted: the 42 (Southbank Road / Edge Lane to Penny Lane via Mill Lane) and the 48 (Penny Lane to Gillmoss via Mill Lane and Muirhead Avenue East). On Saturday 6 September the outer suburban route 49 linking Penny Lane in the south with Muirhead Avenue East by way of Mill Lane, St Oswald's Street and Green Lane operated for the last time. No track was abandoned, although the section from Penny Lane to Edge Lane Drive was only kept to connect the remaining south-end routes with the works.

To cater for new housing estates and growing industrial premises, the routes serving Gillmoss and beyond were revised during 1952/53. On 6 October 1952 the 19A was extended from Lower Lane to the city boundary at Gillmoss, and a new number 19B was assigned to peak-hour journeys terminating on the long wartime loop built to serve the Napier Factory at Gillmoss. This number was also shown on some short-working inbound cars. The Napier sidings were also served at peak hours by cars on other routes. In May 1953 the 19A was extended to a new crossover at an isolated point on the East Lancashire Road known as Southdene; this was also used by the extended 44 from 7 December 1953. Service frequencies on routes 19 and 44 were also improved, although residents in the new estates complained about the trudge across muddy paths to reach Southdene.

The next conversion involved the impressive routes 8 (Pier Head to Garston

Having just passed Garston depot, No.922 heads into St Mary's Road, Garston, on route 33 heading back into Liverpool city centre. R.W.A. Jones/Online Transport Archive

via Smithdown Road and Mather Avenue) and 33 (Pier Head to Garston via Princes Road and Aigburth Road). The proposed abandonment of the Garston Circle was strongly opposed at the Traffic Commissioners' hearing. A ratepayer objected to the loss of recently relaid track; the corporation, however, argued successfully that the losses made by the two routes (£700 a week) more than outweighed interest charges on the cost of the recently relaid track. With only a few days' notice, the two routes were replaced as from 6 June 1953, with the last car along Mather Avenue, No.979, leaving the Pier Head at midnight. With this conversion, Garston depot was closed and trams removed from the south of the city. Miles of recently relaid track were abandoned and the link between Penny Lane and Edge Lane Drive was used for the last time during the following few days by the few cars relocated to Walton depot and by those going into open storage on the west side of Edge Lane works. These were the twenty-four streamlined bogie cars mounted on M&T trucks that had been sold to Glasgow Corporation for £500 each, which made their way north between September 1953 and March 1954 with the trucks and bodies travelling separately.

On 4 July 1953, the peak-hour-only service between Caird Street (serving Ogden's tobacco factory) and Pagemoss was replaced. Although officially un-numbered, the cars sometimes showed 10B on the blind. Withdrawn at the same time was half-hourly route 11 (North John Street to Green Lane via Church Street and West Derby Road, returning via Dale Street). Basically supplementing the 29s on the West Derby Road corridor, this was the last all-day route not terminating at the Pier Head and the last to operate wholly on street track. Following this conversion, just under 220 trams remained.

Yet another depot fire occurred on 1 March 1954, this time at Walton, after which eight burnt or scorched cars were eventually scrapped; three (Nos.151, 170 and 963 on EMB lightweight as opposed to HR/2 trucks) did return to service. The fire was believed to have resulted from an electrical fault on No.983. As a result, buses appeared on 13, 14, 19 and 44 for several hours; also during the rebuilding of parts of the depot, some service trams were stored overnight on the football siding in Walton Lane. The bogie fleet was greater reduced when a further twenty-two 'Liners' on a mix of EMB lightweight and HR/2 trucks were sold to Glasgow; the first, No.878, headed north on 13 May 1954. As a result, some of the remaining non-streamliners enjoyed a short reprieve, including the five EE bogies, 760/62/64-66, housed at Edge Lane. Also soldiering on at Walton, which still needed approximately 100 trams, were a dwindling number of 'Cabins' and 'Marks' bogies. On 27 April fire claimed a further car when No.174 was destroyed on Breck Road while operating on route 13.

The only conversion of 1954 occurred on Sunday 4 April when buses replaced trams on the trunk West Derby Road and Muirhead Avenue corridor: routes 29 (Pier Head to Lower Lane via Dale Street and Muirhead Avenue East), 29A (Pier Head to Muirhead Avenue East via Dale Street) and the short-working 29B. Also replaced were the peak hour 29s to Kirkby and Gillmoss as well as industrial service 47 (Southbank Road to Muirhead Avenue), which ran for the last time during the midday peak on Saturday 3 April. The final 29 to leave the Pier Head was No.891. Following this major conversion, Green Lane depot was officially closed and full operation of the 10B passed to Edge Lane, which had already been supplying some of its additional peak-hour cars. With closure of the centre loop at the Pier Head, the 10B was reassigned to the south loop as from Monday 5 April. A short length of

Only three routes were converted to bus during 1954; one was the 29, from Pier Head to Lower Lane. Here No.944 stands at the Lower Lane terminus. The tram is in the simplified 'Hall' livery.
Phil Tatt/Online Transport Archive

reserved track along Lowerhouse Lane was kept between Lower Lane and Utting Avenue East, which allowed a few cars working to and from Walton depot to use Breck Road and Grant Gardens rather than the more congested route via Walton Hall Avenue and Everton Valley. This arrangement survived until November 1955.

The conversion programme resumed on Saturday 5 March 1955 when the 10B (Pier Head to Page Moss via Dale Street and Prescot Road) ran for the last time. This was the last route along this once extremely busy corridor with its intense peak-hour service. Although needing just four cars during the off-peak, significant numbers of extras still appeared on the 10B during rush hours, most of which boarded at Low Hill, Commutation Row or Clayton Square. Also replaced was industrial route 41 (Southbank Road to Page Moss via St Oswald's Street). This ran for the last time during the Saturday midday peak, although the last 10B to arrive at Page Moss, No.249, returned to Edge Lane depot as a 41. All the surviving non-streamlined cars, Nos.760/62/64-66, 811-13/18/37/41/43/56, were now withdrawn. Eventually they took their place on 'the dump', a series of unwired sidings on the east side of the works where they were either broken up or taken to the 'fire dump' at the back for disposal. Also here were various defective 'Liners' and 'Baby Grands'. However, during 1955, thirty-one 'Liners' were put through the works for major refurbishment, during which leaks were plugged and seats repaired. By this time, no two cars were exactly alike!

From 5 November 1955, two further routes were replaced: the 13 (Pier Head to Lower Lane via Dale Street, Islington and Breck Road) and the 14 (Pier Head to Utting Avenue East via Church Street and Breck Road). Also abandoned were the 13A and 14A, numbers carried by short-working cars or by peak-hour journeys to Kirkby and Napier's sidings. In the city centre, the three-track, peak-hour boarding point at Old Haymarket used by the 6s, 13s and 14s was abandoned, as was North John Street, which still had a couple of scheduled workings. Peak-hour extras on the 6/6A were now diverted via Clayton Square. To prevent overcrowding on trams departing from the Pier Head, the corporation had, over the years, established a number of these peak-hour boarding points in the central area, of which Roe Street, Commutation Row, North John Street and Old Haymarket all closed during 1955. The 13/14 conversion led to the withdrawal of thirty-five cars, nearly all 'Liners' from Walton depot.

At the start of 1956 the fleet consisted of thirty-four 'Liners' and eighty-four

No.953 heads towards the Pier Head with a route 13 car along Lord Street. This tram was one of those scrapped on the Kirkby Trading Estate in early 1957. The tram is showing the wrong route number as the 13s ran via Dale Street. Note the bomb damaged site on the left. R.W.A. Jones/Online Transport Archive

'Baby Grands'. By the summer, Walton depot housed only 'Baby Grands', but for a brief period in August some peak-hour journeys were operated by 'Liners' based at Edge Lane, which worked down to the Pier Head before departing as a 19 or 44. Latterly the 'Liners' tended to appear mostly on the many peak-hour extras needed to transport the hundreds employed in the labour-intensive factories located along Edge Lane. The penultimate phase of the conversion programme saw the replacement of the 19 (Pier Head to Kirkby via Church Street, Robson Street and Walton Hall Avenue), 19A (Pier Head to Southdene via Church Street, Robson Street and Walton Hall Avenue) and 44 (Pier Head to Southdene via Dale Street, Scotland Road, Everton Valley and Walton Hall Avenue) as from 3 November 1956. Also abandoned were their many short workings including journeys on the 19B and 44A as well as the last of the central area peak-hour boarding points in Great Crosshall Street. With these closures trams no longer weaved their way through the maze of one-way workings in Everton where inbound and outbound trams ran in separate streets. The final 44, No.293, carried the inscription 'Scotland Road's Last Tram', the last car from Kirkby was No.206 and the very last car to carry passengers along the fine reservations on East Lancashire Road and Walton Hall Avenue was No.207, which departed from Southdene at approximately 1am. Some forty minutes later it was all over and long sections of reserved track, some opened as late as 1944, had been discarded. During the early hours, Walton's 'Baby Grands' were transferred to Edge Lane and the depot was closed. During the Saturday midday peak on 3 November, some of the surviving 'Liners' made their final runs on the Edge Lane routes, the last to return

Two cars stand at the Southdene terminus: No.956 is on route 19, and No.220 is on the 44. Both services were converted on 3 November 1956. Phil Tatt/Online Transport Archive

to the depot being No.151. As part of this closure, Dale Street was also closed to trams with all journeys on the 6 and 6A now running via Church Street as from 4 November 1956. During the Sunday, the surviving bogie cars, Nos.151-54/56/58/60/65/72/82/86, 870/889, 906/07/09/11/16/17/45/47/48/50/53/56/71/73/74/81/90/92, made the long journey out to Kirkby where they were transferred onto a group of sidings within the Trading Estate. The 19/44 conversion had occurred contemporaneously with the Suez crisis and there was pressure from the local media that the services be restored while the oil crisis continued, but this came to nothing and the stored trams were sold for scrap, the last being No.186 on 26 April 1957.

On 1 January 1957 the active fleet consisted of some sixty 'Baby Grands' with eleven in store together with two snowploughs (Nos.SP1 and SP4) and three works cars (Nos.234/83/87), the latter being owned and maintained by the City Engineers & Surveyors and painted in their two-tone grey livery.

The Suez crisis did prolong the life of the remaining routes. An increased service was introduced on the 40 as from 10 December 1956, a new loading island opened on Lime Street and several cars returned to service; others were repaired and repainted, although sometimes only the lower panels were done. On the debit side, cars with major and minor defects were usually put on the dump with one of the works cars or snowploughs acting as a shunter by using a feed via a bamboo pole to propel cars along the non-electrified sidings.

During summer 1957, it was announced that 14 September was to be the last day of tramway operation and would mark the end of routes 6/6A and 40. The fleet further contracted, but one fascinating tramway anomaly remained – each Sunday morning a hospital extra used part of the former turning loop round the Victoria Monument at South Castle Street. This weekly car picked its way cautiously round the muck-filled rails under the watchful eye of an inspector. No.271 was the final 'special' round the loop on 7 July 1957, after which the hospital working departed from Clayton Square.

During the final week, a tour of the system was held by the Light Railway Transport League (LRTL) on board No.245; souvenir tickets were issued and No.293 ran in public service in a special 'Last Tram' livery of cream and green. On Friday, 13 September some thirty 'Baby Grands' were on the road, of which a few were withdrawn after the morning and evening peak. A more limited service was operated on Saturday, 14 September with trams gradually replaced by buses. The last service car on route 6A was No.293, which left the Pier Head for Bowring Park with a full load of passengers shortly after 1.50pm. The last No.40 was No.274, which left the Pier Head for Pagemoss shortly after 4pm and was back at the depot just before 5pm.

Large crowds gathered at the Pier Head and in various places along the route to watch the final procession of thirteen cars, which departed to a cacophony of ship's hooters at 5.30pm. In the lead was No.210 (bedecked with flags) followed by Nos.264, 214, 235, 213, 226, 266, 260, 296, 245, 207 and 293. At Bowring Park the cars reversed before making the final trip to Edge Lane. By 6.30pm the once mighty Liverpool tram system was defunct and the bus reigned supreme.

The remaining trams had been sold to George Cohen for scrap but two 'Baby Grands' were secured for preservation. The last passenger tram broken up was No.271 on 15 January 1958, and the last tram of all scrapped was rail scrubber No.287, which followed on 27 January 1958.

Saturday, 14 September 1957 saw the final operation of Liverpool's trams. Baby Grand No.293 was painted in a reversed livery to act as official last tram; it is seen at Bowring Park during the course of the day. J. Joyce/Online Transport Archive

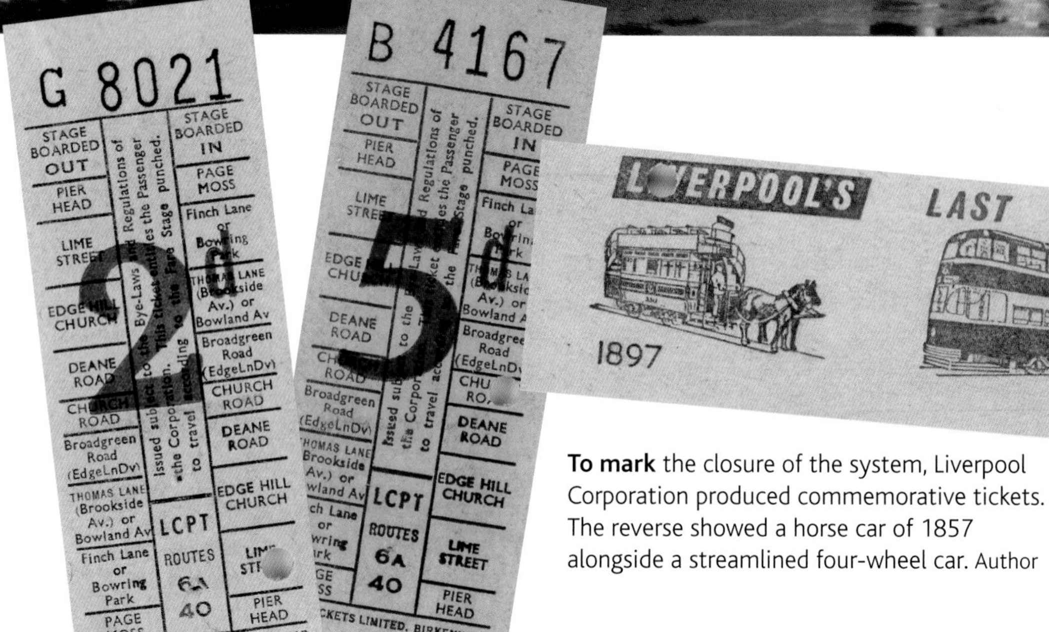

To mark the closure of the system, Liverpool Corporation produced commemorative tickets. The reverse showed a horse car of 1857 alongside a streamlined four-wheel car. Author

Depots

Seven depots served Liverpool's tramways post-war. Replacing an antiquated facility at Lambeth Road, a new depot with capacity for approximately 100 trams opened on part of a large site at Edge Lane in 1926. This was followed by a new works in 1928. This massive complex had more than two miles of track. Scores of new trams were built here and others were rebuilt, refurbished and overhauled. Once employing nearly 1,000 people, Edge Lane served the tram fleet until September 1957.

Dingle depot was opened by the corporation on 16 November 1898 and enlarged in the late 1930s to hold up to 140 cars. Although gradually converted for buses, a few trams were housed here until September 1951 and access was possible until January 1952.

Infamous as the site of several depot fires, especially that of 7 November 1947, Green Lane was originally opened in 1881 by the Liverpool United Tramways & Omnibus Co. Rebuilt in 1901, it housed more than 100 trams. With its awkward entrance directly onto a narrow part of Prescot Road, it survived as a tram depot until April 1954.

Located in the Borough of Bootle, Litherland depot was opened by the Liverpool United Tramways & Omnibus Co in about 1894. It was taken over by the corporation and converted to house electric trams, with the frontage opening directly onto a busy urban street. The building was substantially upgraded and extended in 1939 to hold some eighty cars. Gradually converted to a bus garage, the last trams were displaced in late December 1950.

The large Prince Alfred Road depot opened in 1928. Located a short distance from the earlier Smithdown Road depot, it accommodated approximately 100 cars for most of the south-end routes. Gradually converted, it was cleared of all trams after the closures of 11 December 1949.

Garston depot was opened by the corporation on 21 March 1910. To increase capacity, three tracks were laid without pits in the adjacent bus shed in 1940. Housing more than fifty trams, this depot survived until closure of the 8/33 in June 1953, the last car to leave being No.SP1 on 10 June.

The largest depot was at Walton (known as 'Spellow Lane') with capacity for some 200 cars. Overcrowding occasionally led to cars being parked in the street as well as on a long open siding on Carisbrooke Road. First opened by the Liverpool Tramways Co on 1 September 1870, it was enlarged and converted to house electric trams in 1901. Gradually converted, by November 1956 only five tracks were still used by the trams.

A number of earlier depots had also existed but closed before the war.

Closures

October 1946	43A – Pier Head to Utting Avenue (via Robson Street)
August 1947	16A – Pier Head to Kirkdale station (via Vauxhall Road)
12 June 1948	26/26A – Outer Circular from South Castle Street (via Everton Valley and Oakfield Road) 27/27A – Outer Circular from South Castle Street (via Park Pale and Lodge Lane)
11 December 1948	3 – Walton to Dingle (via Cazneau Street, Lime Street and Park Road)
15 January 1949	43 – Pier Head to Utting Avenue (via Dale Street and Everton Valley)

14 May 1949	15 – Pier Head to Croxteth Road (via Church Street and Princes Road)
21 May 1949	12 – Castle Street to West Derby (via Church Street)
25 June 1949	10 – Castle Street to Prescot (via Prescot Road)
13 August 1949	1/1A/1B – Pier Head to Dingle, Aigburth or Garston (via Church Street, Park Road and Aigburth)
	20 – Aigburth Vale to Aintree (via Park Road, Whitechapel and Scotland Road)
14 October 1949	5A – Pier Head to Penny Lane (peak hours only)
15 October 1949	4 – Pier Head to Penny Lane (via Wavertree Road)
	4W – Castle Street to Woolton (via Dale Street and Wavertree Road)
	5 – Pier Head to Penny Lane (via Church Street, Myrtle Street and Smithdown Road)
	5W – Castle Street to Woolton (via Church Street, Myrtle Street and Smithdown Road)
	unnumbered – Woolton to Gillmoss and Kirkby
5 November 1949	7 – Old Haymarket to Penny Lane (via London Road and Smithdown Road; peak hours only)
	32 – Castle Street to Penny Lane (via Parliament Street and Smithdown Road; peak hours only)
11 December 1949	4A – Pier Head to Childwall Five Ways (via Church Street and Wavertree Road; unnumbered service after 16 October 1949)
2 September 1950	34 – Seaforth to Longview (via Everton Valley and Sheil Road; peak hour only)
	38 – Seaforth to Penny Lane (via St Domingo Road and Smithdown Road; peak hours only)
3 September 1950	30 – Pier Head to Walton (via Dale Street and Netherfield Road)
	46 – Penny Lane to Walton (via Smithdown Road and Netherfield Road, returning via St Domingo Road)
2 December 1950	22A – Pier Head to Fazakerley (via Vauxhall Road; peak hours only)
3 December 1950	16 – Pier Head to Litherland (via Vauxhall Road)
	23 – South Castle Street to Seaforth (via Stanley Road and Rimrose Road)
	24 – South Castle Street to Seaforth (via Stanley Road and Knowsley Road)
	28 – Lime Street to Litherland (via Stanley Road and Bridge Road)
30 December 1950	17 – Pier Head to Seaforth (via Great Howard Street and Rimrose Road)
10 February 1951	18 – Breck Road to Seaforth (via Breckfield Road North and Sandhill Lane)
	18A – Grant Gardens to Seaforth (via St Domingo Road and Sandhills Lane; peak hours only)
	36 – Seaforth to Lower Lane (via Melrose Road and Walton Hall Avenue; peak hours only)
	37 – Seaforth to Utting Avenue East (via Everton Valley; peak hours only)
15 February 1951	35 – Seaforth to Fazakerley (via Melrose Road; peak hours only)
4 August 1951	21 – Aigburth Vale to Aintree (via Mill Street, Whitechapel and Scotland Road)
	22 – Pier Head to Fazakerley (via Scotland Road)
8 September 1951	45 – Pier Head to Garston (via Church Street and Mill Street; returning as route 8)
	45A South Castle Street to Aigburth (via Mill Street)
10 November 1951	2 – Pier Head to Aintree (Black Bull; peak hours only)
4 January 1952	Dingle to Kirkby (unnumbered service)

5 January 1952	25 – Aigburth Vale to Walton (via Princes Road and St Domingo Road, returning via Netherfield Road) 31 – Pier Head to Walton (via Church Street and St Domingo Road)
21 June 1952	10C – Pierhead to Longview (via Dale Street) Unnumbered – Edge Lane (Southbank Road) to Longview
5 September 1952	42 – South Bank Road (Edge Lane) to Penny Lane (via Mill Street; peak hours only) 48 – Penny Lane to Gillmoss (via Muirhead Avenue East; peak hours only)
6 September 1952	49 – Penny Lane to Muirhead Avenue East (via Mill Lane and St Oswald Street)
6 June 1953	8 – Pier Head to Allerton and Garston (via Church Street, Myrtle Street, Smithdown Road and Mather Avenue) 33 – Pier Head to Garston via Princes Road and Aigburth Road)
4 July 1953	11 – North John Street to Green Lane (via Church Street and West Derby Road, returning via Dale Street) Unnumbered (10B) – Caird Street to Page Moss
3 April 1954	29 – Pier Head to Lower Lane (via Dale Street and Muirhead Avenue East) 29A – Pier Head to Muirhead Avenue East (via Dale Street) 47 – South Bank Road (Edge Lane) to Muirhead Avenue East (peak hours only)
5 March 1955	10B – Pier Head to Page Moss Avenue (via Dale Street) 41 – South Bank Road (Edge Lane) to Page Moss Avenue (via St Oswald Street; peak hours only)
5 November 1955	13 – Pier Head to Lower Lane (via Dale Street and Townsend Avenue) 14 – Pier Head to Utting Avenue East (via Church Street and Townsend Avenue)
3 November 1956	19 – Pier Head to Kirkby (via Church Street, Robson Street and Walton Hall Avenue) 19A – Pier Head to Southdene (via Church Street, Robson Street and Walton Hall Avenue) 44 – Pier Head to Southdene (via Scotland Road and Walton Hall Avenue)
14 September 1957	6A – Pier Head to Bowring Park 40 – Pier Head to Page Moss Avenue (via Browlow Hill and Edge Lane Drive)

Liverpool Fleet

1, 6-11, 13-18, 20-27, 29, 30, 32, 34, 36, 39-42, 45-53/55-58, 60-69, 71-80, 82-86, 90, 92-94, 99, 100/02/04/06-13/15/16/ 118-21/23/24/27/29-31/33/35/37/39- 144/46/49, 301/02/06/09/10/13/15/19/20/ 23-27/31/33/39/41/44/48/56/58/59/68/72/73/ 76/78/80/83/87/89, 400/10/15/29/32/41/ 50/62/71, 637-70/72-94/96-720/33/34

In all, some 321 Priestly Standard cars were built between 1922 (when No.358, a handbrake car with enclosed top deck but open vestibules was completed) and February 1933 (when totally enclosed Nos.268 [the last] and 380 entered service). These were the last new trams to enter service in the traditional crimson lake and cream livery first adopted in 1898. All new trams thereafter emerged in green, the first version being olive green and ivory. The majority of the 'Standards' were built at Lambeth Road but the final ninety were completed at Edge Lane. In accounting terms some

Standard No.716 is seen as converted to fully enclosed. Most of the Priestly cars delivered during the 1920s had fully enclosed upper decks but open driving platforms. Following the introduction of enclosed platforms on No.744 in 1927, many of the earlier cars were modified. This has the post-war wood and canvas utility windscreen. Phil Tatt/Online Transport Archive

170 were built on the revenue account as notional rebuilds of older cars (including a number of Bellamy Roof cars), taking the numbers of the trams they replaced. Initially the 'Standards' were fitted with Brill 21E trucks of varying wheelbases, but from 1926 onwards the story becomes ever more complex, with more than 100 being given trucks built from supplied parts, whereas others had radial or pendulum trucks, most being assembled by the corporation. During the life of the 'Standards', there were a number of truck modifications and replacements: some had improved motors, others magnetic track brakes and the body style also evolved with changes to the size and location of the indicator boxes as well as the seating arrangement.

Several were renumbered in 1937 to release numbers for the new series of streamlined cars. These were (with the old numbers in brackets): Nos.1 (168), 6 (151), 8 (154), 111 (171), 127 (186), 142 (199), 302 (208), 310 (219), 319 (263), 320 (265), 324 (268), 326 (271), 331 (281), 333 (288), 337 (296), 339 (297) and 341 (299).

War effectively ended the planned production of further new trams, with the result that many of the 'Standards' had a longer life than expected. During the war and well into the late 1940s, those with open vestibules were given basic 'utility' screens that afforded some protection for the driver. The Green Lane depot fire of 4 February 1942 destroyed Nos.19, 337 and 671, and No.37 was the only 'Standard' scrapped due to enemy action. In 1942 No.41 received the EMB truck salvaged from No.228, which had been withdrawn following damage in an air raid.

At the end of the war some 230 'Standards' remained but no withdrawals occurred until November 1946 when No.733 was taken out of service. During the second Green Lane fire in November 1947, eighteen 'Standards' were lost – Nos.13, 52, 74, 78, 139,

Pictured in front of the Royal Court Theatre, at the peak hour loading point on Roe Street, is No.751; this was one of a number of Priestly-designed cars modernised in the late 1930s as part of the upgrading of the fleet. Phil Tatt/Online Transport Archive

640/41/49/55/57/65/70/86/91/92, 711/13/17 – and thirty-four were withdrawn in 1948. The following year saw forty-four withdrawn, forty-two in 1950 and seventy-six in 1951. This left only fourteen in service at the start of 1952 and all were withdrawn following the conversion of routes 25 and 31 in early January. A few, including Nos.137, 694 and 709, were withdrawn still in the traditional red livery.

After withdrawal, four 'Standards' were converted into snowploughs at Edge Lane, one for each of the remaining depots: Nos.SP1 to SP4 were originally Nos.30, 703, 684 and 646 respectively. These had replaced a group of elderly Bellamy snowploughs. No.SP3 was the first to go after a spell as an Edge Lane shunter and at least one was actively involved clearing snow on Boxing Day 1956. In September 1956 No.SP4 made a special run along Edge Lane so it could be filmed and its motor noises recorded.

5, 12, 28, 31/35/38, 54, 81/87-89, 91/95-98, 101/05/14/26/28/47, 305/16-18/28/29/34/36/38/40/42/ 43/53/67/82/85/86/91/93, 407/20/40/45/51/ 54/59/69, 588, 673, 721-32/45-56

As detailed in his January 1935 report, Marks recommended building 300 new bogie cars as well modernising 162 of the Priestly-designed four-wheelers. The trams selected for this programme were those that had entered service between 1925 and 1930. The majority, except Nos.721-32 and 745-56 (which had radial trucks, the latter supplied by the Kilmarnock Engineering Co), were originally fitted with Brill 21E trucks. No.744 of 1927 was the first Liverpool tram fitted with a partially enclosed driver's vestibule and No.742 with a totally enclosed version. The general manager, Percy Priestly, had previously opposed their installation. The first car in the programme was the three-year old No.440, which was fully enclosed from new and fitted with a replacement M&T swing-link truck. The next car to emerge was No.253, which was fitted with an EMB flexible axle truck. Between 1935 and 1939, when the programme ended, seventy-five cars had been completed. In November 1937 a number of cars in the series between 151 and 299 were renumbered to accommodate the delivery of the new streamlined cars; this involved the following modernised cars (old numbers in brackets): Nos.12 (155), 126 (170), 305 (214), 316 (192), 317 (252), 318 (253), 328 (275), 329 (276) and 343 (233). The refurbishment work included conversion to fully enclosed, when not already in that state, as well as providing new trucks, motors, electrical equipment and a certain amount of bodywork (although the latter tended to be reduced as the programme progressed).

A number of cars were damaged during the war: No.31 in 1941 (it was never repaired and went for scrap in 1948), No.54 in an air raid in February 1942 (it was listed for scrap but was repaired and re-entered service fitted with a Brill 21E truck rather than an EMB flexible axle), No.91 overturned in November 1943 (but was restored to service) and No.317, which was listed for scrap in January 1942 but was restored to service the following year.

Although all the type just about survived the war, the Green Lane depot fire of November 1947 destroyed seventeen – Nos.126, 316-18/29/34/36/40/67/82/85/86/91, 407/20/45, 728 – and damaged others, including No.338, which received a replacement roof. Withdrawals saw a further three cars taken out of service in 1948, seven in 1949, six in 1950 and eighteen in 1951. The remaining cars were all withdrawn by August 1952 having mostly been used latterly for peak-hour short workings from Edge Lane. It is believed that the last survivor was No.747, which had undergone a comprehensive overhaul and repaint as late as February 1951.

33, 43, 70, 117/34/36/38, 303/04/12/14/21/22/30/32/35/63

Between 1920 and 1921 the corporation built twenty-eight open-balcony cars with Brill 21E trucks. Of these, ten incorporated bodies from older trams; these were all withdrawn between May 1934 and early 1939, although the bodies of two (Nos.117 and 126) were reused as vans Nos.9 and 8 respectively. The remaining eighteen cars were notionally rebuilds, although effectively the corporation-built bodies were new. Six of the notional rebuilds, Nos.138/79/87, 230/87 and 321, were rebuilt as fully enclosed in a style similar to the last of the Standard cars. These cars and the contemporary all-new cars (Nos.606-08/34-36) were nicknamed 'Birdcages'. Several were renumbered as part of the 1937 scheme: 70 (187), 117 (179), 303 (209), 304 (212), 213 (230), 314 (236), 330 (280), 332 (287) and 335 (291). One of the type, No.355, was withdrawn during the war, with the remainder withdrawn between 1946 and 1951. No.321 was the last to survive in passenger service, succumbing in August 1951. Nos.122/34 and 303 were converted to snowploughs during the war. Interestingly 303, still in red livery, was employed in late 1947 to tow damaged and burnt-out cars from Green Lane to Edge Lane. When finally withdrawn, No.122 (still in red) of 1921 was virtually in original condition and was the last open-balcony car in the fleet.

151-70/72-88, 868-942/44-88/90-92

During 1936 and 1937, no fewer than 163 high-speed streamlined seventy-eight-seat bogie cars were built in Edge Lane Works to a design by R.J. Heathman. Nos.151-88, 879/81-917/43-52/55/57 were fitted with EMB lightweight bogies, Nos.918-

42 with M&T swing link bogies and Nos.868-78/80, 953/54/56/58-92 with EMB heavyweight 'Jo'burg'-style bogies. No.955 received heavyweight trucks in 1954, and Nos.961/63/67 received EMB lightweight bogies the same year. Nos.171 and 989 were destroyed in the Green Lane depot fire of 4 February 1942. No.943 was withdrawn following an accident in September 1944. There were two withdrawals in 1945: No.910 following a runaway and No.913 was burnt to its frames following a collision on 13 April. The Green Lane fire of November 1947 destroyed Nos.159/63/73, 876/82/88/92/94-96/98, 908/12/15/59/60/80/87/91, and No.176 was withdrawn, in October 1950, again following a fire. Other fire victims included No.988 in 1953 and No.174 in 1954. Following the Green Lane fire, some bogies were salvaged for reuse and a number were sold to Leeds and Glasgow where some appeared under the city's last group of 'Coronations'.

The first of the type withdrawn other than because of accident or fire damage were six condemned in September 1953;

Pictured here awaiting scrapping is No.122; this was the last survivor of twenty-eight trams built between 1920 and 1922. Converted for snowplough use during the war and based at Garston depot, No.122 retained its pre-war red livery until withdrawal. Phil Tatt/ Online Transport Archive

Two of the 163 streamlined bogie cars stand at the Pier Head terminus alongside 'Baby Grand' No.240. R.W.A. Jones/Online Transport Archive

these included Nos.868, 920 and 969. Following the conversion of routes 8 and 33, Glasgow bought 918/9/21-942; these were twenty-four of the twenty-five cars on the M&T trucks at £500 per car (including delivery). The first to migrate northwards was No.927 in mid-September 1953 and all twenty-four had left by March 1954. A further twenty-two were bought by Glasgow in March 1954 at an increased price of £580 each. These all left by November 1954, with No.875 last to make the journey. The 46 cars, on a mix of EMB lightweight and heavyweight bogies, were Nos.869/71/74/75/77/78/80/81/83-87/90/91/93/97/99, 901-04/18/19/21-42.

A second post-war depot fire, at Walton, on 1 March 1954 destroyed three of the type, Nos.965/83/85, and as the system contracted, withdrawals became commonplace. By mid-1956 only thirty-one of the class remained active, all based at Edge Lane and mostly limited to rush-hour use only; the 'Baby Grands', which cost less to operate and maintain, were preferred for all-day operation. The end came on 3 November 1956, after which all the survivors were driven to Kirkby to await their fate; all were scrapped by 26 April 1957. None of the type survived in Liverpool, but Glasgow No.1055 (Liverpool No.869) was secured for preservation in 1959 by the Liverpool

The penultimate of the 100-strong 'Baby Grand' class was No.299. It is seen at the Pier Head showing 6C on the blind. This route number was never officially used although it did appear on a few blinds.
Ronnie Stephens/Online Transport Archive

University Public Transport Society. This car is now restored to Liverpool condition and displayed at the NTM.

201-24/26/27/29-300

Known as 'Baby Grands', the 100 70-seat streamlined double-deckers were built at Edge Lane on EMB flexible axle 9ft wheelbase trucks and fitted with two 60hp motors and recycled controllers from older cars. These cost-effective cars were twenty-five per cent lighter than a Liner but only held ten per cent fewer passengers. The first entered service in 1937 and by September 1939 there were ninety-five. The next three, Nos.296-98, were completed by February 1940 but it was not until January and October 1942 that the last two entered service, each of which differed in detail from the main production run. No.228 had a short life, being destroyed by enemy action in 1941. The only other wartime casualty was No.225, which was scrapped in November 1942 having succumbed to fire in the April – a problem that afflicted a number of this class. In fact, four more cars were damaged by fire in 1945: No.217 on 12 April, No.281 on 3 July, No.209 on 10 August and No.259, following a collision with a lorry, on 6 November. The remains of all were kept until the decision was taken to scrap them in late 1946. This predilection to burst into flames had disastrous consequences when, on 7 November 1947, fire broke out on No.295 in Green Lane depot; ten 'Baby Grands', Nos.233/34/56/82/90-92/94/95, 300, were among the casualties.

By the end of the decade a large number of the survivors were laid up due to their poor condition. Consequently, between 1950 and 1952, the corporation embarked on a programme of returning them to service but even this work was not always successful; the last car treated, No.287, was finished so poorly it had to be taken out of service in July 1953 for a further twelve-month overhaul. During this period, No.201 received two replacement trucks: from No.272 in September 1947 and from No.288 in April 1954.

Following the Green Lane fire, no further 'Baby Grands' were taken out of service until August 1956 when nine were withdrawn; even cars damaged by fire and accident, Nos.235/83/99, were repaired and restored to service. At the beginning of 1957 sixty-one 'Baby Grands' remained operational with a further eleven in store, with the latter being sold for scrap in June 1957 to George Cohen & Sons.

On the final day some thirty cars were in service. The final procession included thirteen 'Baby Grands', including No.293 repainted in a special commemorative livery, and No.210 bedecked with flags. All the remaining trams had already been sold to Cohens with the exception of Nos.245 and 293. No.245 was retained by the corporation and has now been fully restored, and No.293 went to the US and left from Liverpool on board the *American Packer* on 7 May 1958. It reached the Seashore Museum on 23 May.

502-06/07/13/39/40/44/46/53/55/58/64-66/75

Between 1908 and 1913 a total of seventy-four cars, Nos.501-70/73-76, were built by the corporation on Brill 21E trucks. Fitted from new with Bellamy top covers, the cars originally had open vestibules and balconies. These were the first of the Standard Top-Covered cars in that their Bellamy roofs were solid rather than having sliding panels. Nos.504/06/19-32/36-39/47-61/73-76 were designated as first-class cars, with the last of them operating in April 1923. The last two completed, Nos.575/76, were the first Liverpool trams fitted from new with open-balcony top covers (there were 445 Bellamy top cars completed; fifteen were rebuilt as open balcony during 1921 and 1922, eighty-six were rebuilt as Priestly 'Standards', twenty-one were converted

No.566, seen here awaiting scrapping after withdrawal, was one of seventy cars delivered with Bellamy top covers between 1908 and 1912. Converted to a snowplough in 1946, the car survived until last used during January 1952 when it was withdrawn from Walton depot. Phil Tatt/Online Transport Archive

for departmental use (mainly during the period from 1941 to 1943) and 323 were scrapped before the war).

Nos.507/43/58/61/64/66/75 were converted into Air Raid Protection (ARP) cars during the Second World War; the body of No.550 was used as an ARP car and scrapped in 1948. By the end of the war, a number had been or were to be converted into snowploughs: Nos.506/13/39/40/46/65 from 1942, No.503 from 1943 and Nos.507/58 from 1946. No.506 was destroyed in the Green Lane fire of 1947 and No.558 was sold to the LRTL Museum Committee in 1951, but after some time in open storage at Kirkby it was scrapped five years later. Only one of the type, No.565, was repainted green. The last in passenger service, No.544, still in red livery, was based at Prince Alfred Road and survived until 1949, often appearing at rush hours, especially on routes 7, 32 and 48. This historic car was sadly scrapped.

571/77-87/89-96/98-605

In 1912 UEC delivered a single car, No.571, which was one of two experimental cars that the then general manager, Charles William Mallins, was authorised to build. Fitted with a Brill 21E truck, the car had open platforms and balconies plus double staircases at both ends. Following this, Lambeth Road works built a further twenty-three similar cars between 1913 and 1915, Nos.577-99, and a further six cars, Nos.600-05, completed at Lambeth Road during 1919 and 1920. Of these, Nos.603-05 were fitted with only a single staircase at either end from new. When built, a number of the cars were fitted with experimental long-wheelbase radial trucks, although all eventually operated with Brill 21E trucks (Nos.584, 599 and 600 operated, between 1926 and 1930, on reused Brill maximum-traction bogies, and their smooth ride no doubt influenced the decision to invest heavily in bogie cars during the 1930s). In 1920 No.585 was modified to include only one staircase at each end; the remaining cars were so modified between then and the end of 1924 – the last twelve receiving enclosed upper decks at the same time. The remaining cars were later fitted with enclosed balconies. In 1936 No.588 was reconditioned to become a reconditioned EMB car. No.599 received a wartime windscreen and also exchanged numbers with No.61 in June 1948 when it was taken out of service. No.597, having been withdrawn in 1938, was converted into a snowplough in 1942. Of the remaining cars, all received basic

In 1949, No.577 is recorded outbound from the Pier Head and is about to pass under the Liverpool Overhead Railway on route 44. The tram is still in the red livery and is fitted with a wood and canvas windscreen. E. A. Gahan/Online Transport Archive

driver's windscreens by the end of 1947. Withdrawal of the type began in 1946, with Nos.589/90/95. The last withdrawn was No.592 on 19 April 1951. No.594 was also converted into a snowplough on withdrawal in December 1948.

607/08/34-36

In 1921 the corporation took delivery of six completely new open-balcony double-deck cars: Nos.606-08/34-36. These were given corporation-built bodies on Brill 21E trucks. No.634 was the first Liverpool

No.607, new in 1921, is pictured at Old Haymarket in 1947 on a peak hour working to Norris Green. In the background is No.896; this was one of the cars lost in the Green Lane depot fire later in the year. N. N. Forbes/NTM

No.618 was one of nine post-war survivors from a batch of twenty-five cars and was withdrawn during 1948. It is seen here on South Castle Street whilst working a peak hour service to Penny Lane.
C.A. Noon/Online Transport Archive

tram fitted with the more usual Tidswell, as opposed to plough, lifeguards. No.634 was rebuilt as fully enclosed in the early 1930s. No.606 was withdrawn in 1941. Nos.608 and 636 received enclosed driving platforms during the war, with No.608 later receiving enclosed upper-deck balconies and No.636 keeping its open balconies. On withdrawal in 1949 the lower deck from No.636 was reused with the truck from stores car No.Van 8 to create a new City Engineers & Surveyors works car. All were withdrawn by 1950.

614/18/21/25/27-31

In March 1919 a batch of twenty-five open-balcony cars, Nos.609-33, was ordered from EE; all were delivered by early 1920. Fitted with Brill 21E trucks, they remained open balcony and without windscreens throughout their operational careers. No.615 was withdrawn in

No.764 was one of twelve fully enclosed cars built at Edge Lane during 1931 and 1932 and was one of the last withdrawn, in March 1955, with its life extended due to the sale of the bogie cars to Glasgow. It is seen here on Lime Street outbound to Green Lane.
R.W.A. Jones/Online Transport Archive

'Priestly bogie' No 771, inbound from Fazakerley with a route 22 service in July 1951, is recorded on the Longmoor Lane reservation. J. H. Roberts/Online Transport Archive

1937 and a further fifteen had been taken out of service by the end of 1941. This left nine cars in service, of which six were repainted in the post-war green livery. Withdrawals resumed in 1947 with the loss of Nos.628/31. Six more, Nos.614/18/21/27/29/30, followed in 1948 (with Nos.614/27 being the last two in passenger service when they were withdrawn in October 1948), leaving the last survivor, No.625, still in red, to be withdrawn in 1949.

758-769

These twelve seventy-seat cars built by the corporation at Edge Lane during 1931 and 1932 were known as the 'English Electric bogies' and changed the public's opinion of the trams. They were fast, smooth and airy with comfortable seats. They were all originally fitted with air brakes and inside frame 'monomotor' bogies EE equal-wheel bogies. Between 1938 and 1944, Nos.759-62/64-67/69 were reconditioned and fitted with new motors, improved destination displays and EMB lightweight bogies originally intended for use under further new 'Liners'. The remaining three cars, still in virtually original condition, were withdrawn before the war and stored at Dingle depot but not sold for scrap until 1948. The next withdrawn were Nos.759/61/67/69, with the final five, Nos.760/62/64-66, equipped with electro-pneumatic control, surviving at Edge Lane until March 1955. The bulk of the lower saloon from 762 was transferred to the Parks & Gardens Department but the rest were scrapped. After No.762's body was rescued, it was restored by the Merseyside Tramway Preservation Society (MTPS).

770-72/74-81

This batch of twelve fully enclosed seventy-seat double-deck cars, known as the 'Priestly bogies' or the '770' class, was built by the corporation at Edge Lane in 1933 on EMB London-style HR/2 trucks. These were the first of Liverpool's famous 'Green Goddesses', a name given generally to all the modern

As the conductor carefully guides the trolleypole, 'Cabin' car No.789 is in Harlech Street about to enter Walton depot, probably after having worked a peak duty on the Gillmoss/Kirkby services. Cars returning to Walton depot usually showed 'Spellow Lane'. R.W.A. Jones/Online Transport Archive

cars appearing in their new eye-catching olive green and ivory paint scheme. There were differences within the group – for example, the first eight had flat roofs and the last four shallow domed roofs similar to that on London County Council (LCC) No.1 on whose design they were clearly based. No.773 was damaged on 28 November 1940 when it was hit during a bombing raid that killed at least 166 when the Durning Road air raid shelter was hit. The tram was scrapped in September 1943. The remaining cars were still in service in 1945. No.781 was withdrawn following an accident in 1949 and No.780 after its roof was torn off when it overturned in 1950. Nos.771/72/75-77 were sold for scrap during 1952 and No.774 early the following year. The remainder were all withdrawn by the end of 1953.

782-85/87-94/96-817

The thirty-six seventy-seat Robinson 'Cabin' cars, with their domed roofs, were built by the corporation during 1933 and 1934 on EMB heavyweight bogies to a design by Percival J. Robinson (the city's electrical engineer) in the interregnum between the death of Priestly and the appointment of Marks. He was influenced by LCC No.1 and the Middleton bogie cars ordered by Leeds. The cars had 120-degree reversed stairs, folding doors, concealed lighting and a separate driver's cab or cabin, hence the nickname 'Cabin cars' or 'Cabin Cruisers'. No.795 was an early casualty, withdrawn following fire damage on 19 August 1935. It was replaced by a new Marks bogie car. No.786 was another victim of the German bombing of Durning Road on 28 November 1940, with its remains scrapped in 1943. No.809 collided with a US army truck in December 1945; it was not repaired and the remains were sold for scrap in 1947. The next withdrawals occurred in 1951, when Nos.787, 801/05/08/14 were withdrawn; No.805 had been out of service since 1949 following a collision. By the end of 1953 only four of the class remained in service with one withdrawn in 1954 and the last survivors, Nos.811-13, withdrawn from Walton depot in March 1955.

795, 818-67

Once appointed Marks modified the design of the over-heavy Robinson-designed 'Cabin' class. In all, fifty-one of these fully enclosed seventy-seat bogie

No.827, one of the modified 'Marks bogies', is seen in Walton; all bar two of this type survived until withdrawal between April 1951 and March 1955. R.W.A. Jones/Online Transport Archive

cars were built at Edge Lane during 1935/6. They differed from the 'Cabin' cars in having ninety-degree stairs, no driver's cabin, sliding bulkhead doors and a revised destination display. The first group were mounted on EMB heavyweight bogies, whereas Nos.843 to 867 rode on lightweight bogies. However, No.819 was fitted with EE equal-wheel bogies from March 1937, which it retained as non-standard until withdrawal in April 1951. Nos.850/54 (the latter involved in a serious accident on 29 May 1943) were stored in a damaged condition by the end of the war; although there were plans to restore them to service, the decision was made to scrap the remains in late 1946. Of the remaining forty-nine cars, the first withdrawals occurred in April 1951 when eight cars succumbed, with the final five withdrawn from Walton depot in March 1955.

Works cars

Although Liverpool did not have as large a fleet of specialist works cars as other systems of its size, possibly due to track maintenance and repairs being the responsibility of the city engineers and Surveyor Department rather than the tramways department, but there were a number of ex-passenger cars and specially built vehicles serving various non-passenger duties.

There were no dedicated snowplough cars until the war, but bad wartime winters and the bitter winter of 1947 resulted in a number of ex-passenger cars being converted from December 1940 onwards. Initially these were temporary conversions but from December 1942, ten cars were permanently equipped and distributed to depots, especially those serving the miles of reservations. These were Nos.134, 506 (converted into a single-deck car following damage in the 1942 Green Lane depot fire) and 507/39/40/46/53/55/65/97. Further conversions followed as cars were replaced or re-entered passenger service. The last of the wartime and immediate post-war conversions to survive was No.553, which was scrapped in May 1953. It is believed the last Bellamy snowplough to see active duty was during winter 1951/2. The last four snowploughs, SP1 to SP4, formerly Priestly 'Standards' Nos.30, 703, 684 and 646, were available by the end of 1952. As the system contracted the need for snowploughs declined; No.SP3 was the first withdrawn, in September 1955 (but was still used to shunt withdrawn cars at Edge Lane); Nos. SP2 and SP4 succumbed in May 1957, although, No.SP2, was used to shunt withdrawn cars even after the system's closure. No.SP1 was the last to survive and was not scrapped until January 1958.

There were also a number of grinders, vans and scrubbers. In the post-war years these included vans Nos.S1-S4; the last three of these had been originally converted from German-built single-deck cars delivered in 1898, although No.S4 morphed during the 1930s to feature a Bellamy body on a US-supplied truck. No.S4 was last recorded in May 1948; Nos.S1-S3 were slated for scrap in 1947. A rare survivor was a German-built trailer used as a tool van at Garston depot. Never renumbered, this veteran car was secured for preservation (along with No.558) in 1950, but after open storage at Kirkby it was scrapped. Nos.S6, S7 and S9 were rail scrubbers converted from passenger cars Nos.332, 422 and 117 in the mid-1930s; the body of No.S9 was replaced by the lower deck of No.538 in early 1939. This trio was renumbered into the City Engineer's & Surveyor's fleet of lorries, steamrollers, wagons and dustbin carts 273, 283 and 287 respectively in 1948. No.S5 also survived the war; this had originally been converted from No.429 in 1929 with its body replaced from No.354 in 1935, but was scrapped in 1948. No.S8 was another conversion in the mid-1930s, from

By 1952 four ex-passenger cars were converted into snowploughs. No.SP1 was the last to survive, being finally scrapped on 16 January 1958. R.S. Stephens/Online Transport Archive

No.126; in 1949 its body was replaced by that from No.636. Never renumbered, it was scrapped in January 1952. The last totally new tram in Liverpool was built by the CE&S Department in their own workshops. Completed in October 1948, this rail grinder was numbered 234 in the CE&S fleet. It had a purpose-built body housing motor-driven grinding equipment with the underframe, truck and electrical equipment from withdrawn 'Standards'. No.273 was sold in May 1952, and No.287 became a scrapyard shunter in late 1956. The remaining two works cars, Nos.234/83, were the last two trams scrapped in late January 1958.

MANCHESTER

In the pre-war period Manchester Corporation had pursued a tramway conversion programme. This had been agreed on 7 July 1937 with the general manager, R. Stuart Pilcher, producing a plan on 17 August 1938 with a three-year programme. This was endorsed by the council on 8 February 1939 and the first planned conversions took place on 12 February 1939.

However, war meant the programme could not be undertaken, although, on 23 March 1940, converting route 51, from Miller Street to the University, to temporary bus operation was completed, allowing the erection of trolleybus overhead over the route.

At the end of the 1939/40 financial year, the tram fleet numbered 425 cars; some sixty awaited disposal – fifty-two

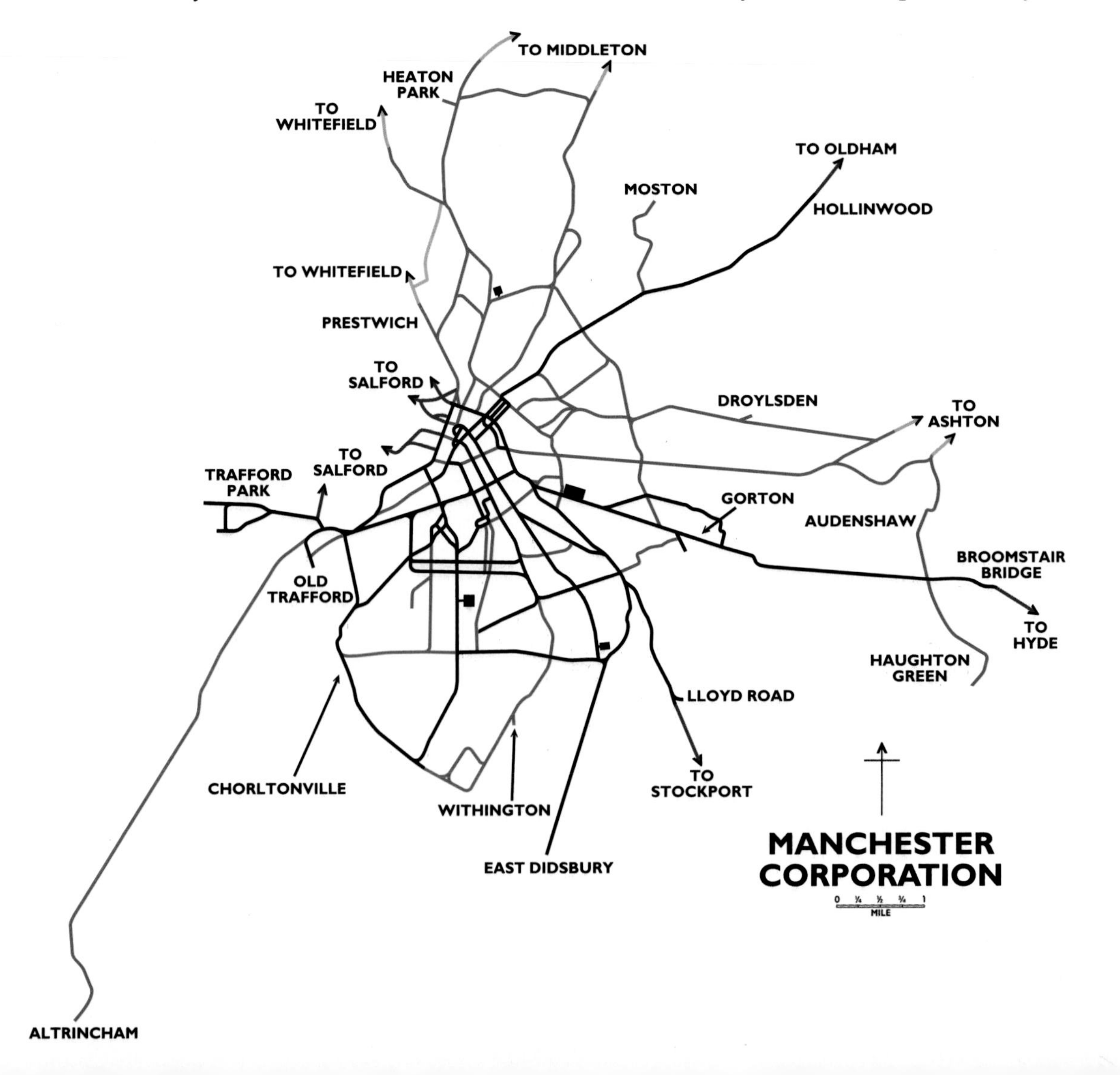

No.962 emerges from Birchfields Road and heads into Moseley Road, heading for Levenshulme. In the background is Birchfields depot. This car survived until the system's closure. F.E.J. Ward/Online Transport Archive

cars were scrapped by 31 March 1941 but, other than nine cars scrapped after damage or accidents, no further trams were scrapped until 1945. The fact that a number of routes had been converted to bus relatively recently meant, during the war, the corporation reinstated a number of services. The first, on 27 May 1940, was route 23, Chorlton to Hollinwood, which had been withdrawn on 2 July 1939. This was followed, on 17 June 1940, by extending weekday-only services on route 38 from West Point to Fallowfield (this section had been withdrawn in 1938); this enhancement was permitted by the earlier withdrawal of route 51 and the release of eight Pilcher cars. There was also an increase in the number of trams on the inner sections of routes 36 and 44 to Wythenshawe. Also during 1940 a new peak-hour service, 42F from Platt Lane to Exchange, was introduced, and, on 17 October, route 37 was extended from Barlow Moor Road to serve a new crossover at Princess Road. The following month, the services to Waterhead and Hollinwood, Nos.20/21, were extended in central Manchester from Stevenson Square to Piccadilly.

In late 1942 the Regional Transport Commissioner demanded bus mileage be cut by ten per cent. This resulted, on 23 November 1942, in restoring route 13 from Chorlton to Albert Square, which was further extended to Southern Cemetery on 20 December 1942. This was the last wartime route restoration. A new local service, the 38B Wilbraham Road to Moseley Road, was also introduced and trams replaced buses on some all-night services.

By 1945 the Manchester system was operated by some 364 trams. On 11 February 1945 the reintroduced routes Nos.13 and 23 were reduced to peak-hour operation only with the 23 curtailed to operate between Piccadilly and Chorlton; off-peak services were replaced by buses. The removal of the all-day service was the consequence of loaned buses being returned to Manchester. Pilcher believed, with peace, converting the tramway would restart; he was correct but, due to problems in the delivery of replacement

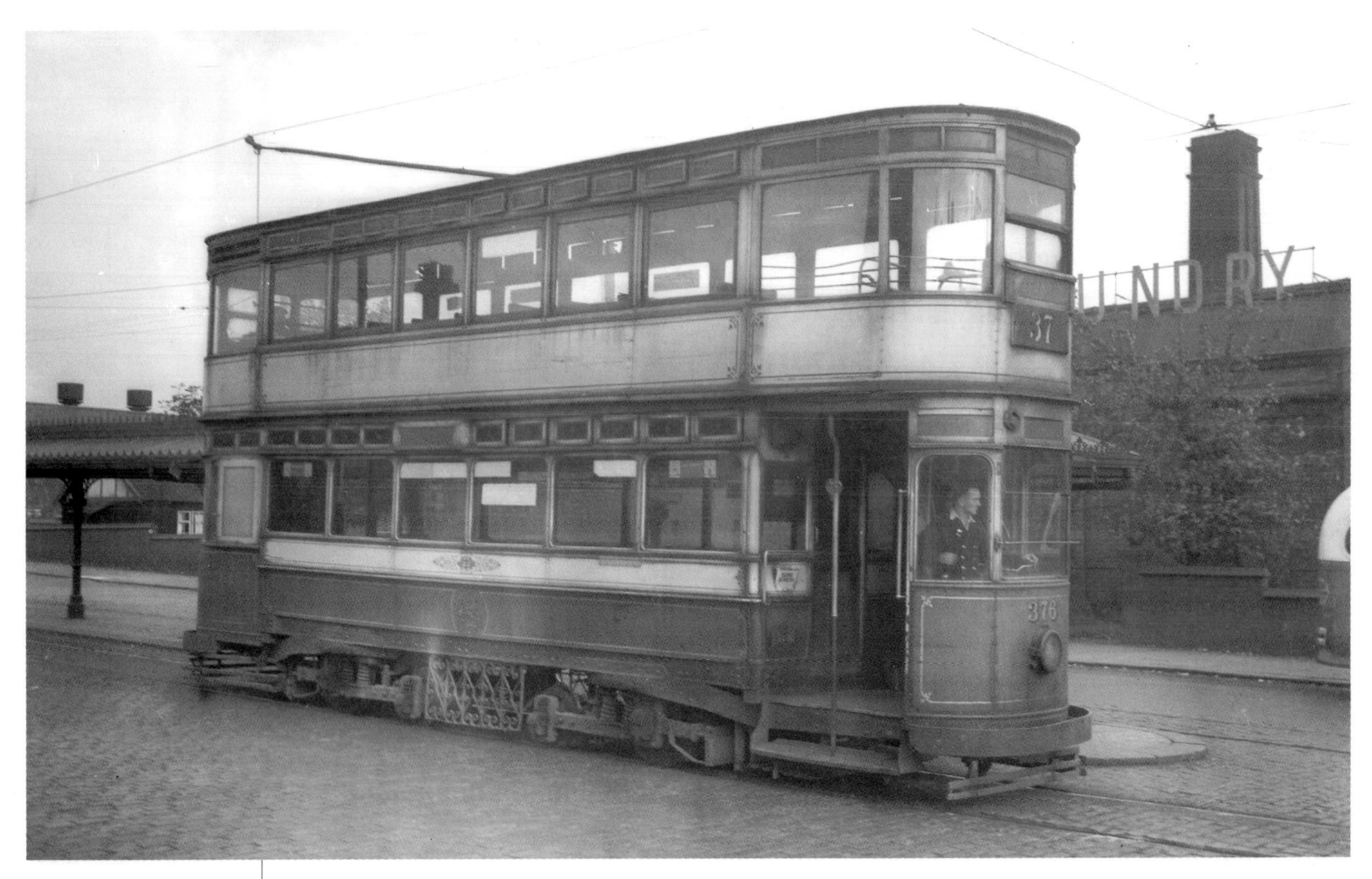

No.376, withdrawn in December 1948, stands at the short terminal stub in Lloyd Road that served as the terminus for route 37 in Levenshulme. F.E.J. Ward/Online Transport Archive

buses, the trams outlived his period in control – he retired on 30 June 1946 and was replaced by A.F. Neal.

Between 8 and 11 May 1945 tram No.639 operated as an illuminated car celebrating the end of the war in Europe; this was the penultimate occasion an illuminated car operated in Manchester. The final run of No.639 as an illuminated car occurred in August 1945 when it was used to mark victory over the Japanese in the Far East. In autumn 1945 two services – the 42F from Exchange to Platt Lane, which had operated for part of the day and for football matches only, and the 27D from Trafford Park to Birchfields depot, which had only operated at peak hours – were both withdrawn to allow the reuse of overhead for the growing trolleybus network. This resulted in the overhead in Great Western Street, Platt Lane and Raby Street, over which route 53 had operated in pre-war years, being recovered by 21 November 1945.

In January 1946 the corporation reconfirmed its tramway conversion policy. With the exception of the route 19 to Hyde, which was eventually converted to trolleybus operation, all future conversions were by diesel bus. The first conversion was the 32 on 17 February. The priorities were eliminating trams in Deansgate, in conjunction with Salford Corporation, and to Trafford Park. The next casualties, on 4 May 1946, were the surviving peak-hour services on routes 13 and 23. Also replaced by buses after this date were the peak-hour services from Trafford Park to Piccadilly via Stretford Road.

The next change occurred on 7 July 1946 when all but the peak-hour service was withdrawn from route 39, East Didsbury to Piccadilly. The same month saw the thirty-eight Pilcher cars offered for sale; withdrawn between October 1946 and June 1948, the trams found new homes in Aberdeen, Edinburgh, Leeds and Sunderland. During summer 1946, frequency was reduced on the 36 and 44 routes to Wythenshawe as extra buses were introduced to the corridor. The terminus of the 44 during off-peak hours was also cut back, from Wythenshawe to Whitchurch Road.

Abandonment of the trams serving Oldham on 3 August 1946 ended the joint service from Manchester to Waterhead via Oldham; Manchester trams continued to operate on the section to Hollinwood, although the Pilcher cars used on the service were transferred to route 19 pending withdrawal and sale. A further reduction occurred on 24 August when peak-hour trams were withdrawn on the services that operated into Trafford Park from Chorlton, Deansgate and Southern Cemetery. This, combined with ending Salford's peak-hours service to Pendleton, closed the lines leased by Manchester from Trafford Park Estates. The next day saw tramway services withdrawn on route 37 between St Mary's Gate and Southern Cemetery, ending tramcar operation in Stretford UDC. At this stage, Manchester trams also ceased operating along Deansgate, except for a short stretch, although Salford's trams were still evident. On 7 November 1946 it was announced that the next conversions would be the routes to Hollinwood and Kingsway. The two services that operated to Hollinwood last operated on 29 December 1946.

The next year saw a considerable contraction in the system. The first casualty, on 2 February, was route 40 from Albert Square to East Didsbury; although the all-day service ended on this date, with No.1007 being the last in service, certain peak-hour services continued. By the end of the 1946/47 financial year, Manchester's tram fleet had declined to only 233 trams.

Following a derailment to No.993 on 6 May 1947, a 15mph speed limit was imposed on any surviving reserved track much of which was in an applalling condition. The investigation resulted in the condemnation of the reserved track along Princess Road and the retention for longer than planned of the section along Kingsway (it survived until 15 November 1947). On 1 June 1947 route 36 operated for the last time; the section of track along Princess Road to Whitchurch Road was thereafter only used during peak hours. Less than a week later on 7 June, the last football cars operated to Manchester City's ground at Maine Road over the former route 36. Also in June, the 'infirmary' service, which operated once-daily between Birchfields Road and Piccadilly via Oxford Road, was withdrawn. On 6 July 1947 route 44 operated for the last time, with buses taking over the next day. A month later, on 10 August, route 33 was cut back in Reddish from Vale Road to the Bull's Head. A further curtailment followed on 16 August when route 38 was cut back from Fallowfield to Moseley Road. The next withdrawal in 1947 occurred on 15 November and cut back the peak-hour-only routes 39X and 40X to Mauldeth Road, marking the end of operation along Kingsway. This was followed, on 13 December, by the reduction in services on route 38 to peak hours only. The next withdrawal of the year, on 20 December, saw the peak-hour-only services 39X and 40X to Mauldeth Road withdrawn. On 30 December, the Hyde service was cut back to Broomstair Bridge.

The first casualty of 1948, on 31 January, was the 38X peak-hours-only service from Albert Square to Moseley Road. The next day witnessed the last tram operation on route 33. A fortnight later, on 15 February, tramway operation in Albert Square ended with the conversion of route 35B to Stockport. On the same day the surviving through service to Stockport, the 35C from Piccadilly, was combined with Stockport's route 4A from St Peter's Square (Stockport) to Hazel

Manchester No.321 stands at the Hazel Grove terminus of the jointly operated through route from Manchester via Stockport. No.321 was withdrawn in October 1948. F.E.J. Ward/Online Transport Archive

Grove, which resulted in a new through Piccadilly to Hazel Grove via Stockport service. The next withdrawal was on 14 March when trams ended operation on route 19 from Piccadilly to Broomstair Bridge; peak-hour trams continued to operate to Belle Vue and Reddish until 1 May 1948 (Stockport Corporation) and 15 May (Manchester Corporation). Hyde Road depot closed as an operational base thereafter, but remained connected to the system via Devonshire Street to facilitate moving trams for scrap.

The Manchester system was now entering its final phase with effectively only three routes still operational. The first converted to bus operation was the peak-hour 37E service from Levenshulme to Grosvenor Street, which operated for the last time on 20 August 1948. Manchester's penultimate route, the 37 from Levenshulme to Exchange, last saw trams on 3 October. The final full day of Manchester tram operation was 9 January 1949 when route 35 from Exchange to Hazel Grove via Stockport was replaced by buses. The last tram from Hazel Grove was Manchester No.940, the last from Mersey Square was No.961 and the last from Levenshulme was Manchester No.243. The next day five cars worked during the morning peak. At 11.30am on Monday 10 January 1949 there was a farewell procession of four cars – Nos.113, 976, 978 and, suitably decorated, 1007 – from Piccadilly to Birchfields depot. This was not the final tramcar movement as the surviving vehicles were driven that afternoon from Birchfields to Hyde Road for scrap. The final obsequies for Manchester's passenger trams came on 16 March 1949 when the last twenty-one were destroyed by fire at Hyde Road; the last survivors, four works cars, suffered the same fate on 4 May.

At the time no Manchester tram was secured for preservation; subsequently two have been preserved: single-deck combination car No.765 and 1901-built No.173. An even more impressive piece of the tramway's survival is Heaton Park Tramway. Based around the terminal stub located in Heaton Park (which closed originally in the 1930s and which lay under a new surface), the original track was revealed in 1976 and was first used for the operation of electric trams in more than forty years when services were inaugurated on 11 July 1976. The line has subsequently been extended.

Although the final full day of tramway operation in Manchester was on 9 January 1949, the following day witnessed the system's final procession of four trams, including No.1007 suitably decorated, from Piccadilly to Birchfields depot. F.E.J. Ward/Online Transport Archive

Depots

The corporation possessed two depots in the post-war era: Birchfields Road, which was originally opened on 24 July 1928 by the corporation and which survived as a tram depot until the system's abandonment (having undergone considerable work during winter 1947/48 to facilitate the changeover to bus operation), and Hyde Road, which dated to 1 December 1902 and which closed as an operational tram depot on 17 May 1948 (although withdrawn trams were scrapped at the site thereafter). The corporation's main workshops, officially opened on 4 October 1905, were also situated at Hyde Road. The complex was rebuilt in the 1920s, with trolleybuses and buses being based there from 1938 and 1940 respectively. The pre-war conversions had seen two other major depots close: Queen's Road, in February 1938, and Princess Road, on 12 February 1939. Unusually none of the horse-tram depots that had served Manchester were converted to electric traction.

Closures

11 February 1945	13 – Albert Square to Southern Cemetery reduced to peak hours only / 23 – Hollinwood to Chorlton reduced to peak hours only between Piccadilly and Chorlton
Autumn 1945	42F – Exchange to Platt Lane (part day and football service) and 27D – Birchfields Road to Trafford Park (peak-hours-only service) – discontinued
17 February 1946	32 – Exchange to Reddish via Clowes Street
4 May 1946	13/23 – Peak-hours services withdrawn
7 July 1946	39 – Exchange to East Didsbury reduced to peak hours only
3 August 1946	20 – Manchester to Waterhead

Closures (continued)

24 August 1946	Remaining Manchester peak-hour tram services into Trafford Park from city withdrawn
25 August 1946	37 – Levenshulme to Southern Cemetery via Deansgate replaced by buses between St Mary's Gate and Southern Cemetery
29 December 1946	21/23 – Piccadilly to Hollinwood
2 February 1947	40 – Albert Square to East Didsbury except for certain trams in peak hours
1 June 1947	36 – Albert Square to Southern Cemetery; Princess Road track beyond Whitchurch Road now used only at peak hours
7 June 1947	Last football cars over 36 from Great Jackson Street to Bowes Street and from City to Wilmslow Road
June 1947	'Infirmary' tram – Birchfields Road to Piccadilly via Oxford road; one tram per day – withdrawn; overhead recovered from Dickenson Road 1 July 1947
6 July 1947	44 – Piccadilly to Southern Cemetery
10 August 1947	33 – cut back from Reddish (Vale Road) to Reddish (Bull's Head)
16 August 1947	38 – Albert Square to Fallowfield cut back to Moseley Road

Closures (continued)

15 November 1947	39X/40X – peak-hour services cut back from East Didsbury to Mauldeth Road
13 December 1947	38 – Albert Square to Moseley Road reduced to peak hours only
20 December 1947	39X/40X – Exchange/Albert Square to Mauldeth Road
30 December 1947	19 – Exchange to Hyde cut back to Broomstair Bridge
31 January 1948	38X – peak-hour services Albert Square to Moseley Road
1 February 1948	33 – Piccadilly to Reddish
15 February 1948	35B – Albert Square to Stockport; end of tramway operation in Albert Square 35C – Piccadilly to Stockport – combined with Stockport route 4A
14 March 1948	19 – Exchange to Broomstair Bridge
1 May 1948	Withdrawal of Stockport peak-hour trams to Belle Vue via Reddish
15 May 1948	34B – Exchange to Belle Vue/Reddish Lane
20 August 1948	37E – Grosvenor Street to Levenshulme (peak-hours service)
3 October 1948	37 – Exchange to Levenshulme
9 January 1949	35 – Exchange to Hazel Grove
10 January 1949	Last Manchester trams operated during morning peak

Taken in Piccadilly with a service towards Reddish, No.499 was completed in June 1925 and remained in service until March 1948. F.N.T. Lloyd-Jones/Online Transport Archive

Manchester Fleet
102/05/08-14/16/17/19/23/27/28/34/37-39/ 147/51/54/57/60/62/64/65/70/71/81-84/86/87, 220/38/39/43/45/46/48/51-53/59/67/77/78/83/ 284/89/90/92/94, 300/10/15/19/21/26-28/30/ 331/36/40/52/53/56-58/60/76/77/79/82/83/88/ 391/93/94/98, 402/04/06/07/10/17/19/21/22/ 424/26/27/29/31/32/34/90/92/95/97/99, 505/06/11

Between 1924 and 1930, 110 replacement fully enclosed double-deck cars were built at Hyde Road using Manchester Corporation Transport Department (MCTD) bogies. Building started with No.128, which emerged in September 1924, and continued until January 1930 when No.319 was completed. All 110 survived through the war, although No.109 was withdrawn during the 1944/45 financial year. A total of fourteen of the type, Nos.102/12/13/39, 243/89/90, 331/48/52/91/94, 490/91, survived until the demise of the system in January 1949.

104/06/21/25/31/41/44/61/63/73/76/96, 217/25/28/31/42/63/66/70/72/74/87, 349/70/80/81/89, 420/93, 502/03/10/38, 610/69/71/76

The 38 Pilcher or Pullman cars delivered between March 1930 and October 1932 represented Manchester's last new trams. Built at Hyde Road using Peckham P35 trucks, the trams were the result of Stuart Pilcher's recommendation to Manchester's Tramways Committee on 21 February 1929 that a batch of four-wheel cars was needed for operation primarily on joint routes where the other operators used four-wheel trams. Post-First World War, the corporation's policy had effectively been to replace four-wheel trams with bogie cars and there was now a need for modern four-wheel cars. Although forty trams were authorised, only thirty-eight were built, with the additional two sets of equipment stored.

All survived through the Second World War; in July 1946 all were offered for sale. Withdrawn between September 1946 and June 1948, the cars were sold to Aberdeen (fourteen at £300 each), Edinburgh (eleven at £210 each, although Nos.173 and 676 had been slightly damaged and so were sold at £173 and £175 respectively), Leeds (seven at £200 each) and Sunderland (six again at £200 each). The last operated in Aberdeen, with the final example, No.49 (ex-Manchester No.106), withdrawn in June 1956. It was offered for preservation at £25 plus £200 transport costs; unfortunately this was not to be and it, like the rest of the class, was scrapped.

No.270, seen here during a tour, was new in October 1930; withdrawn in March 1948, it was sold to Aberdeen. F.N.T. Lloyd-Jones/ Online Transport Archive

Recorded in 1947, No.192 was one of a quartet of 1901-built cars to survive the war. Originally an open-top car, it received an open-balcony top cover before 1915 and an enclosed lower-deck vestibule by 1919. J.H.S. Morris

Between 1924 and 1929, eleven cars, including No.444, supplied during 1902 and 1903 were rebuilt as fully enclosed using wider underframes. All were withdrawn by the end of the 1944/45 financial year. Barry Cross Collection/ Online Transport Archive

192, 219/26/27

These four cars were the only post-war survivors of a batch of fifty, Nos.188-237, that had been delivered as open-top bogie cars in 1901. Built by Brush, they were fitted with either Brush maximum traction or Brill 22E bogies. All were fitted with open-balcony top covers by 1915. No.208 emerged from Hyde Road works in April 1919 rebuilt as the prototype for the standard bogie cars built for Manchester during the 1920s. Between 1919 and 1929, a number were rebuilt; the exceptions were Nos.188/93/96, 200-02/04/5/07/09/11/14/17/18/20/23-25/31/32/34-37. Those rebuilt were fitted with Brill 22E bogies. Nos.192, 219/26/27/29 were rebuilt as fully enclosed between 1924 and 1929. Withdrawals began during the 1927/28 financial year with No.220, one of the unrebuilt cars, and the first of those rebuilt, No.228, succumbing during the 1931/32 financial year. By April 1939 six remained in service, of which Nos.189 and 229 were withdrawn by March 1940. The surviving four cars were all withdrawn between 1946 and 1948.

438/39/43-45/48/49/53/58/71/77

These eleven cars were the survivors of a batch of fifty, Nos.437-86, open-top and open-vestibule bogie cars built by Brush during 1902 and 1903 on Brill 22E bogies. Four of the type, Nos.440/43/45/50, were fitted with short top covers shortly after No.589 was so fitted in November 1904; these cars became known as 'Balloons' as a result. Between December 1907 and December 1916 the remainder were fitted with balcony tops. No.466 was fitted with enclosed vestibules in 1914. Nos.447/50/65/67-70/73-75/78/79/83

No.618 was one of 100 Balloon cars built by Brush during 1904 and 1905. The surviving rebuilt cars were all withdrawn by June 1948. F.N.T. Lloyd-Jones/Online Transport Archive

were rebuilt as fully enclosed on narrow underframes between 1920 and 1923, and Nos.438/39/43-45/48/49/53/58/71/77 were rebuilt as fully enclosed on wider underframes between 1924 and 1929. The first withdrawals occurred during the 1932/33 financial year and, by 1 April 1939, only the eleven rebuilt between 1924 and 1930 remained in service. These were all withdrawn between then and March 1948.

556/59/60/62/67-71/74/75/78-82/86-94/96-98, 602/04/07-09/11/14/16/18-23/26/30/31/33/34/37/39-41/43/48

During 1904 and 1905, Brush supplied a further batch, Nos.549-648, of double-deck bogie cars. Again fitted with Brill 22E bogies, the cars were originally ordered as open top with open lower-deck vestibules. During production, the decision was made to add short top covers; fifty top covers were supplied to the corporation to be fitted to those already delivered, and the final fifty, Nos.599-648, had the Balloon top cover fitted at Brush before delivery. The first of those delivered earlier to be fitted with a top cover was No.589 in November 1904. Four of the covers given were fitted to the four cars of the 437-86 batch, resulting in four of this batch, Nos.553/54/73/88, not being fitted with Balloon covers and operating as open top until late 1907 when balcony top covers were fitted. Of the batch, seventy were rebuilt as fully enclosed; the first eighteen, between December 1922 and December 1923, having external box indicators and the remaining 52, between January 1924 and January 1930, having built-in indicators. Many of the latter batch also received replacement corporation-built bogies. All the non-rebuilt cars (which retained Balloon tops to the end), plus No.583 (which had been rebuilt in January 1923), were withdrawn between 1931 and the end of March 1938. Between April 1939 and March 1940, sixteen of the rebuilt cars were withdrawn, leaving fifty-three of the rebuilds to see service through the war. These were all withdrawn between 1945 and June 1948.

685/86

These two cars survived from a batch of thirty-eight open-balcony double-deck cars supplied in 1910. Built at Hyde Road using Brill 22E bogies, the other thirty-six were withdrawn during 1938 and 1939. No.685 had been rebuilt as fully enclosed in 1925. No.686, keeping its open balconies, was used after 1940 as a works car; its open balconies were ideal for accessing the trolleyheads of disabled trams for repair, particularly on the reserved track sections that were inaccessible to tower wagons. Both were withdrawn in May 1948.

A pre-war view of No.686; this was one of only two of the type that survived post-war. It was withdrawn in May 1948. F.K. Farrell/ Online Transport Archive

812/20/25/30

In 1920 a batch of forty-three fully enclosed double-deck cars, Nos.793-835, was delivered. Of these, Nos.793-97 were given bodies built at Hyde Road with the rest by EE, as successor to UEC, at Preston. All were fitted with Brill 22E bogies but No.182 had these replaced by MCTD-built bogies by 1928. Of the forty-three, twenty-eight were withdrawn in February 1939 upon the conversion of the West Didsbury service and a further eleven, Nos.807/08/10/13/17/19/22/27/29/32/35, were withdrawn between April 1939 and March 1945, leaving four in service. These were all withdrawn by the end of March 1947.

847

Manchester took delivery of twelve single-deck combination cars between November 1920 and January 1921. They were built by EE, although the workload at Preston at the time and other records suggest that five might have been completed at Hyde Road, on Brill 22E bogies. All were withdrawn by the end of 1931, following the conversion of route 53, except Nos.840/43/47 that were kept for rush-hour services. After 1935 the trio were used for moving sand from Hyde Road to other depots. No.843 was scrapped in 1938 and No.840 the following year. The last, No.847, succumbed in 1947.

849/50/55/57/63-65/68-76/83/85/86/88/889/91/92/94-97/99, 903/08-13/19/20/22-25/27-29/32

These forty-five cars survived from eighty-six double-deck fully enclosed bogie cars, Nos.848-933, supplied between 1920 and 1922. All were built at Hyde Road except Nos.860-909 by EE on Brill 22E bogies, although Nos.903/27 had replacement MCTD bogies fitted in 1928. Withdrawal of the type started in February 1939 with thirteen taken out of service, with a further twenty-six following by March 1940. Two succumbed during the 1944/45 financial year, with the surviving forty-five withdrawn between April 1945 and June 1948.

The last surviving single-deck car in the Manchester fleet was No.847; it was withdrawn in 1947. F.K. Farrell/Online Transport Archive

No.924 was one of forty-five survivors post-war from a batch of eighty-six cars, Nos.848-933, delivered between 1920 and 1922. Barry Cross Collection/Online Transport Archive

With the damaged roof of Manchester Exchange station in the background, No.993 was the last of a batch of sixty cars delivered during 1924 and 1925. Although one was damaged during the war, all survived post-war. No.993 was withdrawn in October 1948. F.N.T. Lloyd-Jones/Online Transport Archive

934-93

During 1924 and 1925, EE supplied the bodies for a further sixty fully enclosed double-deck trams. These were all fitted with MCTD-built bogies and all survived post-war. No.983 suffered damage during the war at Chorlton in 1940 but was repaired. Withdrawals started during the 1945/46 financial year but sixteen of the type, Nos.940-42/44/45/47/52/56/60-62/66/76/78/83/85, survived to be withdrawn with the final demise of the system in January 1949.

The last bogie cars acquired by Manchester were fifty built at Hyde Road during 1926. One of the type was withdrawn in 1940, although the remaining forty-nine survived post-war. No.1038 was one of seven withdrawn in March 1948. F.N.T. Lloyd-Jones/Online Transport Archive

Two of the Manchester works cars that survived post-war stand side by side towards the end of their lives. Water car No.8 and sister No.5 were among the last Manchester trams to survive, not being scrapped until May 1949. Freight car No.7 was one of two built by the corporation on Brill 22E bogies. F.N.T. Lloyd-Jones/ Online Transport Archive

1004-46/48-53

A further batch of fifty fully enclosed double-deck trams, Nos.1004-53, was completed in 1926. Again built with EE bodies on MCTD bogies, all survived post-war except No.1047 (withdrawn in 1940). No.1006 suffered blast damage in 1940 and operated for a period with plywood panels in place of the broken window glass; it was eventually repaired. Three were withdrawn between April 1945 and March 1946, with the rest succumbing between then and January 1949; five, Nos.1007/9/29/37/52, remained at closure with No.1007 being the official last tram. The last of the cars were scrapped on 19 March 1949.

Works trams

Apart from a couple of ex-passenger cars that were adapted for works use, Manchester post-war also used a number of dedicated works cars. These included four water cars, Nos.5-8: Nos.5, 6 and 8 were double-tank cars and had been converted between 1928 and 1930 from hopper cars built by Robert Hudson & Co of Leeds supplied during 1912 and 1913; No.7 was an older single-tank car. All were fitted with Brill 21E trucks. In addition, until at least January 1949, the corporation operated a rail-grinder car, No.2, which was used at the end of its career as a shunter in Hyde Road works. Two of the seven freight cars survived post-war: No.5 was fitted with a Brill 21E truck and No.7 operated with Brill 22E bogies. There were also five salt trailers; these vehicles, fitted with Brill 21E-type trucks, originally numbered twenty but had been reduced as the system contracted. Finally there was at least one rail-borne tower wagon; fitted with a Brill 21E-type truck, it was essential for overhead maintenance on the reserved track sections.

MANCHESTER METROLINK

Manchester has always suffered from the fact that the city's main railway stations, now only Piccadilly and Victoria, were to the south and north of the central area and there was no direct connection between them, although there had been proposals for a link. The Picc-Vic plan of the 1970s envisaged building a tunnel linking the rail networks and constructing three new underground stations to serve the centre.

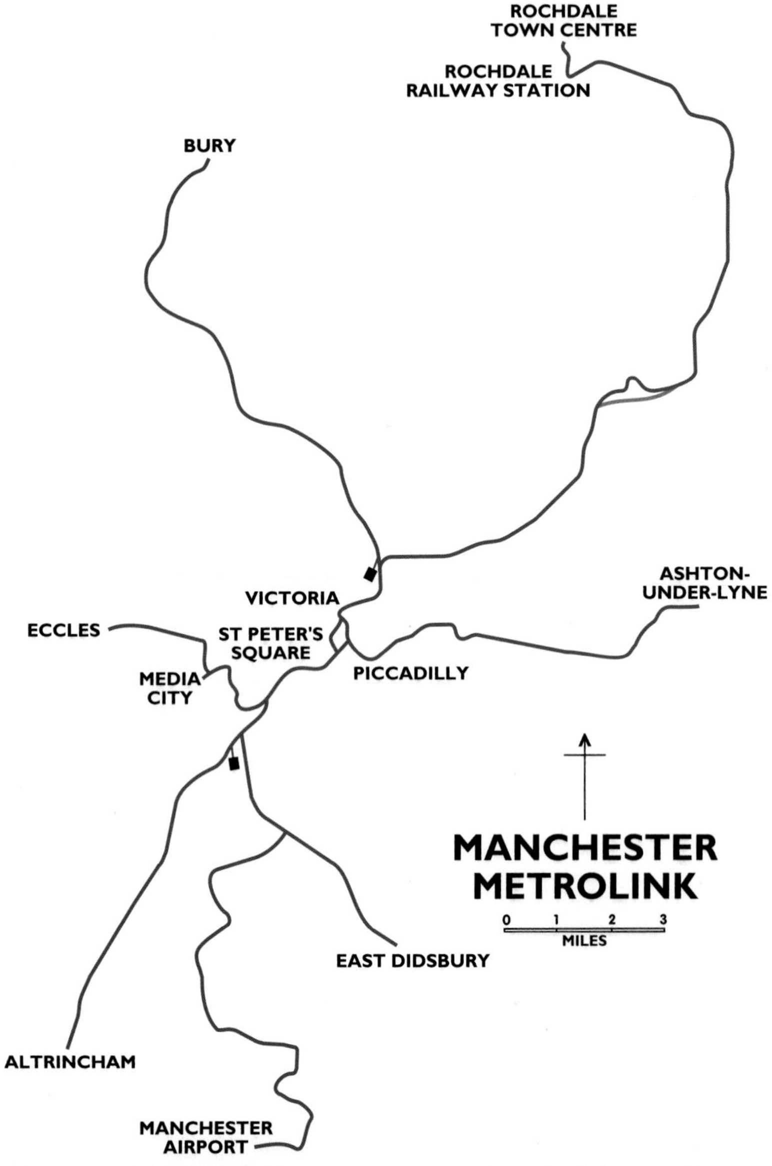

Five years after the abandonment of the Picc-Vic scheme in 1977, Greater Manchester Passenger Transport Executive (PTE) first developed the idea for a surface light-rail connection in 1982. In 1984 detailed proposals for a three-route network were submitted to the government for funding. The routes were: A – Altrincham to Glossop / Hadfield; B – Bury to Marple / Rose Hill; and C – Rochdale to East Didsbury via Oldham. Phase 1, for which funding and powers were obtained in 1987, covered converting the existing British Rail (BR) lines to Altrincham and Bury (both already electrified but with life-expired rolling stock) as well as a cross-city link and branch to serve Piccadilly station. As such, Phase 1 provided a fixed link between the city's two surviving main-line stations (with the Altrincham line passing a third, Central, which had been converted into an exhibition centre after closure).

Following the passage of the Manchester (Light Rapid Transit Scheme) Act in early 1988, work began. A consortium, Greater Manchester Metrolink, was awarded the contract to build and operate the system. Work started on the on-street section in March 1990, and passenger services over the BR routes to Altrincham and Bury were finally withdrawn on 24 December 1991 and 17 August 1991 respectively for conversion. Using the existing railway

With building work on the extension to the town centre visible in the background, M5000 car No.3036 awaits departure from Rochdale Station on 12 April 2013. Author

platforms on these routes meant the new light rail vehicles would need high floors and thus platforms at on-street stations.

The first section of the system to open, on 6 April 1992, was that from Bury to Victoria, which was followed on 27 April 1992 when a suitably bedecked No.1007 inaugurated the section from Victoria through to the erstwhile Central station. Services were further extended to Altrincham on 15 June 1992 and to Piccadilly on 20 July 1992.

The next phase saw work on the Eccles via Salford Quays section start on 25 April 1997. This line opened in two stages: from Cornbrook to Broadway on 6 December 1999 and from Broadway to Eccles on 21 July 2000. Developing Salford Quays as a media centre saw planning permission granted in October 2007 for a 400m extension to serve MediaCityUK; this opened on 20 September 2010.

Passenger services over the railway line from Victoria to Rochdale via Oldham were withdrawn on 3 October 2009 for its conversion. Metrolink services over the line from Victoria to Oldham Mumps began on 13 June 2012. The line was extended to Shaw & Compton on 16 December 2012 and to Rochdale station, via a bridge over the Rochdale-Halifax railway line, on 28 February 2013. Initially services operated through Oldham on the original railway alignment as the route through the town centre was built. The street track through Oldham centre opened on 27 January 2014 and resulted in the closure (and dismantling) of the route on the old railway formation

The extension to East Didsbury from St Werburgh's Road opened on 23 May 2013. No.3004 stands at the new terminus on 25 June 2013. Author

through Oldham Mumps.

Following approval in 1990, work started on building the next phase. The first section to open was the short link from Cornbrook to St Werbergh's Road on 7 July 2011, which was followed by extensions from Piccadilly to Droylsden (opened on 8 February 2013), St Werbergh's Road to East Didsbury (opened on 23 May 2013) and Droylsden to Ashton centre (opened on 9 October 2013). Whereas the line from Piccadilly to Ashton is largely on-street, the route to East Didsbury follows a long-closed railway route. The following year saw two further extensions opened (other than that in Oldham town centre): Rochdale station to centre on 31 March 2014 and from St Werbergh's Road to Manchester Airport on 3 November 2014.

As the system has grown, the capacity of the existing link through the city centre has proved inadequate. The government gave the go-ahead on 8 October 2013 to build a second cross-city route (known as 2cc) – from Victoria to St Peter's Square. Building started in 2014 and the first section, from Victoria to Exchange Square, opened on 6 December 2015 with limited services to Rochdale and Shaw & Crompton. The full city-crossing opened on 26 February 2017.

Pictured on 23 May 2013 as the history of the T-68 class was drawing to a close, No.1007, one of the last two to remain in service, was used for the ceremonial opening of the line through the city centre and, on withdrawal, was preserved. Author

Depots

The Metrolink system uses two depots. The first opened with the system on 6 April 1992 and is situated on Queens Road, Cheetham Hill. As the system expanded, a new facility was needed, which opened on Elsinore Road, Old Trafford, on 5 June 2012.

Opening dates

6 April 1992	Victoria to Bury
27 April 1992	Victoria to G-Mex
15 June 1992	G-Mex to Altrincham
20 July 1992	Piccadilly Gardens to Piccadilly
6 December 1999	Cornbrook to Broadway
21 July 2000	Broadway to Eccles
20 September 2010	Harbour City / Broadway to MediaCityUK
7 July 2011	Cornbrook to St Werburgh's Road
13 June 2012	Victoria to Oldham Mumps
16 December 2012	Oldham Mumps to Shaw & Crompton
8 February 2013	Piccadilly to Droylsden
28 February 2013	Shaw & Compton to Rochdale station
23 May 2013	St Werburgh's Road to East Didsbury
9 October 2013	Droylsden to Ashton-under-Lyne
27 January 2014	Street track through Oldham town centre
31 March 2014	Rochdale station to Rochdale town centre
3 November 2014	St Werburgh's Road to Manchester Airport
6 December 2015	Victoria to Exchange Square
26 February 2017	St Peter's Square to Exchange Square

Closure

27 January 2014	Ex-railway section through Oldham

Manchester Metrolink Fleet

1001-26

To launch the new service in 1992, a fleet of twenty-six T-68 trams was acquired from AnsaldoBreda of Naples in Italy. The single-deck articulated cars followed on from a prototype bodyshell, No.1000, that was built in 1990 and displayed to promote the new system. This bodyshell is now preserved at the Greater Manchester Museum of Transport. The cars first entered service with the opening of the Victoria–Bury route. With the opening of the Eccles route in 2000, three of the type, Nos.1005/10/15, were modified to operate alongside the new 'T-68As'. Eventually all bar Nos.1018-20 were modified and redesignated as 'T-68Ms'. With the decision to order the M5000 type, it was announced that all the original 'T-68s' were to be withdrawn. The first, No.1011, was taken out of service on 19 April 2012. The last of the class, Nos.1007/16, succumbed on 26 May 2014. The majority have been sold for scrap. No.1007 has, however, been preserved and is destined for the Heaton Park Tramway.Nos.1016/22/24/26 were acquired by UK Tram and are currently based at Long Marston. Nos.1020/23 remain in Manchester.

2001-06

To supplement the fleet for the Eccles route six modified T-68s were ordered. Designated T-68A, the cars were again built by AnsaldoBreda and delivered in 1999, with the last, No.2005, entering service on 7 January 2000. The new cars differed slightly from the original class by incorporating all the modifications planned for the original T-68s so as to make them fully suitable for operation on the route to Eccles, but as more of the original cars were modified, the 1999-built cars were seen more widely over the system. For technical reasons, the six T-68As could only operate singly. All were withdrawn in 2013 and 2014; the last two in service, Nos.2001/03, succumbed on 30 April 2014. Nos.2002-06 were all sold for scrap during 2014; currently No.2001 remains in Manchester.

3001-120

With the expansion of the system, further cars were needed. In April and November 2007 twelve articulated trams were ordered from Bombardier to allow operation of the new line to Salford Quays. The new vehicles were to be built at Bautzen in Germany and tested at Vienna before delivery to Manchester. Designated the M5000 series, further orders saw the total reach 120. The first arrived in Manchester on 13 July 2009 and entered service on 21 December 2009. All had been delivered and entered service by the end of 2016. The 'M5000s' can operate singly or in multiple; since the withdrawal of the last of the original 'T-68s' in 2014, the 'M5000s' have been the sole passenger cars in the fleet.

1027/1028

The system has one service vehicle dating from 1991. No.1027 was built by RFS Industries of Kilnhurst in South Yorkshire. There is also a single support wagon, No.1028. No.1027 is a bespoke diesel-powered vehicle with a crane, inspection platform, mobile workshop, and capacity for a driver and three passengers.

To operate the new service to Eccles, six additional trams were acquired. The first of the type, No.2001, is seen on 12 April 2013. Author

OLDHAM

Although Oldham had acquired a batch of twelve fully enclosed double-deckers in 1926, within two years the first route abandonment had taken place and by September 1939 there were only two routes: from the connection with Manchester at Hollinwood to Waterhead and from the town centre to Shaw Wrens Nest.

If war had not broken out, both routes would have been converted to bus in September 1939; as it was, the Shaw Wrens Nest service was only given a short reprieve as it was converted on 2 December 1939 due to the poor track condition.

Consequently Oldham emerged from the war with a single route operated by twenty-seven trams. The corporation obtained sufficient replacement buses for the final conversion and, on 3 August 1946, car No.6 operated the last public service.

The official last car was No.4, which emerged – suitably decorated – at 10.30pm from the depot. It then followed No.16 to the terminus at Waterhead from where it headed west to Hollinwood and then back to the depot, driven by the town's mayor, where it arrived at about 11.30pm.

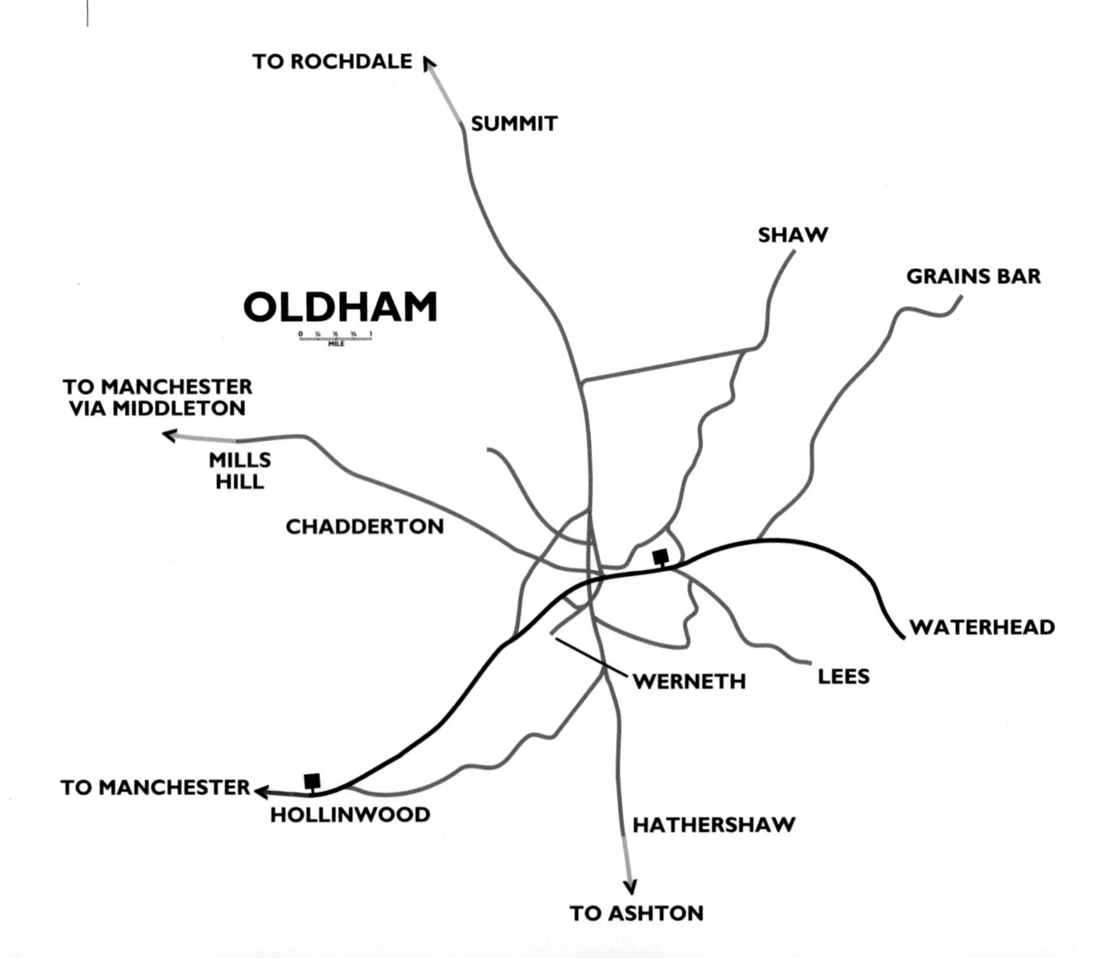

Oldham No.17 was one of six fully enclosed trams acquired in 1924 and one of three of the type sold to Gateshead after the conversion of the final Oldham route on 3 August 1946. Barry Cross Collection/ Online Transport Archive

The closure of Oldham's tram system occurred on 3 August 1946 with No.4, suitably decorated, as the official last car. It and accompanying car No.16 are pictured on the final night. Barry Cross Collection/ Online Transport Archive

In 1921 Oldham took delivery of twelve open-balcony cars, including No.10 seen here heading towards Waterhead, built by EE. All bar one of the batch survived into the post-war era. Barry Cross Collection/Online Transport Archive

Although the majority of Oldham's trams were scrapped following the system's abandonment, six cars were sold to Gateshead for further service. Since closure the body of No.43 has been rescued for preservation. No.43 was the first of a batch of twenty-five open-top double-deckers supplied by ERTCW in

A pre-war view, with Rochdale No.87 in the background, sees No.22 stand at the Summit terminus; this route was converted to bus operation on 6 November 1937 (one of three routes converted that day). J.H. Roberts/Online Transport Archive

1902 with Brill 21E trucks. It was one of two of the type (the other being No.47) that was cut down during 1933/34 for operation over the Oldham to Middleton route; this route was converted to bus on 11 June 1935 and the body spent more than sixty years in private hands.

Depots
Only one Oldham depot survived post-war – Wallshaw Street, which opened originally on 17 May 1902 and had been partially converted for use as a bus garage in 1936. The depot closed with the system on 3 August 1946. A second depot, Hollinwood on Manchester Road (opened 18 August 1910), closed with the contraction of the system on 7 August 1937. There were also four other depots that all closed relatively early.

Closure

3 August 1946	Hollinwood to Waterhead

4-6/8-12/14-16
Between June and August 1921 the first trams delivered to Oldham after the First World War entered service. Nos.4-12 and 14-16 took the numbers of trams sold to Rotherham in 1916 and were built by EE on Brill 21E trucks. These were all open-balcony cars and used initially on the route to Manchester with the exception of No.16, which was slightly taller than the rest of the batch and so could not pass under the railway bridges at Newton Heath. No.7 was withdrawn in December 1939 following the conversion of the Hollinwood to Shaw Wrens Nest route; the remainder survived until August 1946 and final closure.

17/18, 22/24
To replace withdrawn cars, Oldham acquired a further batch of trams from EE in 1924. Fitted with Brill 21E trucks, these were the first fully enclosed trams delivered to the corporation, taking the numbers of the withdrawn trams. Two of the type, Nos.19 and 20, were withdrawn in December 1939 following the conversion of the Shaw Wrens Nest route. The remainder continued in service until the end of Oldham's trams. Following abandonment, Nos.17/18 and 24 were sold to Gateshead & District.

121-32
In 1925 an order for twelve new trams with fully enclosed bodies on Brill 21E trucks was placed with EE. The first three, Nos.121-23, were delivered later that year and the remainder in 1926. All survived in service until the final abandonment of the system in August 1946. On closure, Nos.122/25/28 were sold to Gateshead.

The final tramcars delivered to Oldham were twelve fully enclosed double-deckers supplied by EE during 1925 and 1926. This wartime view sees No.124 operating on the through route 20 to Manchester. Maurice O'Connor/ NTM

SALFORD

Originally it was intended for 1940 to be the last year of Salford's tramway system. In the period before September 1939 the system had contracted significantly and, by the outbreak of war, effectively only three routes – 34 to Weaste, the Docks circular 70/71 and 81 to Irlams o' th' Height plus the connection into Trafford Park for workmen's services – remained operational. The system did, however, gain a fourth route when, in June 1940, route 76 from Deansgate to Weaste via Cross Lane was reinstated; this service had originally been converted in 1939. Routes 34 and 76 were operated by trams based at Weaste depot, and those on the

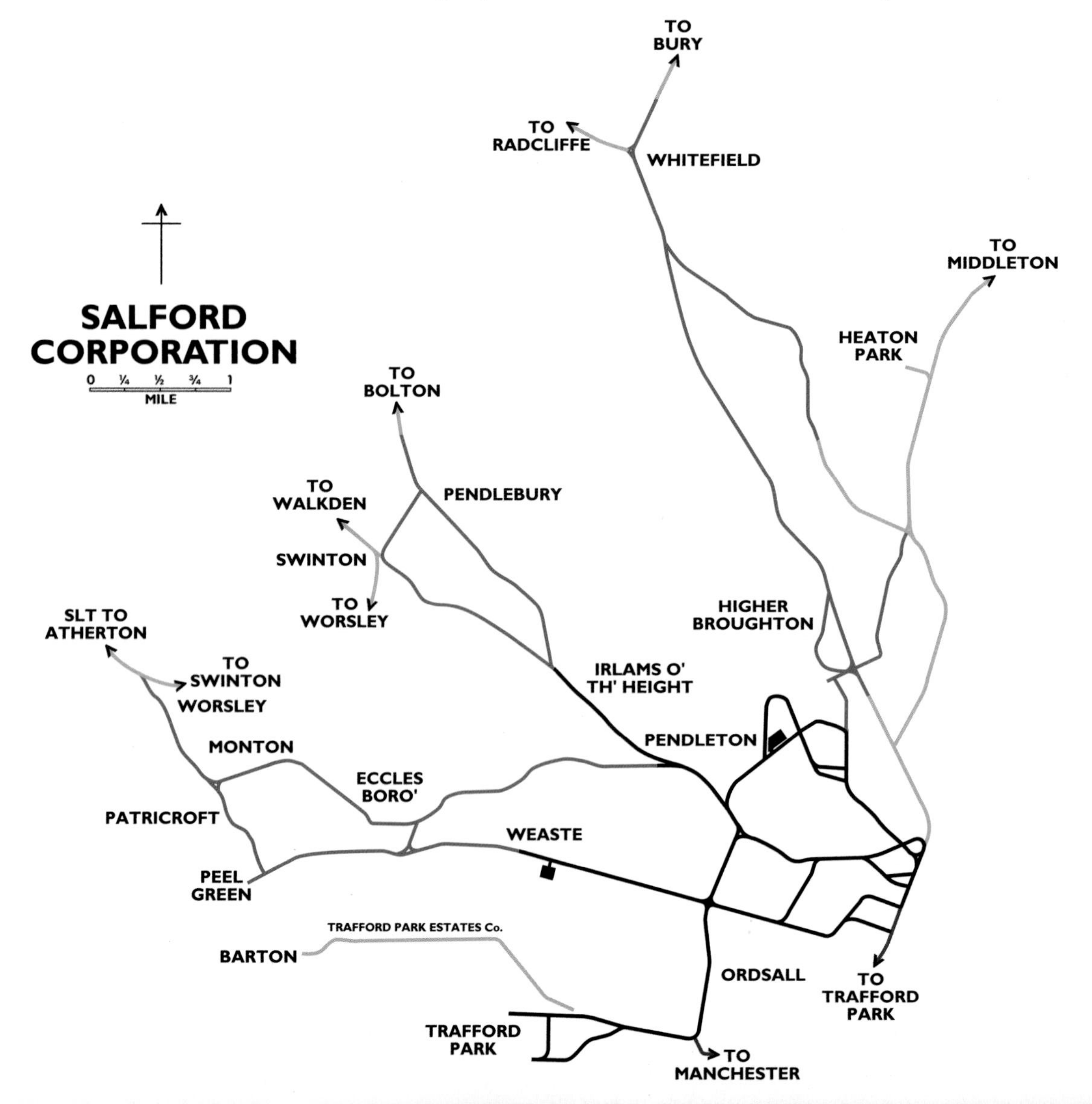

other routes were housed at Frederick Road.

On 29 May 1944 there was an unplanned route suspension when the sewer in Bolton Road, Pendleton, collapsed. This resulted in route 81 being withdrawn between The Woolpack, Pendleton and Irlams o' th' Height. Peak-hour services, however, continued to operate over the section of the route from Deansgate to Pendleton. Route 81 officially became a bus route on 19 November 1945, although the peak-hours service from Pendleton to Trafford Park remained operational.

A change of management occurred in Salford on 10 August 1946 with the retirement of J.W. Blakemore; he was succeeded by C.W. Baroth. He inherited a fleet that included sixty-one trams, of which only thirty-eight with operational. Any possible lack of trams was soon mitigated as, on 24 August 1946, the peak-hours-only service from Pendleton to Trafford Park ended operation. Buses replaced the trams on the following Monday.

January 1947 saw the peak-hours-only service from Cromwell Bridge to Victoria via Lower Broughton Road (route No.69) end. The next conversions occurred on 2 March 1947 when the two routes from

Pictured in its wartime livery is bogie car No.350; wartime liveries were introduced in October 1941 when the urgent need for fleet maintenance became apparent. In all six cars were painted in grey during 1941 and 1942 and a further nine appeared in a dull maroon between then and the end of 1944. Barry Cross Collection/Online Transport Archive

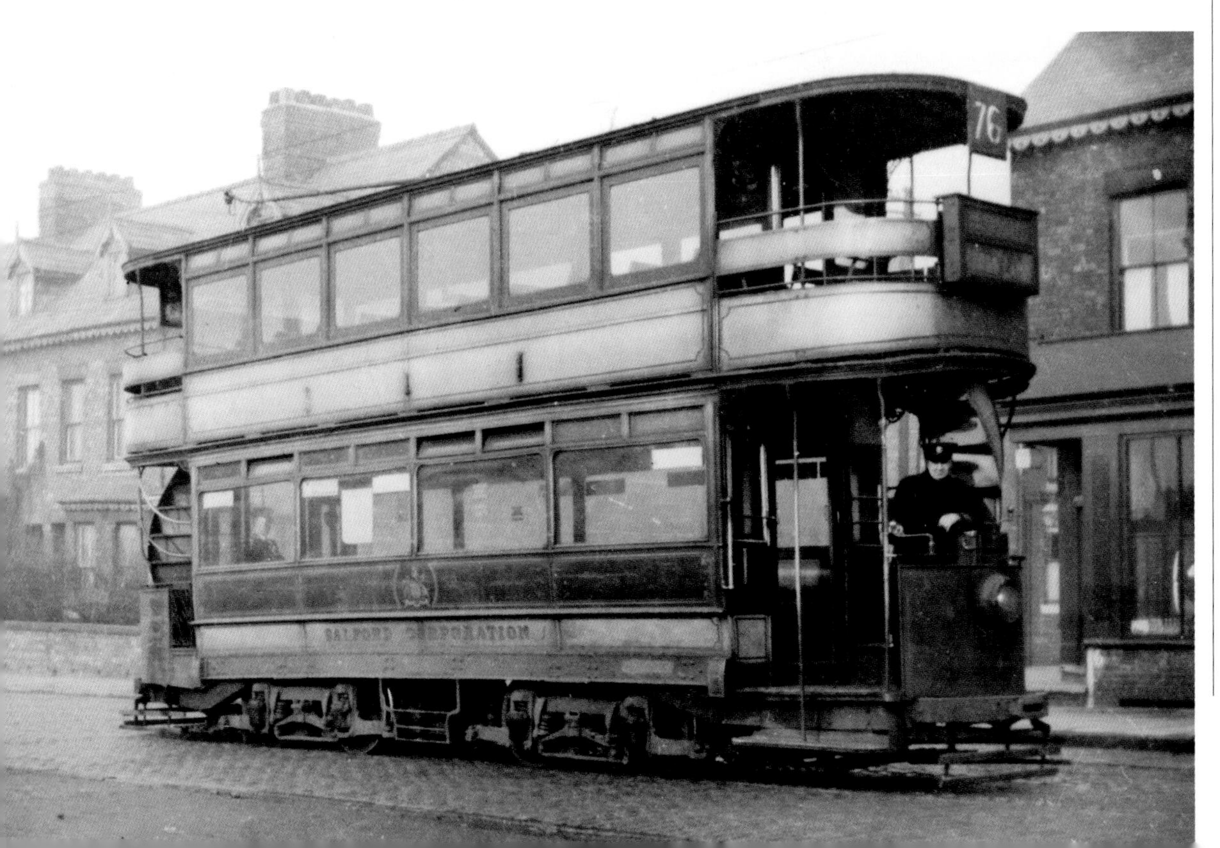

Seen on 1 March 1947, this open-balcony bogie car is clearly living on borrowed time. Salford's fleet at the start of the war included twenty-one similar open-platform bogie cars. R.B. Parr/NTM

Deansgate to Weaste operated for the last time. Time was now running out for Salford's trams; conversion of the last route occurred on 31 March. The final service was operated by No.350, which was the official last car. Following closure, the surviving trams were taken to Hyde Road, in Manchester, for scrap, with a number being towed by No.350. The last trams made this one-way journey in early June and no Salford tram survives in preservation.

Depots

There were two depots serving the electric tramcars of Salford. These were Frederick Road, where the workshops were also located, which opened originally on 4 October 1901 and closed with the system on 31 March 1947, and Weaste, which opened on 29 October 1929 and closed on 2 March 1947 with the conversion of routes 34 and 76. There were also three earlier horse-tram depots that closed in 1902 and 1903.

Closures

18 November 1945	81 – Deansgate to Irlams o' th' Height
24 August 1946	Peak-hour trams linking Pendleton with Trafford Park
January 1947	69 – Victoria to Cromwell Bridge via Lower Broughton Road
2 March 1947	34/76 – Deansgate to Weaste
31 March 1947	70/71 – Deansgate and Docks circular

Salford Fleet

154-56/58

Built by Brush in 1913/14 on Brill 21E trucks, these four cars were the survivors of a batch of ten, Nos.151-60. Originally delivered as open-top cars with enclosed lower-deck vestibules on Brill 21E trucks, all were fitted with open-balcony top covers during 1923 and 1924. Only one of the type was fitted with enclosed balconies – No.154 in 1931. In about

No.155 was one of four survivors post-war from a batch of ten cars originally delivered during 1913 and 1914. The Salford system was noted for its heavy industrial traffic, to the Docks and to Trafford Park, but it was reputed to be in a very poor condition post-war with some cars in a 'state of semi-collapse'. Barry Cross Collection/ Online Transport Archive

In 1915 Brush supplied a batch of twelve open-balcony cars to Salford; all survived post-1945. J.H. Roberts/Online Transport Archive

1931 No.151 exchanged numbers with No.161, the ex-Trafford Park Estates car. Of the ten cars built, four survived into the war years; the remaining six were all withdrawn during 1939. Of the four, No.156 was withdrawn in November 1946 and No.158 in January 1947. The last two survived until final closure.

201-12

This batch of twelve cars was built by Brush in 1915 on Brill 27G maximum-traction bogies. Delivered with balcony top covers and enclosed vestibules, these cars were never rebuilt as fully enclosed. All survived the war, but the first withdrawal occurred in June 1946 with No.201. No.205 followed five months later. Of the remaining ten, all survived to final closure except Nos.202 (early March 1947) and 209 (January 1947).

214-19/21/22

Supplied by Brush in 1915/16, Nos.213-24 were open-top cars with enclosed vestibules on Brill 61E maximum-traction bogies. These were designed for the routes that passed under the low railway bridges at Besses o' th' Barn and Monton. They were all rebuilt as fully enclosed in 1923 and transferred away from the routes affected by the low

Originally delivered as one of a batch of twelve open-top cars in 1915, No.222 was, along with the other eleven cars, rebuilt as fully enclosed in 1923. Eight of the batch survived into 1945 and six remained operational until the end. J.H. Roberts/Online Transport Archive

The last new trams delivered to Salford were a batch of six supplied by Brush during 1923 and 1924. No.228 was the penultimate of the batch to survive, being withdrawn in February 1947. Maurice O'Connor/NTM

bridges (although No.220 was damaged in 1927 when a driver forgot this). Nos.213/20/23/24 were withdrawn in 1939. No.219 was withdrawn in February 1945 and No.216 in November 1946. The other six cars survived until the system's closure.

A pre-war view sees No.349 standing alongside No.368 in front of Frederick Road depot in April 1939. No.349 was withdrawn in December 1946. W.A. Camwell/NTM

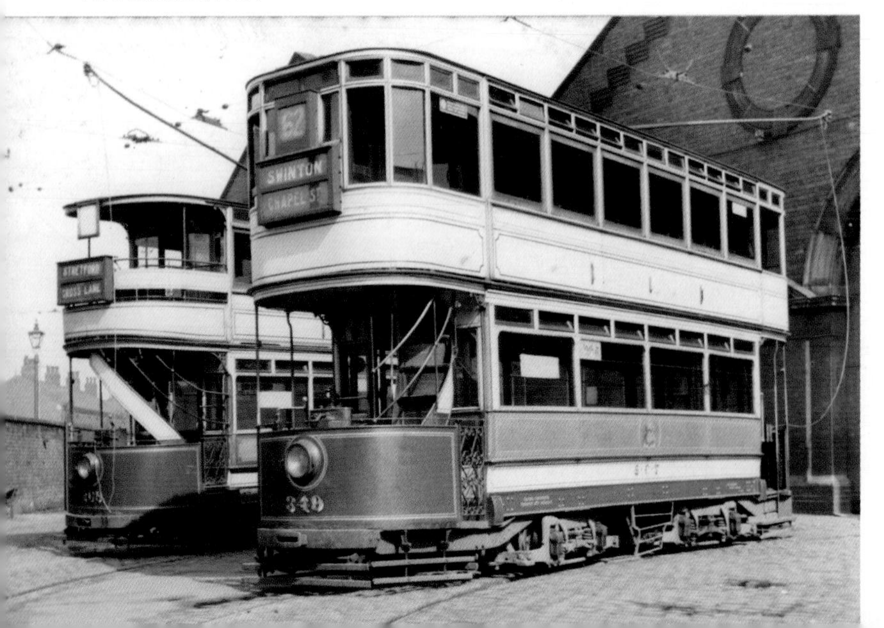

225-30

The last trams delivered to Salford were six, Nos.225-30, that were supplied by Brush in 1923/24. All were fully enclosed from new and fitted with Peckham P22 trucks. All survived the war; four were withdrawn during 1946 (Nos.225-27/29) with the last two in 1947 (Nos.228 in February and 230 at final closure).

333-35/38/39/41/44/46-53/56-9

In 1902/03 Milnes supplied thirty open-top trams, Nos.101-30; these had Brill 27G bogies. In 1912 No.130 was the first to receive an open-balcony top cover; it retained an open lower-deck vestibule until withdrawal. A further twelve, Nos.101-05/07-09/11/18/22/26, received open-balcony top covers during 1923. Another twelve, Nos.106/10/13-17/20/21/23/25/29, received enclosed top covers in 1924; Nos.110/21 were also fitted with enclosed lower-deck vestibules (the remainder of the 1923-24 conversions retained open lower-deck vestibules until withdrawal). Nos.112/19/24/27/28 were all rebuilt as fully enclosed in Frederick Street between October 1920 and March 1922. In 1935 the batch was renumbered 330-59. Withdrawals began in 1939 with Nos.330-32/36/37/40/42/43/45/54/55 all succumbing that year. Nos.333-35/41/44/46/49/51/52/57-59 were all withdrawn in 1946, leaving seven to serve into 1947. Two of these, Nos.338 and 347, were withdrawn in early March, leaving Nos.339/48/50/53/56 to soldier on to the end.

361/63-65/67/69-71/73/76

These ten cars were the survivors of a batch of cars, Nos.131-50, supplied by British Electric Car Co (BEC) in 1903. Fitted with Brill 27G maximum-traction bogies, the cars were originally open

No.367 was one of ten survivors post-1945 from a batch of twenty cars, originally numbered 131-50, that BEC supplied in 1903. Maurice O'Connor/NTM

top and unvestibuled. In 1910/11 No.132 was fitted with an experimental top cover and enclosed vestibules. The remaining nineteen cars were fitted with open-balcony top covers in 1912 but never received enclosed vestibules. During the 1930s, No.132 was used an illuminated car for a royal visit in 1934, for the jubilee of King George V in 1935 and for the coronation of King George VI in 1937. Stored thereafter, the tram returned to service in 1942, surviving until the system's closure. The entire batch was renumbered 360-79 in 1935. Nos.360/62/66/68/74/77-79 were all withdrawn in 1939, and No.372 succumbed in March 1942. The first post-war casualties were Nos.364, which had been fitted with enclosed lower-deck vestibules in early 1940 (the only one so treated), and 371 in March 1945. Five were withdrawn in 1946, Nos.365/69/70/73/76, with two others surviving into 1947: No.363 was withdrawn in February and No.367 in January.

380

Originally built for Trafford Park Estate Light Railway, as No.10, in 1903, No.380 was built by BEC on Brill 27G bogies. Similar in design to the corporation's own Nos.131-50, it passed to corporation ownership in 1905, becoming No.161. It exchanged numbers with No.151 in about 1931, having been rebuilt as a fully enclosed car in 1925. It became No.380 in 1935 and survived until March 1947.

The only car inherited from the Trafford Park Estates Light Railway to survive post-war, No.380 was new in 1903. It is pictured here on 29 March 1947. J.E. Gready/Barry Cross Collection/Online Transport Archive

SHMD

The once extensive system of SHMD had gradually contracted from 1928 and, in 1936, powers were obtained by the board to operate trolleybuses. Although the board never operated trolleybuses itself, the Act facilitated converting the through service from Stalybridge to Manchester via Ashton. This service was inaugurated on 1 March 1938.

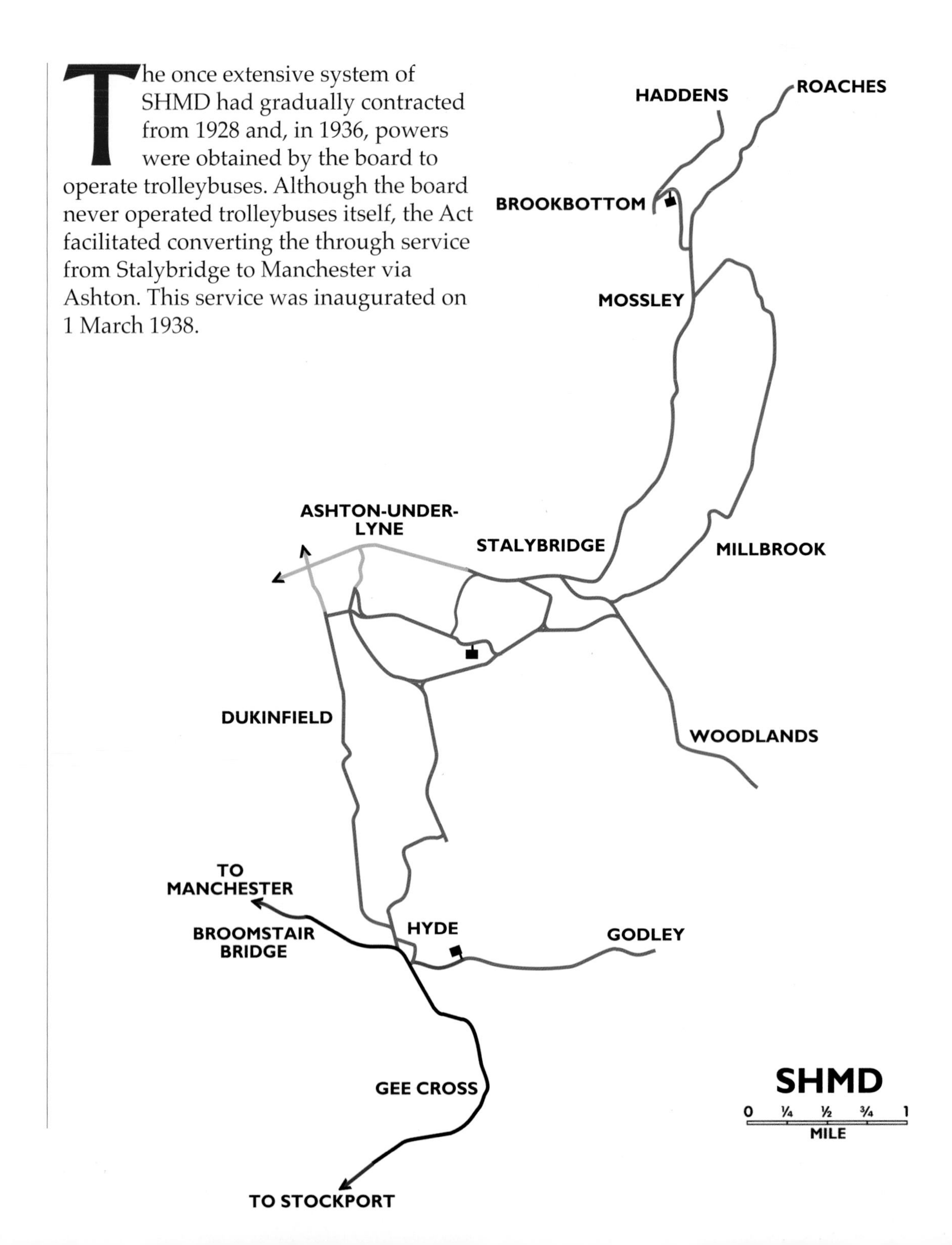

The bulk of the SHMD network had been converted to bus operation before the war, but the through services to Manchester and Stockport remained. The fleet comprised six cars, of which four, such as No.61 illustrated here, were open-balcony cars built in the operator's own workshops during 1924 and 1925. Barry Cross Collection/Online Transport Archive

The result of this conversion and the abandonment of the track to the town was that SHMD's main workshops in Stalybridge were no longer accessible by the remaining trams; for the final seven years of SHMD operation the trams were all maintained at the depot at Mottram Road on the route out to Godley, with any major work undertaken at Stockport; passenger services over the route to Godley had been withdrawn before the war but a half-mile section was kept for accessing the depot.

At the start of the war, SHMD operated effectively only over the routes to Broomstair – the through service to Manchester had been operated exclusively by Manchester Corporation since 1935 – and via Gee Cross on the through service to Stockport. Undoubtedly the war prolonged the life of the SHMD system but the physical condition of the track was poor. In November 1943 concern over the track led the board to recommend converting the through service to Stockport to bus operation, but this was rejected by Stockport.

From 2 March 1944 the six surviving SHMD cars were restricted to operating the weekday shuttle from Hyde to Gee Cross, leaving the through service to Stockport and Edgeley to be operated exclusively by Stockport trams. As the shuttle did not operate on Sundays, SHMD cars continued to operate through to Stockport on Sundays only until 20 September 1944.

From September 1944 onwards SHMD trams were limited to weekday operation of the Gee Cross shuttle and in May 1945 the board again sought to obtain permission for withdrawing its final trams 'in the interests of public safety'.

No.18 was the sole survivor post-war of a batch of ten trams delivered by BEC in 1904. It is seen here in front of Mottram Road depot in Hyde. Barry Cross Collection/ Online Transport Archive

Although the Ministry of War Transport permitted the board to end operation, having condemned the six surviving cars, it ordered that the track be maintained for the continued operation of Manchester and Stockport trams on the through services.

The last day of SHMD normal tram operation occurred on 12 May 1945, but this was not the final running of an SHMD tram as, on 29 May 1945, No.18 operated for the last time in connection with a BBC sound recording. Following closure, the surviving six trams were all scrapped.

Although SHMD operation ended in May 1945, this was not the end of tramway operation within the board's area as Stockport continued to operate through to Hyde via Gee Cross until 1 March 1947 and Manchester Corporation continued to operate the through service via Broomstair Bridge until 30 December 1947. The track and overhead from Broomstair Bridge through to Hyde remained extant until after it was formally abandoned on 14 February 1948.

Depots

The SHMD possessed three depots, one of which opened in 1904 and the other two in 1905. The first to open on 22 May 1904 was Tame Valley in Stalybridge; SHMD's main workshops were also located here. The depot became inaccessible to the surviving trams from 1 March 1938 with the conversion of the route to Manchester to trolleybus operation and the abandonment of the track in Stalybridge itself. Of the two depots that opened in 1905, Stamford Road in Mossley closed in 1931, leaving Mottram Road depot in Hyde to accommodate the fleet through to closure on 12 May 1945.

Closure

12 May 1945	Hyde Market Place to Gee Cross (track used by Stockport until 2 March 1947. Manchester trams also terminated in Hyde Market Place on route 19 from the boundary at Broomstair Bridge until 30 December 1947)

No.42 was one of a batch of fifteen trams originally supplied by Hurst Nelson in 1905 and was one of two of the batch that received a replacement Peckham P22 truck; it is seen at Mottram Road depot. Barry Cross Collection/ Online Transport Archive

SHMD Fleet

18

A second batch of cars, Class B Nos.11-20, were ordered from BEC in December 1903 and delivered the following year. Built as open-top cars, they were fitted with McGuire 21EM trucks. All were fitted with open-balcony top covers by 1919. Of the ten cars, all bar No.18 were withdrawn before the Second World War, with the sole survivor succumbing in 1945, being the last SHMD tram to operate when it was recorded for a BBC broadcast on 29 May 1945.

42

In 1905 Hurst Nelson delivered fifteen open-top trams, Nos.41-55. Designated Class E, they were fitted with M&G 21EM trucks. In 1914 No.42 was fitted with an experimental balcony top cover built at Park Road, and a glass windscreen. The latter innovation proved shortlived and was soon removed. All were eventually fitted with open-balcony top covers. No.42, which had had its original truck replaced by a Peckham P22 (as had No.51, which had been withdrawn before the war), survived until the system's demise on 12 May 1945.

61-64

During 1924 and 1925, four trams were built in the board's workshops at Park Road. Nos.61 and 62 were completed in 1924 with Nos.63 and 64 coming in 1925. All were open platform and balcony-top cars, with three fitted with Brill 21E trucks and the fourth receiving a Peckham P22 truck. All survived until the final closure of the system in 1945 and were subsequently scrapped.

The last new trams supplied to SHMD were a quartet – Nos.61-64 – built in the board's own workshops in 1924 and 1925. J.H. Roberts/Online Transport Archive

STOCKPORT

Stockport entered the war with its system largely intact; the only conversion pre-war was the section from Cheadle to Gatley but there was no planned programme of closures.

The war years were relatively quiet in the town; during 1944, there was a partial renumbering of the fleet. This resulted in the trams being numbered in three sequences: Nos.1-29 for low-bridge cars used on the joint service through to Hyde; Nos.30-45 were normal-height open-balcony cars; and Nos.46-83 for fully enclosed normal-height cars. The low-bridge cars were further distinguished by the use of the letter 'H' either side of the headlight on the lower-deck dash; the 'H-H' designation indicated those trams capable of passing under the low bridge at Bredbury on the route to Hyde. Later in the same year it was rumoured that the through service to Manchester was under threat; however, considerable opposition resulted in the Ministry of War Transport refusing the conversion. As a result, on 31 October 1944 the council undertook relaying the track along Wellington Road. Work started during summer 1945 and was a significant undertaking. It lasted for about eight months and meant

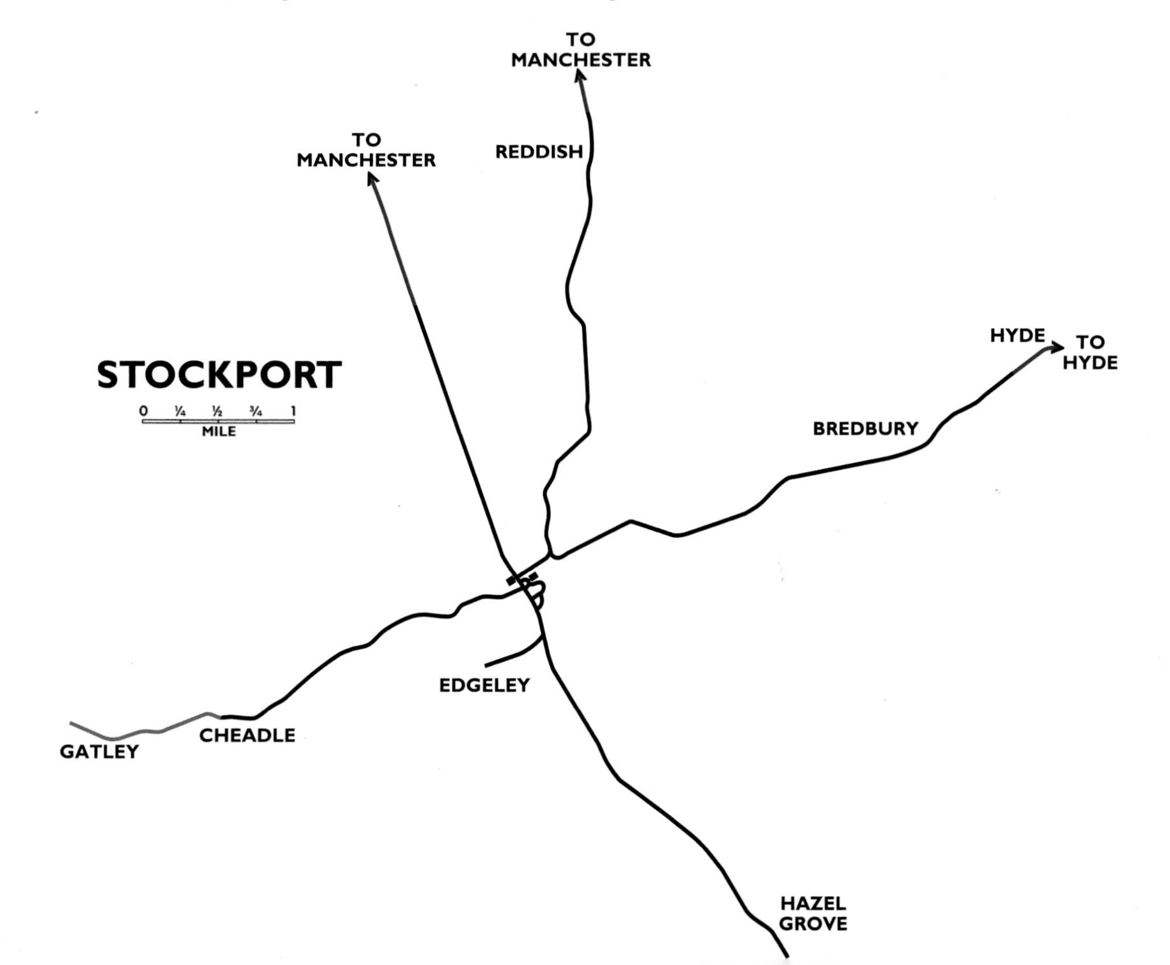

certain sections operated as single track at times. It also included building a new crossover at Belmont Bridge. This was not the only remedial work undertaken. On the route to Hazel Grove, the feeder cable was replaced as far as the borough boundary; the southernmost section was left unaltered as the line was only leased to the corporation by Hazel Grove UDC.

The hub of the Stockport system was Mersey Square. Here No.82, one of ten fully enclosed cars delivered in 1925, makes its way through the complex track en route to Reddish. F.E.J. Ward/Online Transport Archive

As Stockport relaid the through route, the threat to the service in Manchester meant the Stockport Planning Committee noted 'it is anticipated that the tramway track will be removed'. It was also noted that Stockport was considering conversion to the motorbus 'because Manchester will not have anything else'.

In April 1946 Stockport trams that had previously served Gorton Library were diverted to serve Belle Vue; this was because Manchester removed the overhead along the erstwhile route No.32. The following year was one of contrasting fortunes for Stockport's trams. On 1 March the through service to Hyde, which had used the surviving ex-SHMD track, was withdrawn. Services, however, continued to operate all day to Vernon Park with a peak-hours extension to Bredbury Bar. The peak-hours extension survived until 3 May 1947. The closure of the line beyond Bredbury to Hyde rendered redundant the 'H-H' on the tram dashes as the service no longer passed under the low railway bridge. On the other hand a certain amount of track repair work was undertaken and tram No.16 was repaired after sustaining serious damage. Indicative that Stockport did not anticipate the imminent conversion of its remaining routes was comment in the contemporary press that trackwork had been obtained to replace the complex Mersey Square layout; in reality this proved a false dawn – events in Manchester meant the days of Stockport's trams were numbered and the work was never undertaken. As late as 1950 it was reported that the replacement track was languishing behind the depot.

On 15 February 1948 the 35B from Albert Square to Stockport was operated by trams for the last time; the same day route 35C from Piccadilly to Stockport was combined with Stockport's route 4A from Hazel Grove to St Peter's Square with through cars now running from Hazel Grove to Piccadilly via Stockport.

This meant trams no longer served St Peter's Square in Stockport. In addition, Stockport's trams continued to operate peak-hour services to Belle Vue and to Reddish until 1 May 1948.

Operation of route 35 ended on 9 January 1949, although Stockport cars continued to operate over the section from the town centre to the boundary at Crossley Road. Converting the Manchester system was perhaps the final nail in the Stockport system's coffin; on 8 July 1949 the town council bowed to the inevitable and agreed that the surviving tram routes would be replaced by sixty-eight new buses.

The first consequence of this policy occurred on 14 January 1950 when trams operated for the last time on the routes to Hazel Grove and to Crossley Road. The fleet was now reduced to some forty-five cars and maintenance gradually declined. The last car repainted, in March 1950, was No.53; this was then used on an enthusiasts' tour of the surviving system on 12 March 1950. Elsewhere there was evidence of lack of maintenance; there were reports of traction columns having rusted through with span wires being affixed to adjacent poles or even to trees.

The system survived for more than a year; the next conversions did not occur until 3 March 1951, when the routes to Vernon Park and Edgeley succumbed, and 10 March 1951, when the service from Mersey Square to Cheadle followed. Following this conversion, the one remaining service was curtailed to terminate at Princes Street, rather than Mersey Square, with the result that the once complex network of lines that served Mersey Square was abandoned other than for access to and from the depot. With the conversions of March 1951, the town's second depot, at Heaton Lane, stopping being used by trams. The remaining thirty

The fate of the Stockport system was inextricably linked with its northern neighbour, Manchester. Here No.54, one of the EE-built cars of 1920, stands in Piccadilly, Manchester, with a route 35 service to Hazel Grove. F.E.J. Ward/Online Transport Archive

No.72, one of the ten cars delivered from Cravens in 1923, stands at Reddish on 13 August 1950. Peter N. Williams/ Online Transport Archive

cars in the fleet, Nos.50-61, 65-68 and 70-83, were all based at Mersey Square for the last few months of the system's life.

The final closure of the Stockport system came on 25 August 1951 with the conversion of the route from Princes Street to Reddish. The official last car was an illuminated No.53; ironically the following day would have witnessed the fiftieth anniversary of electric tram operation in the town.

Although no Stockport tram survived into preservation at closure, the body of No.5 was subsequently rescued and has now been restored.

Depots

Stockport used two depots during the electric era. The first was Mersey Square, which opened on 26 August 1901. The original depot and workshops were extended in 1929 and the enlarged depot survived until the final closure of the Stockport system on 25 August 1951. The second depot, Heaton Lane, opened on 31 January 1924. This depot, damaged in an air raid in 1940, closed on 10 March 1951. A third depot, Dialstone Lane, was used by the horse trams of the Stockport & Hazel Grove Carriage & Tramway Co and closed in 1905 with the end of horse-tram operation.

Closures

1 March 1947	Vernon Park to Hyde
3 May 1947	Vernon Park to Bradbury Bar (peak hours only)
15 February 1948	Alterations to services in Manchester allowed Stockport to withdraw trams from St Peter's Square, Daw Bank, Lord Street and Wellington Street; services now operated through to Hazel Grove
9 January 1949	End of through service to Manchester
14 January 1950	Crossley Road (Levenshulme)
14 January 1950	Hazel Grove
3 March 1951	Vernon Park to Edgeley
10 March 1951	Mersey Square to Cheadle
25 August 1951	Princes Street to Reddish

1, 25/27(i)/28, 64

In 1903 ERTCW supplied a batch of six open-top cars, Nos.25-30, fitted with Brill 21E trucks. No.28 was rebuilt following an accident in 1916 and received a Brush top cover three years later. Nos.25/29 and 30 were rebuilt with top cover and enclosed vestibules in 1923, 1922 and 1920 respectively; four years later No.29 was rebuilt as fully enclosed using the top cover from No.9 and fitted with a replacement Cravens truck. No.30 was rebuilt as fully enclosed with a replacement Cravens truck in 1931. No.26 was converted into a breakdown car in 1925 and became No.101 four years later. No.27 became an illuminated car in 1935 and was cut down to single deck in 1941. Nos.29 and 30 were renumbered 64 and 1 respectively in 1944. No.27

With the 'H-H' designation prominent on its dash, No.25 is seen rebuilt as fully enclosed in 1923. F.N.T. Lloyd-Jones/Online Transport Archive

Originally No.48 when delivered in 1907, No.7 was one of a batch of five cars rebuilt as fully enclosed during 1931 and 1932. It was one of three withdrawn in 1950. F.E.J. Ward/ Online Transport Archive

was withdrawn in 1945; the remaining passenger cars were taken out of service in 1949 (Nos.1 and 28), 1950 (No.64) and 1951 (No.25).

2, 4, 7, 16, 27 (ii)
Originally numbered 46-50 when new in 1907, these top-covered double-deck trams were built by UEC on Brill 21E trucks. All were rebuilt as fully enclosed during 1931 and 1932. They were renumbered 4, 16, 7, 2 and 27 respectively in 1944 and were withdrawn in 1950 (Nos.2, 4 and 7) and 1951 (Nos.16 and 27).

No.49 stands at the junction of Kenilworth Road with Stockport Road in Cheadle Heath. No.49 is in the condition that resulted from its rebuilding in 1924 when it also received a Cravens-built replacement truck. F.N.T. Lloyd-Jones/ Online Transport Archive

Seen shortly before its withdrawal in Castle Street heading inbound from Edgeley with a service to Vernon Park, No.6 had originally been numbered 61 when delivered in 1919. F.E.J. Ward/Online Transport Archive

3, 5, 8, 30, 42, 49, 62
The system opened with ten trams, Nos.1-10, that were supplied as open-top double-deckers by ERTCW in 1901. All were fitted with Brill 21E trucks. Nos.2, 4, 7-10 were fitted with UEC top covers during 1911 and 1912. In 1921 Nos.3, 5, 8 and 10 had top covers supplied or replaced by new Brush-built top covers. No.2 was rebuilt with a top cover reused from No.25 and fitted with a Cravens-built truck in 1924. The UEC top cover from No.2 was fitted to No.9 in 1925 at the same time as a replacement Cravens truck was provided. No.6 was converted into a works car by 1925. No.1 was withdrawn and converted into a snowplough in 1927; refurbished and fitted with a top cover in 1941, it was restored to public service. Nos.7 and 10 were withdrawn in 1933. Nos.1, 2, 4 and 9 were renumbered 30, 49, 42 and 62 respectively in 1944. Withdrawals started in 1948 (Nos.3 and 5), with Nos.30 and 42 following in 1949, No.8 in 1950 and Nos.49 and 62 in 1951. Although not preserved on withdrawal, the body of No.5 was subsequently rescued and restored.

6, 9-11, 29
Originally numbered 61-65 when delivered during 1919 and 1920, these five cars had lower-deck bodies supplied by EE and were originally fitted with Brill 21E trucks. They were fitted with UEC top covers reused from Nos.10/15, 27, 8 and 30 respectively. All were rebuilt with enclosed vestibules and replacement Cravens trucks during 1929 and 1930. The cars were renumbered 6, 9, 11, 29 and 10 respectively in 1944 and were withdrawn in 1949 (No.6), 1950 (Nos.10 and 29) and 1951 (Nos.9 and 11).

On 15 January 1950 No.12 is recorded on Wellington Road South with a southbound service. No.12 had been rebuilt as fully enclosed in 1929; at the same time, the tram's original Brill 21E truck was replaced by one manufactured by Cravens. John Meredith/Online Transport Archive

12/15/17-24, 43/45, 63
In 1902 ERTCW supplied a batch of fourteen open-top double-deck cars fitted with Brill 21E trucks – Nos.11-24. During 1911 and 1912, Nos.11/12/15/16/19 were fitted with UEC open-balcony top covers. Nos.14/18, 20-24 were fitted with Brush open-balcony top covers by 1921. Nos.15/17 were rebuilt as fully enclosed in 1923 and fitted with new Brill 21E trucks. No.13 was withdrawn in 1927 and converted for use as a snowplough; it was refurbished and fitted with a top cover – the last Stockport tram so treated – in 1945 before being restored to service as No.45. Nos.12 and 19 were rebuilt as fully enclosed with new Cravens trucks in 1929 and 1928 respectively. No.14 was withdrawn in 1944, the only example of the type not to see service post-war. Nos.11 and 16 were renumbered 63 and 43 respectively in 1944. Withdrawals started with No.43 in 1947; Nos.12/18, 20-22/24 and 45 followed in 1949 and Nos.17/19, 23 and 63 in 1950. The last survivor was No.15 (withdrawn in 1951).

The last new tram to enter service with Stockport was No.26; built in the corporation's own workshops on a Cravens-built truck, it was new in 1929. Barry Cross Collection/Online Transport Archive

26
The last new tram to enter service, No.26 was built in the corporation's own workshops in 1929 and fitted with a Cravens-built truck. Fully enclosed from new, No.26 remained in service until withdrawal in 1950.

31-40
In 1905 Brush supplied a batch of ten open-top double-deck cars fitted with Brill 21E trucks. All were fitted with UEC open-balcony top covers during 1907 and 1908. In 1941 No.39 received a replacement Brush-built top cover that had previously been used on No.27. The first of the batch withdrawn, in 1947, was No.35. No.40 followed in 1948 and Nos.37/39 in 1949; the remaining cars were withdrawn in 1950.

41/44/46-48
In 1906 UEC delivered a batch of five open-balcony cars, Nos.41-45, on Brill 21E trucks. Nos.43 and 45 were rebuilt as fully enclosed in 1936 and 1933 respectively; No.45 also received a replacement Cravens truck. Nos.42/43/45 were renumbered 46-48 respectively in 1944. All survived until 1951 apart from Nos.41/44, which were withdrawn in 1950 and 1948 respectively.

50, 65, 76-83
The Cravens Railway Carriage & Wagon Co of Darnall in Sheffield supplied a batch of ten fully enclosed double-deck cars, Nos.76-85, in 1925; all were fitted with Cravens trucks. Nos.84/85 were renumbered 65 and 50 respectively in 1944. All were withdrawn in 1951.

51-60
Built by EE on Brush trucks, Nos.51-60 were delivered as fully enclosed in 1920.

With the depot in Mersey Square forming a backdrop, No.39 is pictured towards the end of its life. No.39 received a replacement top cover in 1941. F.N.T. Lloyd-Jones/Online Transport Archive

No.78 is seen awaiting departure from Hazel Grove showing the Crossley Road destination. This was used by Stockport's trams that operated on the once through service to Manchester that terminated at the borough boundary between January 1949 and January 1950. F.N.T. Lloyd-Jones/Online Transport Archive

Seen alongside No.77, No.46 was one of a batch of five cars supplied by UEC in 1906. Originally No.42 when new, the car was renumbered 46 in 1944. F.N.T. Lloyd-Jones/Online Transport Archive

Recorded in the late 1940s heading into Stockport along Gorton Road in Reddish, No.59 was one of a batch of ten cars built by EE in 1920. F.N.T. Lloyd-Jones/Online Transport Archive

No.55 received a replacement Cravens truck in 1927; the rest were so equipped by 1930. All survived until 1951.

61

Delivered in 1928 and fully enclosed from new, No.61 had been No.6 until the 1944 renumbering. The body was built in the corporation's own workshops on a Brill 21E truck. It was withdrawn in 1951.

66-75

This batch of ten cars was supplied as fully enclosed double-deckers by Cravens in 1923 on Cravens-built trucks. The first of the type withdrawn was

Pictured awaiting departure from Victoria Street in Manchester is No.61 with a service to Hazel Grove. No.61 dated originally to 1928 and had been built in the corporation's own workshops. Originally No.6, the car survived in service until 1951. R.B. Parr/NTM

Also pictured in Gorton Road, Reddish, in the late 1940s, No.70 was one of a batch of ten fully enclosed double-deck cars supplied by Cravens in 1923. F.N.T. Lloyd-Jones/Online Transport Archive

No.69, in 1950, with the remainder succumbing in 1951.

100-102

These were three works cars. No.100 was a water car built by Dick Kerr on a Brill 21E truck in 1902. No.101 was converted into a breakdown car in 1925 from 1903-built open-top double-deck car No.26. This had originally been built by Brush on a Brill 21E truck and was renumbered 101 in 1929. No.102, built by ERTCW in 1901 as an open-top double-deck car, was converted to a single-deck salt car by 1925. It was also fitted with a Brill 21E truck and was renumbered 102 in 1929. All three works cars were withdrawn for scrap in 1951.

Works car No.101, pictured outside Mersey Square depot, had been open-top passenger car No.26 (new in 1903). It was converted into a breakdown car in 1925 and was renumbered 101 in 1929. F.E.J. Ward/Online Transport Archive

PRESERVATION

Aside from being able to ride on historical trams at Blackpool, when the heritage fleet is in operation, there are two working museum tramways in the north-west of England: Heaton Park, in Manchester, and Birkenhead.

The former is home to preserved trams from the region. Appropriately there are two ex-Manchester cars based at Heaton Park: 1901-built open-top car No.173 (in store awaiting restoration) and 1914-built California single-deck car No.765.

The operational fleet also includes two ex-Blackpool single-deck cars: the modern toastrack No.619 and one of the 1937 Brush-built railcoaches No.623. In addition, two Blackpool Balloon cars, Nos.702 and 708, are in store, as is 1920-built railgrinder No.1 (ex-752). Trams from a further three local systems – single-deck Oldham car No.43 (new in 1902), Rawtenstall No.23 (a 1912 single-deck car) and Stockport No.5 (originally an open-top car delivered in 1901) – are either undergoing repair or are long-term restoration projects. The collection also houses one of the first generation of Metrolink cars, No.1007. Two trams from the collection are on loan: Manchester Carriage & Tramways Co No.L53, the only Eades Reversible horse tram to survive, is at the Bury Transport Museum, and Blackpool No.680 is, appropriately, on loan to its home town.

The Wirral Tramway has operated from the Wirral Transport Museum to the ferry terminus at Woodside since 1995. The first trams to operate were built for the line in Hong Kong and were numbered 69 and 70 to follow on from the highest-numbered Birkenhead car. In terms of historic trams, the collection includes a number from the north-west. There are two ex-Liverpool cars – bogie car No.762 and Baby Grand No.245 – along with one each from Birkenhead (Milnes-built open-top car No.20) and Wallasey (Brush-built Bellamy-top No.78) that have been fully restored. One of the Brush-built Blackpool railcoaches, No.626, is also at Birkenhead, and Warrington No.2 is currently under restoration. In addition, the collection possesses two horse trams: Birkenhead No.7 and Liverpool No.43.

The NTM possesses a single tram from Liverpool, No.869, which was acquired following its withdrawal from Glasgow, as well as a number of ex-Blackpool trams. These are No.4 (one of the original conduit cars of 1885), single-deck Blackpool & Fleetwood No.2 of 1898, Dreadnought No.59 of 1902, Blackpool & Fleetwood enclosed single-deck car No.40 of 1914 (currently on loan to Blackpool Transport), two 'Standards' (open-balcony No.40 and fully enclosed No.49; both date to 1926), Toastrack No.166 of 1927, Pantograph No.167 of 1928, Boat No.236 and Balloon No.249 (both of 1934), Brush-built 'Railcoaches' No.298 and 630 (both of 1937), and 762, one of the two rebuilt double-deck cars completed in the early 1980s. In addition, Blackpool railgrinder No.2 and 1927-built electric locomotive No.717 are also owned by the NTM.

These are all electric trams; the NTM also houses MBROT No.84 from 1886. This is a Wilkinson Patent vertical boiler steam tram built by Beyer Peacock. Used in industry between 1905 and 1954, it was preserved, until transferred to the NTM, by the Manchester Museum of Science & Technology.

Beamish has three ex-Blackpool cars: 1901-built four-wheel car No.31, Brush-built railcoach No.621 of 1937 and Balloon No.703, which operates in the guise of a spurious Sunderland No.101. Two Blackpool cars are also preserved at Carlton Colville: Standard No.159 and VAMBAC single-deck car No.11.

Across the pond there are a number of ex-Blackpool trams preserved as well as ex-Liverpool Baby Grand No.293, which is based at the Seashore Trolley Museum at Kennebunkport. This museum is also home to one of the two Blackpool Standard cars preserved in the US – open-balcony No.144. Fully enclosed No.48 is based at the Willamette Shore Trolley, Portland, Oregon. There are also four 'Boats' in the US: No.226 is based at the Western Railway Museum, California; Nos.228 and 233 with the San Francisco Municipal Railway; and No.606 at the National Capital Trolley Museum in Maryland. Also based in the US is

Although no Stockport tram was preserved when the system closed, the body of one – 1901-built No.5 – was recovered and fully restored. Owned by the Stockport 5 Tramway Trust, the car is currently on loan to the Heaton Park Tramway. The tram is seen at Heaton Park on 4 August 2012. Les Folkard/Online Transport Archive

The only museum street tramway in the UK is the Birkenhead Heritage Tramway. One of the Merseyside Tramway Preservation Society's fleet of trams is Wallasey No.78. This Bellamy-roofed Brush-built car, seen here on 16 August 2014, dated originally to 1920 and was the highest-numbered car in the Wallasey fleet. Author

illuminated car No.731, the *Blackpool Belle*.

There are no fewer than six ex-Blackpool trams based at the North Eastern Electrical Traction Trust in Sunderland. These are 'Balloon' No.721, twin-car set Nos. 674/84 and Centenary No. 647.

The largest concentration of historic Blackpool trams is undoubtedly still in Blackpool. Apart from the surviving and modernised Balloon cars that form the operator's 'B' fleet (Nos.700/07/098/11/13/18-20/24), there is also the heritage fleet. This comprises some thirty historical cars, not all owned by the operator, including two 'Standards' (Nos.143 and 147), six 'Balloons' (Nos.701/04/06/15/17/23), two Centenary cars (Nos.642 and 648) and four twin-car sets (Nos.671/81, 272 [672]+T2 [682], 675/85 and 676/86). Also included are four of the historic illuminated cars (Nos.732 *Rocket*, 733+734 *Western* train, 736 *Frigate* and 737 *Trawler*). These remain based at Rigby Road.

The East Anglian Transport Museum possesses two ex-Blackpool cars. One is the sole-surviving VAMBAC car, No.11, and the other is Standard No.159; the latter is pictured here on 5 June 1995. Author

BIBLIOGRAPHY

Blackpool Coronation Cars; Martin Wilson; Lancastrian Transport Publications; undated
British & Irish Tramway Systems since 1945; Michael H. Waller and Peter Waller; Ian Allan Publishing; 1992
British Bus, Tram & Trolleybus Systems: 12 – SHMD Joint Board; W.G.S. Hyde and E. Ogden; TPC; 1990
Liverpool Transport – Volume 2 1900-1930; J.B. Horne and T.B. Maund; TPC/LRTA; 1982
Liverpool Transport – Volume 3 1931-1939; J.B. Horne and T.B. Maund; TPC/LRTA; 1987
Liverpool Transport – Volume 4 1939-1957; J.B. Horne and T.B. Maund; TPC; 1989
Manchester Tramway Diary 1940-1951; I.A. Yearsley, J.H. Price, C. Taylor; Manchester Transport Historical Collection; 1961
Manchester's Transport: Part 1 Tramway & Trolleybus Rolling Stock; C. Taylor; Manchester Transport Historical Collection; 1965
Oldham Corporation Tramways; Arthur Kirby; Triangle Publishing; 1998
Modern Tramway/Tramways & Urban Transit; LRTL/LRTA; 1937 onwards
Salford's Tramways: volume 1; Edward Gray; Foxline; undated
Salford's Tramways: volume 2; Edward Gray; Foxline; undated
The Classic Trams; Peter Waller; Ian Allan; 1993
The Directory of British Tramway Depots; Keith Turner, Shirley Smith & Paul Smith; OPC; 2001
The Manchester Tram; Ian Yearsley; Advertiser Press; 1962
The Manchester Tramways; Ian Yearsley and Philip Groves; TPC; 1988
The Pilcher Pullman Cars built 1930-1932; Ian Johnson; Manchester Transport Museum Society; 2010
The Trams of South Lancashire and North Wales; J.C. Gillham and R.J.S. Wiseman; LRTA; 2003
The Tramways of Salford; Edward Gray; Manchester Transport Museum Society; 1967
The Tramways of South-East Lancashire; W.H. Bett and J.C. Gillham; edited by J.H. Price; LRTL; undated
Tramway Review; Light Railway Transport League; 1950 onwards
Tramways and other historic 'ways' in and around Stockport; Raymond Keeley; Foxline; 1990